Kevin Townley has written a delightful and quirky book, which I thoroughly enjoyed. His book is structured around two interlocking discussions. He gives readers a great introduction to the Buddhist five Buddha family teachings, and he brings the reader to an intuitive connection with those teachings by means of art and in particular through the work and life stories of 26 accomplished female artists. His writing is fresh and accessible, and so tender. As soon as I started reading it, I immediately started thinking of friends I'd like to give it to.

JUDITH L. LIEF, BUDDHIST TEACHER, EDITOR OF *THE PROFOUND TREASURY OF THE OCEAN OF DHARMA*

In this book, Kevin Townley pulls off the impossible. He finds, grabs, holds on, and interweaves with lightning speed dexterity the threads of Mandala, Mindfulness, and Marshall McLuhan into a brilliant magnum opus on art, the art world, and the meaning of life. Bonus, it's hilarious. Without a doubt, he is the Fran Lebowitz of Buddhist writing.

JOHN HODGMAN, HOST OF THE *JUDGE JOHN HODGMAN PODCAST*

Kevin Townley is a seasoned meditator who, in recognizing the emotion of each of the Five Wisdom Energies of the Buddha families, is able to see how these essential qualities are evident in specific works of great female artists ranging from Artemisia Gentileschi to Marilyn Minter. It is an inspired book that opens both the mind and the heart, filled with enough art history, poetry, and philosophy to delight the intellect, and enough laugh-out-loud lines to instigate sudden enlightenment. A true treasure map for Buddhist art lovers, or a fabulous introduction to both art and Buddhism for the curious. It is a delightful, impressive accomplishment.

CINTRA WILSON, AUTHOR OF *FEAR AND CLOTHING: UNBUCKLING AMERICAN FASHION*

If, like me, you agree with John Ruskin's assertion that "all that is good in art is the expression of one soul talking to another," this book will facilitate conversations that once seemed beyond your grasp. *Look* led me to cast aside ideas about how making or absorbing art "should" feel and welcome its more visceral effects. By uncovering links between Buddhist practices and creative processes, Kevin Townley demystifies that daunting link between art and spirituality while leaving room for the divine. By weaving artists' histories with his own, he makes the reader feel comfortable drawing connections between heady concepts and personal experience. Through a unique blend of compassion and curiosity, Kevin Townley has given readers a more intimate, spiritually minded *Ways of Seeing*.

Everywhere we look, we see the harmful effects of human confusion on the world's ecologies. Townley explores the architecture of Buddhist mandala practice through the lens of 26 artists and unequivocally reveals that the solution to our deleterious confusion lies in unflinching intimacy with our own inner mandala. He helps us look, shows us what to see, and inspires our own creative potential through the obstacles, insights, and creative workarounds of his chosen artists. This book has much to teach us about the nature of mind and how it actually affects the physical world.

This book is beautiful and illuminating, sure to make you laugh and feel all kinds of feelings. Townley makes art and Buddhism sing out at us from the pages, making it impossible not to share his wonder at and appreciation of the pieces he looks at, again and again.

This book will change you. It's a rare feat, but with generosity, wit, and wisdom, Townley shifts your perspective so that when you look, you can actually see clearly. I cannot emphasize enough the profound effect this book has had on me. If you feel lost, confused, caught in the self-help craze, do yourself a favor and read this book, chock-full of ancient wisdom that will enhance your life and awaken your imagination.

Kevin Townley's new book is beautiful, smart, funny, provocative, and disturbing in the best possible ways, just like Kevin himself. I love the way Kevin writes so much, he could probably write cereal box copy and I'd still be riveted, but

I'm glad he chose to write about art and Buddhism instead. If you have interest in either subject, you'd be a fool not to read this book. And if you have interest in both subjects and still don't read it, then color me enraged even though the fact that I just said that is proof enough I have many miles to go on my own spiritual journey.

DAVE HILL, COMEDIAN AND AUTHOR OF *DAVE HILL DOESN'T LIVE HERE ANYMORE*

Look, Look, Look, Look, Look Again is a kaleidoscope of a read: endlessly fascinating, deftly recursive, and wickedly funny. Weaving together Buddhist philosophy and art history, Kevin Townley achieves a real high-wire feat here. And since the idea of self is an illusion, I'll go ahead and congratulate all of us.

APARNA NANCHERLA, COMEDIAN

From the inside scoop on a delicious portrait of Madame du Barry to a quick and incisive take on contemporary multimedia shaman Laurie Anderson, these explorations of the nature of creativity will delight anyone with an interest in the merging point of art, psychology, and buddhadharma. I particularly liked the ease and adventure of bopping around from artist to artist and Buddha family to Buddha family. It is a fine journey. Kevin's take on various artists, their work, and Buddha family influences, and his encouragement to go deep with our own interpretations is a spot-on challenge. There is delight in the invitation to take what we're learning and immediately apply it and look, look, look, look, look again. There's no question that when finished I found myself thinking that Kevin would be a delightful companion with whom to wander the halls of the Met. But if that's not possible, then having this book in your back pocket might be the next best thing.

GAYLE HANSON, BUDDHIST TEACHER AND ARTIST

An excellent work bringing out a deeper understanding of the Five Buddha families. Kevin Townley sets up an awareness dynamic that allows you to actually enter into the energies. The images he evokes help us proceed on a journey into the underbrush of our own society and from the underbrush right into the museums, into the galleries, into artistic production of artists...and right into *our* lives. These are brilliant commentaries on the artwork and artists. Needless to say, I learned a lot. Very entertaining, funny, and fantastically good.

SOKUZAN, ABBOT, SOKUKOJI BUDDHIST MONASTERY

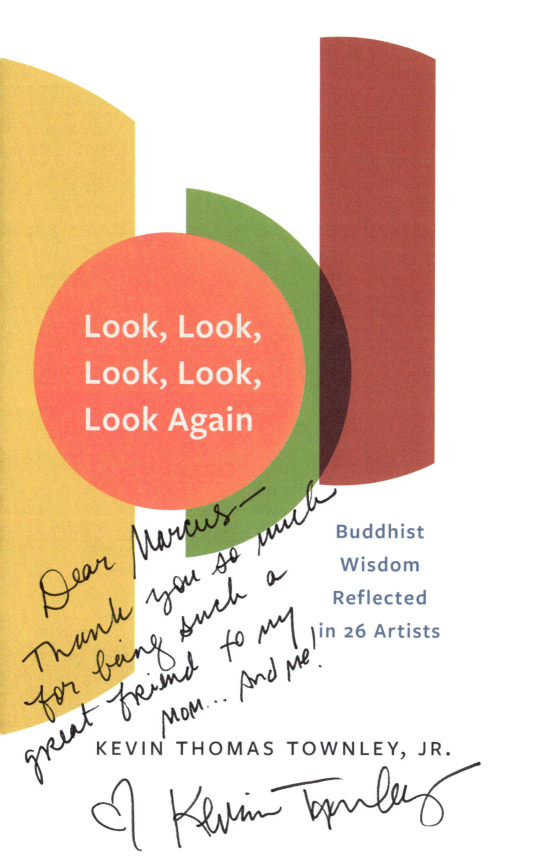

Look, Look, Look, Look, Look Again

Buddhist Wisdom Reflected in 26 Artists

Dear Marcus—
Thank you so much
for being such a
great friend to my
mom... And me!

KEVIN THOMAS TOWNLEY, JR.

♡ Kevin Townley

Lionheart Press, Somerville, MA, USA
lionheartpress.net

Library of Congress Control Number: 2021924103

ISBN 978-1-7369439-0-8 (paperback)
ISBN 978-1-7322776-9-4 (e-book)

Cover images by Nuala Clarke, Elisabeth Louise Vigée Le Brun, Hilma af Klint,
Sophie Taeuber-Arp, and Laura Wheeler Waring
Excerpts of interview, "Laurie Anderson and Mohammed el Gharani: Habeas Corpus"
reprinted with permission from The Laura Flanders Show.
Cover and text design by Jazmin Welch (fleck creative studio)

Look at your life. Look at the ways in which you define who you are and what you're capable of achieving. Look at your goals. Look at the pressures applied by the people around you and the culture in which you were raised. Look again. And again. Keep looking until you realize, within your own experience, that you're so much more than who you believe you are. Keep looking until you discover the wondrous heart, the marvelous mind, that is the very basis of your being.

TSOKNYI RINPOCHE

If the doors of perception were cleansed, everything would appear to man as it is—infinite.

WILLIAM BLAKE

She made the world her book, took a piece of coal and marked a blank white wall.

DANIELLE DUTTON, *MARGARET THE FIRST*

The eye of man hath not heard, the ear of man hath not seen, man's hand is not able to taste, his tongue to conceive, nor his heart to report what my dream was.

WILLIAM SHAKESPEARE, *A MIDSUMMER NIGHT'S DREAM*

Contents

Padma

Karma

For Sokuzan, a true teacher.

In memory of Francis Mirai Nishida, a true artist.

TRÉ GALLERY, *FRANCIS AND ANA*, 2009

Dear Reader,

I ask that you indulge a brief word regarding the themes and content of this book.

As you will discover, I have chosen to write about female artists from various time periods, styles, and backgrounds. While life is difficult for everyone, I don't think I'm being controversial in saying that, historically, women have had a harder time of it than men, who, in large part, have gone out of their way to subjugate them.

The Five Wisdom Energies (or Buddhist mandala teachings) explored in this book contain both shadow and light. For women artists, as human artists, no subject matter is off-limits, and contrary to sexist clichés, they have not relegated themselves to quilt-making and painting portraits of babies (though they have done both splendidly). This book examines an array of artwork created by women inspired by the spectrum of human experience—from nature, beauty, and sexuality, to imprisonment, rape, and murder. Dark subject matter indeed. In quite a few of the essays I also explore the lives of these artists as a means of better understanding their work. Some of their biographical details are quite distressing.

I have done my best to approach this material with frankness and honesty, but without being egregious. I, too, am sensitive to how intense human suffering can be. That being said, the following artists' work contain particularly challenging, even devastating, topics: Howardena Pindell, Niki de Saint Phalle, Laurie Anderson, and Artemisia Gentilischi. The book can accommodate hopping around—after all, the sacred mandala and its Five Wisdom Energies are not linear.

Thank you so much for taking the time to read this book and for accompanying me on this fascinating journey.

Your friend,
Kevin

Sawblade Sunrise

Mira Dancy

2019 | COURTESY OF THE ARTIST

Even an Abstract Has Eyes

remember the day I fell in love with art. I was in preschool and our minders introduced us to the great masters. They held up reproductions of paintings and explained that people from long ago had made these pictures to express something about themselves and the world in which they lived. Somehow these pictures had survived for me to look at. A taste of art was also a taste of immortality. The only image I distinctly remember was Rembrandt's *Self-Portrait* of 1660. It wasn't that I liked the picture, it was that it seemed to be looking at me as much as I was looking at it.

An interest in art was not something anyone particularly valued in Boulder, Colorado, where I grew up. This is partly why I moved to New York City after graduating high school. I was too terrified to apply to college, so I made what seemed the simpler choice at the time: just pack up and move to New York City at seventeen. I never did end up engaging in higher education, at least not on its terms.

In the big city I quickly realized that being able to look at art and articulate an opinion about what one saw was a status symbol. Glamorous people were magnetized by art galleries, not necessarily lured by the objects they displayed but because of the money, privilege, and power that the art objects were portals to. So to be able to have even a superficial insight about, say, Cindy Sherman or Jean-Michel Basquiat was unexpectedly cool.

At nineteen, I learned that art could be more than a parlor trick. My roommate at the time, a German expat named Cóline, worked at DK Publishing. DK specializes in large-format art books and, one day, Cóline gifted me one being released in conjunction with Sister Wendy Beckett's television docu-series, *The Story of Painting*. It was through Sister Wendy's off-kilter insights into great masterpieces that I understood how art went beyond money and aesthetics. Fundamentally, it is an expression of what it means to be a human being. I realized how, by taking time to really look at the work of another person, I could also learn something about myself.

A decade and a half later, I attended a workshop called "Opening the Eye-Mind," led by a Zen monk named Kyoun Sokuzan. I was already versed in meditation and had grown into a serious practitioner, but the idea that one could directly connect art with meditation had never occurred to me. Sokuzan was a student of both Chögyam Trungpa Rinpoche and Kobun Chino Roshi. He was also a graduate of the Art Institute of Chicago. The workshop took place at the Metropolitan Museum of Art, where Sokuzan sat us down in front of some of the world's creative masterworks. While many spiritual practices engage the breath or a mantra to stabilize the mind, here we used the paintings of Robert Motherwell and Susan Rothenberg as the objects of our meditation.

A 2001 study concluded that museum visitors spend an average of seventeen seconds looking at an artwork.[1] Sokuzan asked us to look at a painting for fifteen to twenty minutes at a go. In doing so, he was giving us techniques with which to strengthen our awareness and realize that, despite vision's sensory primacy in humans, we rarely see what we're looking at. His instruction was for us to rest our eyes on some central shape or color on the canvas. Keeping our eyes anchored in place, we would then be directed to move our visual *awareness* around the canvas (blinking allowed). He prompted us to move that awareness to all of the blue areas on the canvas, then to all of the yellows, or to anything triangular. We might then be prompted to move our awareness to just outside the frame of the canvas, or to the back of our own necks, all the while never moving our eyes themselves.

As frustrating (and surprisingly exhausting) as this exercise was, it was also astonishing. Somehow, the strange combination of a sustained, fixed gaze in counterpoint to the playful engagement of awareness had the effect of dislodging self-centeredness from the visual sense faculty. In spending so much time with the artwork, the ego-mind had basically thrown its hands up in bored exasperation and retired to the porch swing for a snooze. We had traveled beyond concerns of personal preference and aesthetics, out past the carnival grounds, and into an open visual field. There, colors and shapes came alive, conversing and vibrating and rearranging themselves. The landscape we were entering was the mind-state of the artist at the time of the work's creation. The energy that the artist was (perhaps unwittingly) a conduit for was still present in the work itself, and by paying the toll of time and attention, I was included in it. I flashed on my childhood reaction to Rembrandt's *Self-Portrait*. I had assumed it was his penetrating gaze that made me feel like he was staring back at me, but now I saw that this can be true of all art. Even an abstract has eyes.

By applying meditation techniques to art appreciation, the Opening the Eye-Mind practice helped to strengthen my overall awareness, and further allowed me to realize the non-conceptual nature of the visual sense. I also realized this insight could be applied the other way around: the enthusiasm I have for looking at art could be directed toward examining the contents of my mind during meditation. Rather than seeing my moods and discursive diatribes as problems to solve, I could regard them as a touring exhibition, curated by someone with very eclectic—and very strange—tastes.

After falling in love with art, I obviously developed an abiding soft spot for Tortured Artists. You know, the poor individuals for whom the protective membrane that buffers the nervous system from the beauty and abrasions of life is frustratingly, gloriously absent. They appear saturated by the vibrancy of the world, causing them to overflow into poetry, painting, needlepoint— pursuits which are largely met with derision by a callous, unsophisticated public. This then leads to any number of tragic ends, from suicide (Sylvia Plath) to customs inspector (Herman Melville). We've all heard stories like that before.

Aside from devoting my own free time to feeling misunderstood and a strong predilection for emotional aggrandizement, what is most beguiling to me about this trope is the notion that the very energy which, in one iteration can lead to creation, in another form can lead to self-destruction. How can the same energy lead to such drastically different results even in the same person?

For many artists, what's most torturous is to begin, meeting space without any idea of what will happen next. We yearn to honor the creative impulse by expressing ourselves, and yet many of us, when met with the imagined edge of our own inner abyss, slink backward, and, adding insult to injury, feel ashamed by our cringing. We cannot bear the intimacy of our own brilliant minds, and so we look away. Looking away can show up in behaviors as myriad as diverting our creative energy into gossip, house cleaning, manicures, masturbation, and volunteer work. Mythologists might grandly refer to this as "the refusal of the call," but it is also a completely understandable response to meeting the charnel ground of one's psyche. There are instances when approaching a blank page or canvas feels more like visiting a crime scene, where a daub of VapoRub under the nose would be more appropriate than a daub of paint on the canvas.

In his brilliant book *From Where You Dream*, Robert Olen Butler describes the creative process as entering one's White Hot Center. This radioactive unconscious realm feels like hell, because, for most of us, it *is* hell. Like scaffolding erected around treacherous architecture, our entire personalities are deliberately crafted to avoid descending into the underworld of missed opportunities, traumas, and gears from obsolete machinery. And yet this is precisely what we must do, whether we are on the creative or the spiritual path (and I would hazard to say they are the same thing). By keeping that portal open through constant visitation, we may not only find our endurance for entering that zone strengthened but also come to be quite adept at navigating its sinkholes and topiary. But you don't get to choose what you discover.

The Artists
Included Herein

You may wonder how I came to select the artists I have included here. In some cases, I chose artists whose work has affected me strongly or whose art-making practices I have found inspiring. I relished the opportunity to find out what exactly I loved about them through the process of writing. Other artists I discovered in the process of writing the book. For example, in the case of Tayeba Begum Lipi, I knew I wanted to include a work that was capable of slicing and dicing in order to evoke Vajra energy. In other cases, some artworks just kind of appeared on their own.

My intention going into the project was to include works that were diverse in style, period, and culture, while staying within a budget (I won't bore you with the esoterica of licensing fees). The depressing reality is that, given the oppressive nature of colonial capitalism, most artists whose work is in the public domain are white, and most of the non-white artists who managed to break through are hugely famous and their usage fees thus (rightfully) prohibitive. I also set myself the challenge to use only female artists, which further narrowed the playing field. In the case of living artists, I reached out to many directly or through their galleries; some graciously agreed to have their work included, while others graciously declined, and many others never replied. So in the end I ended up where I ended up, with a largely choiceless collection of brilliant artists.

The images in this book are ones that I felt were good emissaries of these five energies. They may or may not resonate for you—maybe an image I use to evoke Ratna energy will seem more evocative of Padma to you. That's good! There are no right or wrong answers in this exploration, no conclusions to come to. The images are meant to jog your own contemplation, not to be doctrinal. It is my hope that, looking deeply at these images and the profound human energies they contain, we will not only be better able to intuit how these energies show up in our lives, but also feel encouraged to look at art in new ways. Because one thing art and the Dharma have in common is that there are times when we think we "get it" and walk away feeling some solace (if not a little pleased with ourselves), but other times we feel completely stymied, even to the point of directing our frustration at its apparent cause, whether that's a painting by Helen Frankenthaler or the Thirty Verses of Vasubandhu. Anything not immediately "gettable" is banished to the realm of elitism. In a culture that celebrates rugged John Wayne-esque self-reliance, we tend to equate the experience of Not Knowing with being talked down to, feeling stupid, or worse, that our lives are in danger. And so we reject spirituality and art, accusing them of causing our feelings of inadequacy when, in reality, the feeling of uncertainty always was and always will be there. Macho posturing is itself a pitiable grab at girding oneself against vulnerability, which ironically is our greatest strength. We can forget that even John Wayne himself (b. Marion Morrison, 1907–1979) was a work of creative expression by a tortured artist.

Mandala

Mandala of Vairochana Buddha

CENTRAL TIBET, CA. 1300–1399

Cryptographer and squid enthusiast Bruce Schneier once said, "If you think technology can solve your security problems, then you don't understand the problems and you don't understand the technology." This sentiment applies to the spiritual path as well: If you think getting rid of negativity is going to solve your problems, then you don't understand your problems and you don't understand negativity. One of the distinguishing features of Tibetan Buddhism is this: IT IS PRECISELY THE THING YOU WANT TO GET RID OF THAT YOU REQUIRE IN ORDER TO BE FREE. Sorry for shouting, but negativity and positivity are not two separate things. They are, instead, contrasting experiences of a natural vitality that gets warped relative to the degree of our own personal fixation.

My first direct exposure to Buddhism was in 1999, when my father brought me to a fundraiser in Boston where a group of Tibetan monks presented an evening of sacred dance called *Cham*. The Cham dancers, wearing ornate brocade robes, moved in low elliptical twirls, accompanied by rumbling trumpets, cymbals, and drums. They wore startling masks portraying three-eyed demons, deer, and other spirits, which seemed more appropriate for a heavy metal concert than a religious function. To a young actor with a macabre sensibility, it was enormously appealing. Afterwards, we joined a roomful of maroon-robed monks to receive a practice transmission from His Holiness Drikung Kyabgön Chetsang Rinpoche. Although he spoke entirely in Tibetan, some seed lodged in my mind. Years later a friend gave me a book to read by the American Buddhist nun, Pema Chödrön. I remember that one of the chapters was called, "Hopelessness and Death." These, it turned out, were meant to be positive qualities on the spiritual path, and I remembered laughing out loud—both because it seemed such a brazen thing to say and because I knew it to be true. Still, what the heck kind of spiritual path would advocate such a crazy notion?

I discovered that Pema Chödrön was connected with the same lineage of Buddhism as the monks I saw in Boston. To a lifelong fan of mystery novels, this seemed a thread worth following. I was led from Pema Chödrön to her teacher, Chögyam Trungpa, and eventually to my teacher, Sokuzan. The wisdom offered to me was access to my own mind through the simple yet profound meditation practices *shikantaza* and *shamatha-vipashyana*. To whatever degree I have experienced personal transformation in my life or am able to impart any insight in this book, it is directly related to the sitting practice of meditation and not just a theoretical pursuit of Buddhism's many intellectual riches.

Chögyam Trungpa (1939–1987) was a refugee from Tibet after the Chinese invasion of 1959 and is largely responsible for reframing ancient Buddhist wisdom for a contemporary Western audience. He is a controversial figure because, in addition to being a meditation master, he also drank heavily, used drugs, and had sex with many of his students. When I first heard of his behavior, I was a little surprised because, like, if you're a spiritual leader, shouldn't you *not* be doing all of the worldly things my Irish Catholic grandma said would send you to hell? Well, not exactly.

There is an ancient Indian tradition of the *mahasiddha* ("great achiever" in Sanskrit), who is basically a person who managed to realize their enlightened nature in the course of their everyday life. Mahasiddhas were colorful individuals whose eyebrow-raising lifestyles included, but were not limited to, alcohol abuse, prostitution, murder, and ferryboat operations. As a heavy drinker myself at the time, I found all of this highly encouraging—not because I needed to have my personal addiction condoned by long-dead Indian eccentrics, but because the stories of the mahasiddhas confirmed that my drinking habits were not fundamentally at odds with my spiritual pursuits. So however people try to justify or decry Chögyam Trungpa's behavior—he undeniably harmed people and quite literally saved the lives of others—I felt the freedom to explore the veracity of his teachings for myself and to incorporate what was nourishing to me and set aside what was not.

Weirdly, the upshot of this was that I got sober, thanks to the teachings of a person who drank himself to death. There is some poetry in that, and more than anything else, it seems to me that Chögyam Trungpa was an artist. After all, he emphasized the arts as practice modalities with his students: calligraphy, photography, flower arranging. I mention all of this not to convince you of anything—for some, the very mention of his name is a non-starter, which I totally respect (this book is likely fully refundable)—but in the Buddhist tradition it is important to honor the lineage of the teachings, which are said to be offered from warm hand to warm hand down through the ages.

Tibetan Buddhism has *a lot* to say about the vibrant energies we humans encounter. These energies are visually represented in the sacred image of the mandala. Mandala is a Sanskrit word meaning, simply, "circle." Mandalas are a symbol of all states of being, meant to encapsulate all energies existent in the universe. They function a bit like sacred blueprints. The structures they suggest could be any of a wide array of assemblages—from a temple, to a community, to our own body, to the unabridged cosmos. Despite its contemporary association with "mindfulness" coloring books, the mandala is a very ancient form, rich and complex.

I once made a pilgrimage to the American Museum of Natural History, in New York, where a group of Tibetan monks were building a gigantic sand mandala. A platform had been erected around their workspace where we spectators could gather and observe their progress as in an old surgical theater. The level of detail they were able to achieve through such a finicky medium as sand was amazing. More amazing still was when, after weeks of exacting work, the monks destroyed the mandala. The gasps from the crowd seemed to delight them and they giggled as they swept away any evidence that they had been there at all. *What an interesting psychological insight about impermanence and joy!* I remember thinking, or something along those lines. Contemporary Buddhist studies attract many psychotherapists who find in the Dharma resonant psychological metaphors. I recall an early exchange I had with a more seasoned practitioner in my Buddhist community—we had just heard a talk on the Six Realms, a classical teaching that describes the possible places one might be reborn—and I said, "Oh, I get it! The Six Realms are like psychological states! So like when you're consumed by anger, you're in the Hell Realm, and when you're overrun by craving, you're in the Hungry

Ghost Realm." My companion looked at me wryly and said, "Try telling that to a Tibetan. For them those realms are as real as the room we're standing in."

Not long thereafter, I attended another workshop (I was going through a workshop phase), an introduction to the Five Wisdom Energies (the energies that manifest within the mandala) led by Judy Lief, a close student of Chögyam Trungpa and one of the original Western recipients of the teachings from the Tibetan Buddhist point of view. We were handed a printout of a mandala, a shape I was by now quite familiar with: a circle divided into four quadrants with a smaller circle at its hub. We were informed that while this was a sacred shape, it was also completely ordinary. We were invited to consider it a map of who and where we already were, a light reference point to orient us as we engaged with meditation practices and movement exercises that would bring the mandala alive in us. I realized that up to that point I'd managed to hover over the Dharma like a clown perched on a carnival dunk tank. But the teachings Judy Lief offered us had the effect of a knuckleball pitched right at the bullseye, sending this clown splashing into the heart of the mandala. Thereafter I couldn't unsee how the energy I experience as emotion also threads through music, my wardrobe, architecture, heated conversations, and the colors of the weird decorative cabbages planted along the sidewalks of New York (themselves a mandala). Mandala is the through line of the universe, although the narrator is unreliable.

I received the Buddha family teachings herein presented from Judy Lief, Sokuzan, and Lama Tsultrim Allione, all of whom received them from Chögyam Trungpa, who received them from his teachers, and so on. While it is up to you to determine whether any of this is true, I cannot take credit for making up any of it.

I find the mandala teachings particularly helpful because not only do they articulate the nondual nature of positivity and negativity, they also translate what could be very heady material into color, texture, emotion—the language of art. If you have even lightly scratched the surface of Buddhist teachings, you've likely encountered the eye-crossing array of lists that lie in wait for the practitioner: the Four Noble Truths, the Six Paramitas, the Eightfold Path, the Ten Bhumis, the Fifty-Nine Lojong Slogans of Atiśa. The possibility of getting sucked into analytical sinkholes in pursuit of the Dharma is very real. But the beauty of the language of art is that it helps us to leap from a purely intellectual understanding of the Dharma and back into our senses. As Robert Olen Butler points out, an artist may have a lot of conceptual underpinnings in their work, but the medium itself naturally cuts through the falderal because clay, sound, movement, paint are all sensual media and therefore inherently non-conceptual (the exception to this is writing, whose medium *is* conceptual, but that's another kettle of fish).

In broad terms, some traditional Himalayan mandala paintings are depictions of five cardinal energies known colloquially as the Five Buddha Families. Each Buddha family represents a wisdom energy, which corresponds to an element, direction, color, season, and so on. These energies also describe the way in which our difficult emotions can be transformed into wisdom—or perhaps more accurately, already *are* wisdom. While all living things do their best to get less of what they don't want and more of what they do, we in the West mostly think that to be happy, we have to get rid of negativity to "make room" for abundance and positivity and non-toxic brand ambassadorships or whatever.

Most people who embark upon a spiritual path don't do so because they're feeling fabulous. If you're *not* suffering (or aren't acutely aware of your suffering), why try to get out of it? The Hindu mystic Sri Ramakrishna went so far as to advise us, "Do not seek illumination unless you seek it as a man whose hair is on fire seeks a pond." The implication being that if you don't want to be given the bum's rush out of your comfort zone, then it is better not to start. Don't go looking for trouble. But sometimes, of course, trouble finds us in the form of heartache, stress, ambivalence, or loss, and we yearn for some means of excising the pain.

As with a smoke alarm, the unpleasant shriek of emotion alerts us to the fact that something is awry, enabling us, we hope, to make our way in a swift and orderly fashion to the emergency exit. The very energy of the trouble is what alerts us to the need for a new way of being. Fire is not something you want in your hair but isn't bad in and of itself. Fire can be experienced positively or negatively, depending on the context. It is merely a neutral energy. In Ramakrishna's simile, it is actually the fire itself that is catalyzing the search for the pond. The negative experience of the transcendent energy of fire is precisely what drives us choicelessly onto the path of awakenment. When we pay heed to the message of negativity in our lives, it not only has the opportunity to become the ambassador for wakefulness, it *is* awake.

The Five Buddha Families symbolize the five ways of looking at and understanding the strengths and difficulties in our lives. They describe a continuum of five painful emotions and their attendant wisdoms. At the center of the mandala, the hub of the wheel, is the first Buddha family, conveniently known as...the Buddha family. Appropriately, the classical image that symbolizes this family is the eight-spoked Dharma Wheel, which represents the teachings set into motion by the historical Buddha himself, Siddhartha Gautama. The color of the Buddha family is white; it represents open space, and, similarly, its corresponding wisdom is called "all-encompassing space." However, spaciousness has a way of devolving into spaciness, and in its confused state Buddha family energy manifests as "ignorance." You could say that ignorance is the root cause of all of our problems. From the get-go we are off on the wrong foot, thinking that we are somehow separate, independent individuals who are free to go where we want and do what we choose. No matter how convincing this drama may be, it is demonstrably false. Unfortunately, as is the case with pernicious misperceptions, rather than humbly reassessing how we got ourselves into this pickle in the first place, we tend to double down, even going so far as to finagle an identity out of our confusion.

The other four Buddha Families describe the various tactics we employ to maintain the illusion of separateness, and they also provide a map back to sanity. They are correlated with cardinal directions to further reinforce the map-like nature of the depictions.

The Vajra family resides in the east, its color is blue, and its element is water. Vajra's emotion is anger. It can only take so much incompetence, ugliness, and waste before it blows its stack. When people willfully ignore the itinerary, Vajra is not above whacking someone. Anger can be treacherous, but when we try to cast it out completely, we discard along with it "mirror-like wisdom." I recently watched a clip of Dr. Martin Luther King, Jr., giving a speech with the sound off. If I hadn't heard the speech before, I might have assumed, given King's fiery demeanor, that he was angry. And I'm sure that on some level he was, but whatever relative rage he felt wasn't suppressed; it was transmuted into the impassioned words he uttered with that thundering voice. That cutting quality of anger, minus hatred, is called compassion.

Ratna lives in the south. Its color is a rich, golden yellow, and its element is earth. There used to be a kitschy gift shop in Manhattan's East Village called Too Much Is Not Enough, which perfectly sums up Ratna energy. The Ratna family is about excess and amassing bling to prove what a hotshot you are. Aside from its tendency toward hoarding, in its confused state, this energy shows up as pride and arrogance. Because we fundamentally think we're pieces of shit, we start swanning about, giving orders, and engaging others in hydraulic relationships. However, Ratna's wisdom energy is called "equanimity": on some deep level, we know that, no matter what our circumstances, we have enough. Through a dedicated awareness practice, we may begin to see that we have access to an inner richness at all times. But in the meantime we have personalities like RuPaul to look up to: a fabulous, glimmering drag queen who has fortified her wealth through fracking. Doesn't get more Ratna than that.

To the west, we find Padma, the red fire lotus. This energy is all about seduction. Unlike Ratna, which is occasionally sated as it sleeps off a binge, Padma is always aching, always striving for what's just over the horizon. This is the American Dream, and it is killing us. While its confused aspect is called "craving," its wisdom energy is called "discriminating awareness." In other words, all of the *Play Misty for Me* stalker energy that knows the placement of each hair follicle on the object of desire can actually apply that discerning eye to compassionate ends. Instead of seducing everyone into your world view, you might use your powers of assessment to bring Nomi and Cristal together on the Doggie Chow campaign, or feng shui your home.

Lastly, the Karma family in the north. Karma is the element of air, and its color is green. Green with envy, as this is the energy of competition and jealousy. It is always compare-and-despair time for the Karma family person. You've always been more talented than everyone else, but somehow you've been left behind on the ladder of success and everyone else is laughing at you from their hot tub in Malibu! But you'll show them! You dig down deep and come up with a highly personal scripted series to pitch to NBC, only to be informed that they *just* purchased a show *just* like it...from your ex-wife! And so on and so forth. The fever of competition is cooled by Karma's enlightened energy: "all-accomplishing wisdom." In other words, competition is a circular fantasy, and when we are truly awake there is nowhere else to be, nothing else to do. Everything is already accomplished.

The tradition also describes four skillful actions one might employ in any given situation. Known as the Four Karmas, they are pacifying (Vajra), which allows us to step back, cooling the flames of anger; enriching (Ratna), where we dive into a situation, invigorating it with our presence; magnetizing (Padma), which connects disparate elements; and destroying (Karma), which wipes the slate clean for a fresh start.

While these teachings first appeared in the late eighth century, in the *Guhyasamāja Tantra*, the wisdom they describe is not bound by history or culture. As sacred circles have appeared throughout human history, the mandala can't be said to have been invented so much as discovered, or maybe remembered. That said, the tradition from which I am drawing is the Vajrayana or Tibetan Buddhist one. When you walk into New York's Rubin Museum of Art, you will be overwhelmed by the beauty of the paintings and sculptures, many of which depict the Five Buddha Families. However, unless you happen to be well versed in the symbology of medieval Tibet, the message of these beautiful works can remain remote. Or you might assume, given their provenance, that whatever they're describing was specific and exclusive to the time and place from which they came. This got me wondering if, given that these wisdom energies are meant to be timeless and elemental, it might not also be possible to look at a Dutch still-life or an Abstract Expressionist painting as a spiritual metaphor. Can art from different periods, cultures, and genres help us to intuit the inner truth of these spiritual teachings? The answer, I would hazard to say, is yes.

The teachings on the Five Buddha Families provide an access point to these inquiries. By learning to recognize how these energies appear as seasons, shapes, colors, and the elements, I have been better able not only to recognize how they show up in my body and mind, but also to regard my emotions with the same dispassionate respect I have for a mountain or a particularly striking shade of purple. In doing so, I find I am suddenly afforded an enormous amount of mental space in which I can rest or react, based on awareness rather than compulsion. This isn't to say that emotions won't still show up and hurt like hell or titillate me, but when I can hold my thoughts and feelings as elemental building blocks of the universe, I tend not to take them so personally. I mean, I'm sure the furnace of a star nursery isn't a particularly pleasant environment to be in, but I wouldn't try to improve it. And yet we arrogantly treat ourselves in this manner all the time, imbuing what amounts to an inner electromagnetic field or meteorological front with a permanent identity that can win or lose, based on getting more of this and less of that. By placing emotion in the non-conceptual realm of texture and color (the language of art), the Buddha families help us to see that, by virtue of their transitory nature, thoughts and feelings not only aren't "who we are," but—and more to the point—there isn't actually a solid person who is experiencing them.

Although the mandala teachings were not intended to be the equivalent of a ninth-century personality quiz, the Five Buddha Families are a helpful lens through which we might understand our own personal tendencies a little better. Like astrology or the Enneagram, the Buddha Families elevate seemingly personal hang-ups into the realm of the archetypal. This invites us to examine our feelings and behaviors as classic human attempts to navigate the uncertainty of life, rather than browbeating and pathologizing ourselves. As you read the essays in this book, you may recognize some of your own personal tendencies described as characteristics of a particular Buddha family. You may identify with more than one family. For example, some people might manifest strongly as a Padma person, while someone else might be more Buddha/Karma. Or you might notice that you exhibit the wisdom of, say, the Vajra family, but when the going gets tough your "exit energy" might be in the style of the Ratna family. Again, these Five Wisdom Energies are meant to be taken not as yet another way to clamp down on a solid identity, but instead as a means of seeing that the components of that apparent identity are dynamic and always in play. In this way, the mandala could be considered an ancient technology, not in the irritating #lifehack sort of way but as a means of applying insight and knowledge to our baseline experiences. It thereby provides us with a fresh vantage point and more breathing room in our lives. The mandala invites us to look and look again.

One of my all-time idols is someone who probably doesn't immediately jump to most people's minds when discussing the Dharma. Nevertheless, the great media mystic and philosopher Marshall McLuhan (1911–1980) has a lot to offer regarding the spiritual ramifications of art and technology. McLuhan was a Canadian literature professor who, early in his career, realized that he wasn't communicating with his students. So he threw out his lesson plan in favor of examining the advertisements that were all around them, as though they were (and he argued that they *were*) modern-day myths. Marketing firms attempt to reduce human psychology to its unexamined base elements in order to reconstitute them as tantalizing ad images that encourage sales. Through deconstructing the advertisement and its effect on us, McLuhan said that we would not only learn about the unconscious values of our society but also learn to be one step ahead of the marketing manipulators. If we understand how the machine works, we can turn it off. Today, he is mostly remembered for the aphorism "the medium is the message," which suggests that we shouldn't obsess over content so much as the medium by which that content is conveyed to us. The psychological and physiological effects of learning about a devastating mudslide, say, are completely different if you read about it in print, hear it on the radio, or watch it on television. By emphasizing the *effect* of the medium rather than the content, McLuhan was encouraging an intuitive, embodied contemplation of our plugged-in, simultaneous, electric world.

The Buddha Families, similarly, don't moralize about positive and negative emotions, but rather ask us to familiarize ourselves with the somatic effects of the experience, to take another look, and then to look again. McLuhan also encouraged this approach toward the myriad electric media in our lives. He even formalized a means by which we could take a fresh look at our technology, a method he called "the Tetrad," which is also a mandala and which echoes the Four Karmas. McLuhan posited that all technology has four simultaneous properties: they "extend" or enhance some physical part of the body or psyche; they "obsolesce" an old way of doing things; they "retrieve" something from our past; and, when pushed to their extreme, all technologies "reverse" on themselves and do the opposite of what they were intended to do. The Tetrad is an invitation to look at the environment created by our gadgets with some curiosity and openness. "There is absolutely no inevitability as long as there is a willingness to contemplate what is happening," McLuhan said.[2] That's as good a summary of the Buddhist path as any.

More than anything, what I hope you take away from this book is a half-step toward the realization that negativity is not a problem or something to vanquish. Again, the thing we think we need to get rid of is the very thing we need to wake up. You might also get a glimpse of how these five energies show up in your life, and perhaps even some creative freedom in working with them. If you're an art person, I hope this will inspire you to look at your favorite works with fresh eyes—and if you're not an art person, I hope, if not to convert you, at least to instill in you a sense of permission to look, receive, and share in the creative expression of your fellow human beings. If you have any experience with the sitting practice of meditation, then you're already well trained to look at art. As Sister Wendy said, "All you need to appreciate art is time and a place to sit."

Buddha

White. A blank page or canvas. His favorite. So many possibilities...

JAMES LAPINE, *SUNDAY IN THE PARK WITH GEORGE*

Ignorance is like a delicate exotic fruit; touch it and the bloom is gone.

OSCAR WILDE, *THE IMPORTANCE OF BEING EARNEST*

Before anything there is space.

A blank canvas.

An open dimension in which maybe anything can happen. At times, we experience this vast expanse of possibility as a nurturing, amniotic sea. At other times, it feels more like walking into a fiberglass whitewash—disorienting and abrasive.

Buddha energy is Peter Cushing in *The Abominable Snowman*, high in the Himalayas, out of his depth and on unfamiliar ground, uncertain of what form will emerge from the veil of the blizzard. Friend or fiend? Monster or monad? Will he come face-to-face with the Yeti or with his own mind?

Settled, our experience of space shimmers like snow-blanketed hills. Light dances off the ice. Unable to prioritize any one color, the feeble human eye is overwhelmed with the spectrum; what seems to be an absence of color is actually the inclusion of all color to brilliant, blinding effect.

Buddha energy sits at the center of the mandala like a crystal. When it is activated by light, it refracts into the rainbow of the other four energies. It is the white static on the baby monitor that paranormalists use, attempting to contact "the other side." It's the few seconds in the darkroom after slipping the photo paper into the developer, before the image emerges.

In the delicate moment when artists endeavor to begin their work, they meet this energy. Like Igor atop Frankenstein's castle with his kites, we invite lightning to strike, hoping it will bring our creatures to life. The question is whether we can endure this ozone-charged space long enough to receive the spark, or if we'll bolt, spooked by the animating gap. It is only in space that form arises.

The creative act tests our stomach for the vulnerability we feel in spaciousness. Can we truly own up to our human desire to be intimately known?

For some of us, this situation is so fraught that, rather than soaring on the warm updraft of Not Knowing, we opt instead to crash down through space, leaden with our ultimatums, protocols, and assumptions. We often make demands of the creative process, proceeding as if it were an intellectual gambit. Fear of space turns it into concrete; all-encompassing space becomes ignorance. The artist's challenge is precisely the same as the meditator's: to train in resting with restlessness.

In its unblemished state, Buddha energy is called "all-encompassing space." Space doesn't move, so it doesn't miss much and doesn't mind anything. In Tibetan it is called *Sangye Namparnanzad*, or "perfect knowledge of all things as they manifest." Without identifying as the perceiver, perception is merely a receiver. With the attitude of the consummate hostess, anything that arises in this directionless gaze is welcome and accommodated just as it is, no agenda, no preference. One could imagine a transcendental Donna Reed passing cosmic canapés around, whether it be to Sidney Poitier, Marlon Brando, or Charles Manson; Marry, Fuck, Kill, with equal graciousness.

When we get caught up in the feedback loop of our own thoughts (known as the "self-centered mind" in Buddhism), rather than appearing as a fertile ground of potentiality, space seems like a problem to be solved or a void to be filled. Conventional wisdom dictates that if you don't know what to do, just do *something* and see what happens next! Aside from being bad advice, this is also possibly psychotic. Taking action from a state of confusion pretty much guarantees a confused result—sure, you might even get lucky, relatively speaking: you were a confused, high-powered ad exec, you flailed around, dropped out, and accidentally started a successful baby food empire (see Diane Keaton in *Baby Boom* for details). But that success is relative to the failure you felt yourself to be when you were flailing, and since nothing lasts, the confusion that the relative success temporarily covered up eventually finds a way of bobbing back up to the surface like a corpse in a Swedish police procedural.

My teacher, Sokuzan, advocates, "Don't do anything unless you have to." Our ploys to jolt ourselves out of confusion-induced paralysis tend to be preludes to, if not catastrophe, then at least an irritating afternoon of picking goat cheese out of the carpet. The disappointing fact of the matter is that, despite what our advertisement-addled nervous systems would have us believe, life is not composed of a zillion moment-to-moment do-or-die decisions. There's a lot of downtime. A lot of breathing room. A lot of space. It's just that we don't really like downtime because it's then that the critters come creeping back in; all of the stuff our busy-ness occludes from awareness. It's not long after the last businesses abandon the mall that the deer move in, and when the tourists stay home, the dolphins return to Venice. Not only are there not a lot of decisions to be made, there actually might be none.

Once you're able to clearly assess the situation, there really might be no "choice" to be made at all. No decisions. No choices ever. Simply the next step as inspired by the moment. The editorializing that goes up to the point of the "choice" is really just killing time in an attempt to ignore the fact that you're terrified that you don't know what will happen next. You wind up like Mrs. Peacock in the movie *Clue*, shouting, "If I wasn't trying to keep the conversation going, we'd just be sitting here in an embarrassed silence!" Next thing you know, you've blasted off on the propulsive fuel of your preconceptions, eager to colonize the solar system and beyond with your own egocentric Space Force. When your personal identity is insinuated upon open space, you wind up with Ignorance with a capital *I*. And it is from Ignorance that all subsequent afflictive emotions discharge. It is Ignorance that permeates all the other Buddha Families.

Martin

(1912–2004)

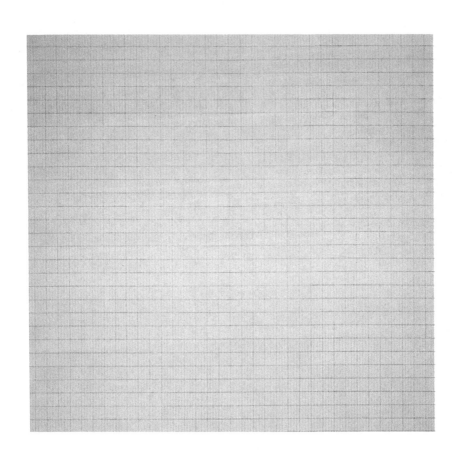

Morning
Agnes Martin

1965 | TATE

Creative impulses arise within the all-encompassing space of Buddha energy. The earnest impulse to create results in a range of neuroses, from antic squirreliness to suicidal mania. All we wanted to do was make some crafts! It's just that in order to express something, one requires the ability to sit in the discomfort of not knowing what that something will be. The ego mind, which wants credit for being "the artist," will rush to back-fill the space with the intellect and its preconceptions. Paving paradise with the parking lot. True creativity begins with receiving, not producing.

To me, no artist better exemplifies this energy through process and temperament than the legendary abstract painter Agnes Martin. A fairly late creative bloomer by most standards, Martin began painting when she was in her thirties and did not have a solo show until she was forty-seven years old. Sitting in a little chair in her Taos, New Mexico, studio, she would wait and wait, sometimes for weeks on end, for inspiration to arrive. And arrive it would, as if delivered by the U.S. Postal Service. For Martin, inspiration showed up as a fully formed mental image of a painting about the size of a postage stamp, communicating simple, elusive concepts like "Beauty," "Hill," or "Innocence."

"I'm an empty mind," Martin said. "So when something comes in you can see it." Her only real duty was to find a way to translate that mental picture into a physical one by way of a series of complicated mathematical equations that allowed her to scale up the stamp-sized image on her six-by-six-foot canvas.

As she described it, "Every day for twenty years I would say, 'What am I gonna do next?' That's how I ask for inspiration. I don't have any ideas myself. I have a vacant mind. In order to do exactly what the inspiration calls for. And I don't start to paint until after I have an inspiration. And after I have it, I make up my mind that I'm not going to interfere, not have any ideas. That's really the trouble with art today. It seems to me the artists have the inspiration, but before they can get it on the canvas they've had about fifty ideas and the inspiration disappears."[3]

Born in Saskatchewan, Canada, in 1912, Martin said she came out of the womb with a little sword, ready to conquer the world...until she met her mother, from whom she suffered one defeat after another. They never got on. Later, Martin narrowly missed placement on the Canadian Olympic swimming team and wound up banging around as an elementary school teacher, eventually completing a degree in arts education at Columbia University's Teachers College.

She landed in Taos, New Mexico, where she became a part of the vibrant local art community. Well into her thirties, she resolved to become a successful painter and began producing works with a ferocious ambition. Her personal standards were exacting, and rather than rework paintings she felt weren't good enough, she destroyed them, a practice she would maintain into her eighties.

During her time in Taos, her work caught the eye of gallerist Betty Parsons, who offered to show her in New York City on the proviso that she, too, move to New York and enter the art scene. This was the New York of the great Abstract Expressionists—Jackson Pollock, Willem de Kooning, Philip Guston— pugnacious personalities who brawled with each other at the Cedar Tavern and then with their canvases in their studios. While some women certainly held their own in this kind of environment (see Joan Mitchell, page 257), this was not Martin's vibe. She wound up living and working in Coenties Slip, an area at Manhattan's southernmost point. At the time, it was still an active seaport, and there was already a small enclave of gay artists living and working there. Among them were Robert Indiana, Ellsworth Kelly, Jasper Johns, and Lenore Tawney (with whom Martin had a relationship). Not only was Coenties Slip free from uptown's blustering testosterone, but there was also not an inordinate amount of socializing. Each artist had their own studio and largely kept to themselves.

This kind of setup appeals to the antisocial aspect of Buddha energy and certainly suited Martin's predilection for solitude. She once said to a friend, "I have no friends, and you're one of them."[4] She was able to keep her own hours and, at times, the only human contact she had was with the sailors she could see aboard the ships passing by her window. While solitude can be conducive to productivity, it can also harden into isolation, and in Martin's case, any harbingers of psychotic episodes might have gone unnoticed. She was diagnosed as a paranoid schizophrenic in early adulthood, which, along with the constant company of what she called "her voices," manifested at their worst as catatonic states in which she didn't know who or where she was.

In one harrowing episode, she was picked up on Park Avenue in a catatonic state, unable to give her own name. She was brought to Bellevue Hospital, where she underwent multiple rounds of electroshock therapy. Luckily, the doctors discovered a scrap of paper in her coat that had Robert Indiana's name on it, and they contacted him. Along with Lenore Tawney, Indiana rescued Martin from Bellevue and arranged for her to go into private care.

This anecdote is, of course, highly personal and unique to Martin's experience, but it serves to elucidate what can be an extreme manifestation of Buddha energy: a dissolution of self into space to the degree that the relative functionality required to navigate the world as a human becomes impossible; the permissiveness of space can at times render us immobile.

During this period, she saw the Zen master D.T. Suzuki at Columbia University, and, along with her friend, painter Ad Reinhardt, Martin began exploring Buddhist and Christian mysticism. While she never formally followed Zen Buddhism, she did find solace in the precise forms for which it is known. Later in life, however, she was less likely to be found reading Dogen Zenji than she was Agatha Christie. My own first literary love affair was with Agatha Christie, and it seems to me that Martin's affinity for her novels is instructive. The Golden Age of detective fiction (1920–1940) served a specific psychological role for its readers. In the face of seismic cultural shifts and two catastrophic world wars, readers could take comfort in an Agatha Christie novel, knowing, as P.D. James put it, "All the mysteries will be explained, all the problems solved, and peace and order will return to that mythical village which, despite its above-average homicide rate, never really loses its tranquility or its innocence."[5] Perhaps Martin, who struggled to maintain her own inner tranquility, found a similar solace in the dependable formalism of Christie's work. Or maybe she considered Christie a creative kindred spirit in their shared use of structural repetition as a backbone of their respective work.

An odd parallel is the fact that both Agatha Christie and Agnes Martin had episodes where they, in effect, vanished. Christie's disappearance was for only eleven days and created a tabloid furor, whereas Martin went off the grid for about eighteen months, to little fanfare. Still, not much is known about what transpired for either of these women in those gaps. That both managed to pull off a disappearing act in the face of personal anguish (the collapse of Christie's marriage and the death of Martin's friend Ad Reinhardt) is an extraordinary accomplishment given the social strictures placed on women, which denied them the privilege of risking personal safety in the pursuit of their own mental health.

Ten years on in New York, Martin emptied out her studio, destroyed some paintings, gave the rest away, crammed her belongings into a van, and took off. She showed up a year and a half later outside Cuba, New Mexico, where she began living more or less like a homesteader. She built an adobe house for herself, lived off the land, and, according to some accounts, even took in work salting bear hides.[6] After a three-year hiatus she began painting again.

While a fresh canvas is a great metaphor for Buddha energy, I do not mean to suggest that Martin's sparse paintings are blanks or that they lack something. Her canvases, all six-foot-square of them, are chock-a-block with paint, and they go as far as anyone can to communicate the ineffable essence of Buddha energy. She claimed to have even gone beyond nature into pure abstraction. Unlike most other large abstract works, you can't really step back from a Martin painting in hopes of seeing what it is. On the contrary, they require you to step not just toward them but *into* them. At such close range you find yourself holding your breath for fear that a sharp exhalation would send the mirage quivering back into the ether. Depending on your proximity to the canvas, the grid rises and falls like gooseflesh on the back of your own neck when you notice that a stranger has been staring at you for a few moments too long. These paintings totter at the edge of minimalism, but they are still abstract down to their canvas stretchers. These are not paintings that gratify our roving eyes' desire for flashy entertainment or narrative, and any tatty grabs at an easy answer only inflame frustration. Martin herself often commented on the fact that in music (which she considered the highest art form) "people accept pure emotion, but from art people demand an explanation."[7] There is no *Reader's Digest* version of a Martin painting.

Martin's retrospective at the Guggenheim in 2016 highlighted not just the perfection of the work, but the imperfection of my eye. Between the bright lighting in the museum and the shimmering of the paintings themselves, I was dishearteningly aware of the number of floaters in my eyes. At times, her stunning work became little more than a background scrim for the dance of my own ocular entropy. I even began to sense the onset of a migraine, my eye muscles frantically over-flexing, trying again and again to grasp something solid—a pretty good descriptor of the mind twisting in all-encompassing space. Every effort of my gaze to take something tangible home was rebuffed. Materialist impulses of that sort would need to be sated in the gift shop.

Though her work is timeless, we cannot remove Martin from her time, when a justifiable self-preservationist paranoia abounded as a result of the systemic and institutionalized oppression of queer people. While deeply in the closet, Martin also bristled at the suggestion that she be included in exhibitions of "Women Artists" and rejected the notion that her career was in any way informed by being a woman. "I'm not a woman," she insisted to journalist Jill Johnston, "I'm a doorknob, leading a quiet existence."[8] Whether she was taking umbrage at the limits of the gender binary, or just resentful of being identified as anything at all beyond her creative output, is an open question—and none of our business.

Olivia Liang draws the connection between Martin's diagnosis of paranoid schizophrenia and the contemporaneous inclusion of homosexuality as a mental illness in the DSM[9] (it wasn't fully expunged until 1987[10]). As if Western culture wasn't homophobic enough, now there was a pseudo-scientific pretext for the continued persecution of queer people. Perhaps Martin feared that by being outed she might not only lose funding and be publicly defamed, but also be subjected to further brutalities in the name of psychiatric healing. A therapist friend pointed out that not only would Martin's homosexuality not be diagnosed as a disease today, she probably would not be diagnosed with paranoid schizophrenia at all. Given the perennially murky waters in which mental illness tends to be diagnosed, it's no wonder Martin reviled categorization. And while, of course, countless people have been helped by psychiatric care, it does lead one to wonder if perhaps what needs to be expanded is not our labeling arsenal, but rather our accommodation of what a human being is allowed to be.

The impulse to bridle at any personal qualifiers as incarceratory is a fascinating manifestation of Buddha energy. Buddha family folks might not have an issue with amorphous space in the way many people do, but they can become quite defensive—perhaps even anti-territorial—rebelling against anyone cordoning off space and imposing false boundaries on them. Given the state-sanctioned persecution of queer people, it's no wonder Martin rejected that descriptor. And once one has refused the descriptor of "homosexual," it stands to reason that "gender" might next come under serious scrutiny—even "non-binary" becomes a self-referential millstone around one's neck, and the next thing you know, calling oneself a "person" seems a bit of a stretch. Perhaps it was in this spirit that Martin claimed to be a doorknob. When asked for biographical information to be included in the catalog for a solo exhibit at the Whitney Museum in New York, Martin canceled the show. Burned by luminosity, Buddha energy throws its lot in with emptiness.

Martin often inveighed against "ideas" and "intellect" as an approach to making and experiencing art, instead advocating what she called "true feelings." The kind of emotion Martin conveyed in her work was akin to the feeling that might overtake you as you approach the vastness of the ocean: a spontaneous rush of energy that defies language. She wanted viewers of her work to feel improved for the looking. She wanted us to feel happy and free. It's interesting that the form that enabled her to attain this freedom was a grid—not quite Cartesian, as she preferred what she considered the more inviting rectangle to the boxy, bossy square, but a grid nonetheless. And yet through the grid she achieved something Descartes never could: intimacy, warmth, and transcendence.

Despite her paintings' undeniable lightness, there is also a hum of hyper-vigilance. There is a kind of Presbyterian rectitude in Martin's work, evoking for many viewers the vast Canadian prairies of her youth (an interpretation she rejected). I could see her paintings in bonnets and dun-colored frocks, just getting on with things because by the time the hay is threshed and the stables mucked and you've had your simple dinner, all you're left with is a well-earned exhaustion, which leaves no fuel for lighting the wick of existential dread. The happiness Martin espoused seemed a practiced attitude rather than a feeling, the kind that will brook no idle chatter, the kind that is hard-won in the face of unimaginable chaos. For a mind that has known such darkness, this joy is a rebuke—bracing, like a plunge with the Polar Bear Club, which leaves you ecstatic, not because something wonderful has happened but because your nervous system has met the indifference of nature head on and cannot believe its good luck at still being alive.

Photographer Donald Woodson wrote a memoir about his time as a young man living and working with Martin. He chronicles the warm, erratic, and sometimes abusive treatment he received from her, a stark contrast with her more mythologized image as the inscrutable mystic of the mesas. Our instinct when confronted with these paradoxical contrasts, particularly with figures whose work elicits spiritual introspection, is to discount the wisdom manifestation as a put-on or a con; how else can we reconcile the bitchiness, the stinginess, the madness? But to paraphrase George W.S. Trow, the difference between a flirt and a con is that we walk away from a flirt with more than we went in with, while a con leaves us with less than we had when we arrived. While it's hard to imagine Martin flirting (though I'm sure she did!), it is harder still to imagine exposure to her work leaving anyone defrauded.

Martin said she was thinking about the innocence of trees when the grid first appeared, which may or may not be true. Artists, like the rest of us, tend to craft some mythology around why they do the things they do. Perhaps Martin wasn't so much abstracting trees and roses down to their essence as abstracting them as she herself was abstracted. To stare at a Martin painting is to fall, not into the trance of the tree or the rose, but into the trance of Martin. To accept the invitation of such a courageous gesture is the height of generosity.

Her long-time dealer, Arne Glimcher, recounts a visit his granddaughter paid to her apartment. Martin noticed the girl was mesmerized by a rose she had on her table and asked, "Is this rose beautiful?"

"Yes, this rose is beautiful," the girl replied. Martin then took the rose and hid it behind her back. "Is the rose still beautiful?"

"Yes, the rose is still beautiful."

"You see?" Martin replied. "The beauty is not in the rose. The beauty is in your mind."[11]

DeFeo

(1929–1989)

The Rose
Jay DeFeo

1958–1966 | PHOTOGRAPH BY BURT GLINN

J ay DeFeo was twenty-nine years old when she began *The Rose* (alternately titled *The White Rose* and *The Deathrose*). Her inspiration was to create something with a center, a quest that would become the center of her life for nearly a decade.

It was 1958, the height of the Beat Generation, and the apartment she shared with her husband, artist Wally Hedrick, on Fillmore Street in San Francisco, was its epicenter. They hosted parties and salons, socializing with musicians, painters, and poets (she attended the first public reading of Allen Ginsberg's "Howl"). Yet she was no mere satellite to the heavenly Beat bodies. Her work as a jewelry designer and painter quickly gained traction and, in 1959, visionary curator Dorothy Miller included several DeFeo paintings in MoMA's landmark exhibition *16 Americans* (Louise Nevelson was the only other woman in the show). Miller wanted to include her most recent work, *The Rose*, but DeFeo declined; it wasn't yet done.

While still in process, *The Rose* garnered a lot of interest in the art world and had already attracted interest from several buyers, but still, it wasn't yet done. At the time, DeFeo couldn't afford dedicated studio space, so she worked in the bay window in her living room. The enormous canvas eclipsed all sunlight, like a lumbering planetoid. What began as a nine-by-seven-foot canvas metastasized into a behemoth nearly eleven feet tall, eight feet wide, and, most strikingly, one foot thick. Bruce Conner, an artist friend, noted that the piece wasn't confined to the canvas: as DeFeo worked, paint accumulated on the floor, her stool, her body.[12] The entire *environment* became the work. As the years passed, layers of oil paint mixed with glittery, powdery mica were added to the canvas in ever-thickening, flesh-like deposits; wooden dowels were added to fortify the work as paint was slathered on, sloughed off, chiseled, molded, and scraped into a sculptural escarpment. DeFeo's process evolved into something more akin to erosion than painting. Like a wrathful goddess, she locked into making this juggernaut, tapping into a primal creative force, so hungry to exist that it became an ouroboros, cannibalizing its own conduit.

The color of the Buddha family is white. Through the ages, whether it be to kiss a seascape with a glistening crest of foam, or working undercover as an underpainting, white has always been fundamental to the painter's palette. White pigments are known by many different names and derived through many different recipes. The opaquest of the whites (and the most treacherous) is lead white. A perennial health hazard, there is record of lead white as far back as 4 BCE. The philosopher Theophrastus even described the process (called "stacking"), which went largely unchanged for millennia. Basically, a special dual-chambered clay pot was designed to hold coils of lead on one side and vinegar on the other. Thousands of these pots were then buried in air-tight sheds, stacked one on top of the other amidst layers of cow shit in a hellish lasagna. After a solid month of fuming and fermenting in CO_2 and god knows what else, the process was complete and the poor bastard who drew the short straw had to go into the shed to retrieve the lovely frothy cakes of white lead. These were then ground into a pigment that was popular for its thick opacity; a little went a long way and was relatively inexpensive. But even in ancient times, people knew something wasn't quite right with this pigment, remarking on the odd ailments and ghastly pallor that befell the artisans who created it and the artists who used it.[13] [14]

There is a delicious dissonance here: a luminous, virginal white pigment whose vibrant opacity can cause delusions, brain damage, tooth loss, and internal bleeding. In retrospect, the combination of Europe's association of white with holiness and its penchant for religious-themed artwork was a disaster just waiting to happen. Many artists, including Michelangelo and Goya, were said to suffer from "artist's colic," a catch-all diagnosis used to describe the strange maladies that befell them. Even Van Gogh, whose myriad mental troubles may well have been congenital, could not have been done any favors by his habit of sucking on the end of his paintbrushes as he worked, enjoying the sweet anise-like taste of the lead paint. Delicious indeed.

The Asian association of white with death and mourning might have acted as a warning flare—that is, until we recall that the Chinese and Japanese loved to mix lead into their cosmetics to get that superior coverage. Maybe she's born with it, maybe it's lead poisoning. Lead white remained in use up until 1994, at which point the U.K. banned the sale of it, sending the painter Lucien Freud into a tizzy. Cremnitz white, the lead carbonate-based paint Freud considered integral to achieving the harrowing hues of his gloppy portraiture, was about to become contraband and he swiftly began stockpiling the pigment before the cut-off date.

One of the prevailing themes of Vajrayana Buddhism is the utilization of poison as medicine, which is the essential instruction of the mandala. In ancient times, the peacock symbolized this concept, as it was believed to get its colorful plumage by eating poison. While this is not exactly true, the ancient rajas of India would keep peacocks to help protect against cobras, as they are deft snake killers, happy to consume their slithery victims.

Despite its poisonous qualities, lead also has its positive applications. It lines the weighted aprons we wear to be X-rayed, protecting us from radiation. In metaphysical terms, lead symbolizes an impenetrable container, protecting us from dissolution into space. In Western astrology, it is said that lead is ruled by the planet Saturn, which takes its sweet time tooling around the sun (approximately twenty-nine and a half years). Its return to its exact placement at the time of birth heralds an individual's Saturn Return. When that Big Daddy Energy swings back into town to check up on us, we may experience an energetic headwind if we are on the right course, but if we are not prepared, we need only take a gander at Goya's painting of *Saturn Devouring His Son* for a glimpse of what is in store for us. Or, as David Lynch says in *Twin Peaks: The Return*, "Fix your hearts or die."

The dates of *The Rose* are listed as 1958–1966, but DeFeo never really finished it. Rather, it was stopped by "an uncontrolled event," as described by Conner. "She kept changing it. Using black and white paint. White lead. And as time went by it was the only identity she had with any kind of exterior reality. And I think the white lead paint had an effect."[15]

DeFeo and her husband were eventually evicted from their apartment. "Probably because Jay had gotten so crazy,"[16] Conner mused. In any case, *The Rose* had to be removed and by this time it was estimated to weigh one ton. The work was so large it could not fit through the door. When the men in white coats finally came (in this case, Bekins movers), they had to remove the street-facing wall of the apartment so that a forklift could haul the painting out. Conner, who was a filmmaker, documented the proceedings in a film called *The White Rose*. Conner filmed as the painting was pried off the wall and crated, all the while keeping an eye on DeFeo, for whom this experience could only have felt like an unspeakable violation. As her creation was lifted out the window, Conner expressed concern that she might jump out after it. "It was the end of *The Rose* and it was the end of Jay,"[17] he said. It might just be a strange story if it all ended there. It doesn't end there.

Not long after its removal, *The Rose* was shown at the Pasadena Art Museum and the San Francisco Museum of Modern Art. In the eight years since DeFeo had started *The Rose*, the art world conversation had moved on from abstraction and minimalism to Pop. Even though it had become infamous, there were no buyers for *The Rose* and DeFeo couldn't afford to store it. The practical question of where to put the damn thing loomed heavily.

A friend arranged for it to be hung in a conference room at the San Francisco Art Institute, but unfortunately the painting began to crack and buckle under its own weight. As a protective measure, it was encased in a layer of plaster, but soon students started graffitiing it like the wall of a bathroom stall. Needless to say, DeFeo wasn't thrilled with how her masterwork was being stewarded, but she had still no funds to store it elsewhere. In addition, *The Rose* had been so bulked up with plaster that the SFAI literally could not get it out the way it had come in. A stop-gap solution was struck upon—namely, to erect a false wall in front of the painting. In essence, mummified in plaster, *The Rose* was entombed in a wall like a heretic pharaoh.

DeFeo never saw *The Rose* again. She went on to create stunning work in photography, painting, and drawing, but nothing matched the grandeur of *The Rose*, *The White Rose*, *The Deathrose*. In 1989, she died of lung cancer. There are, of course, countless mitigating factors, from smoking to genetics, that can contribute to such an illness, but when I read about her fate I thought, *That painting killed her.*

In 1995, the Whitney Museum of American Art disinterred *The Rose*. The plaster casing was removed and it was remounted on a reinforced backing. The current estimate is that the painting weighs about three thousand pounds, though no one has ever really properly weighed it. After acquiring the work, the Whitney employed yet another forklift to hoist the painting into the museum through yet another window. It is not yet fully dry and probably won't be for another hundred years.

Thomas Hoving, the former director of the Metropolitan Museum of Art, wrote a book called *The Greatest Works of Art of Western Civilization*, in which he describes the objects that completely bowled him over at first sight: Van Gogh's *Starry Night*, Michelangelo's *David*, Goya's *The Third of May 1808*. He includes DeFeo's *The Rose* in this company. Hoving describes it as "a sort of 'angel' in abstraction, trumpeting the birth of all matter...an illustration for the Book of Genesis."[18]

The first time I saw *The Rose* at the Whitney, Bach's Toccata and Fugue in D minor wafted in from a neighboring gallery. To me, it looked less like an angel and more like a nuclear blast site. Instead of the Bible, a few lines from the old Scottish ballad, *The Daemon Lover*, came to mind:

"O what a bright, bright hill is yon,
That shines so clear to see?"
"O it is the hill of heaven," he said,
"Where you shall never be."

Leah Levy, director of the Jay DeFeo Trust, recounts a moment toward the end of DeFeo's life when they discussed the prospect of rehabilitating *The Rose*. Registering her fatigue, Levy suggested they continue the conversation the next day. "Oh no," DeFeo said. "I'm listening to every word you're saying, but right above your head I see this scenario...I'm in another life and I'm walking in a museum and I come upon *The Rose*. And I see someone looking at it and I walk up to them and nudge them and say, *I did that*."[19]

Fini

(1907–1996)

Les Aveugles (The Blind Ones)
Leonor Fini

1968 | PRIVATE COLLECTION

Artist Alberto Savinio imagined Leonor Fini as "the prototype of a species" he called the "Fini-ans." He captures a quality of Buddha energy when he writes, "The 'Fini-ans' have roots that are not buried in the ground but that float in the free air, and this means they are not earth-bound, on the contrary, they can move about as the wind takes them."[20]

Today, Fini is mostly remembered as a painter (one article[21] credits her with creating the first erotic male nude painted by a woman, which can't possibly be true), but she was also an illustrator, author, experimental filmmaker, and theatrical designer. Freedom of personal expression was always paramount to her, but maintaining an identity was never a priority. Buddha energy skillfully engages identity as a malleable tool to meet the needs of a given moment. We already do this naturally in that we don't speak to our bosses like we do to our partners, or behave the way we might in a tavern at a tabernacle (though there are exceptions and we know who you are).

Before Fini turned two years old, her mother, Malvina, realized she had made a bad marriage. Although he was rich and good-looking, Herminio Fini was a violent and tyrannical man. Malvina could not raise a daughter in that environment, and so she bundled up little Leonor and escaped Argentina for Trieste, Italy. Herminio's pride was badly bruised and he vowed to get his daughter back. He dispatched some heavies to Trieste, hoping to kidnap Leonor and take her back to Argentina, but Malvina, suspecting such a ploy, disguised her as a little boy to throw the kidnappers off. The use of disguise succeeded in protecting Fini, as well as instilling in her a lifelong fascination with roleplay and gender fluidity. "To dress up is to have the feeling of changing dimension, species, space," she would later say. "You can feel like a giant, plunge into the undergrowth, become an animal, until you feel invulnerable and timeless, taking part in timeless rituals."[22]

When she was twelve, Fini contracted rheumatoid conjunctivitis, which temporarily blinded her. She credited the two and a half months she spent blindfolded with the cultivation of a vibrant inner world. Once her sight was restored, she was eager to chronicle these visions in paint. With no formal artistic training (she was a rebellious child and had been expelled from every school she had been enrolled in), she taught herself what she wanted to know. As a teenager, she voraciously read Nietzsche, Freud, and Jung. She also taught herself to draw and paint, learning anatomy by sketching corpses. Fini recalled, "At the age of twelve or thirteen, I fell in love with dead people. I would go to the morgue of a hospital in Trieste, which was divided into two halls. One was a stately viewing room: the dead were dressed up...very sumptuously, elegant, bejeweled, adorned with flowers...The attendant, who was fond of me, allowed me to enter."[23] By the time she was seventeen, Fini had outgrown Trieste and moved to Milan to make a name for herself. There she befriended the great metaphysical painter Giorgio de Chirico, who saw in her a kindred spirit. But with fascism on the rise in Italy, de Chirico encouraged Fini to leave Milan for Paris, where a vibrant avant-garde community was blossoming.

Fini really hit the ground running in Paris. Her flamboyant personality and style won her many admirers among the Surrealists, including Max Ernst, whom she took as her lover. With her sophisticated grasp of philosophy and psychoanalysis and her uncanny painting style, the group must have seen this brilliant young woman as a Surrealist ready-made. Her work, with its dark, erotic theatricality, perfectly encapsulated the Surrealist aesthetic and she was quickly included in their group shows. However, the group was presided over by the punctilious André Breton. "I hated his anti-homosexual attitudes and also his misogyny," said Fini. "It seemed that women were expected to keep quiet in café discussions, yet I felt that I was just as good as the men...I refused to join the group."[24] After all, she had already seen first-hand the havoc wreaked by controlling men.

Fini had no truck with persons or ideologies that in any way hemmed her in. She rejected traditional marriage, instead preferring to live in "a big house with my atelier and cats and friends, one with a man who was rather a lover and another who was rather a friend. And it has always worked."[25] Like many women of her generation, she loathed the label of "female artist." "I am fascinated by the androgyne, for it seems to me to be the ideal," Fini stated. "I would like to think of myself as androgynous."[26] Nevertheless, she did participate in Peggy Guggenheim's seminal 1943 exhibit *31 Women*, which proved to be instrumental in exposing America to her unique brand of Surrealism. On occasion, Fini even bridled at being referred to as a painter. For her, the notion that you would segregate your art-making from the rest of your life was asinine. As the curator Lissa Rivera observed, "If she depicted it in her art, she lived it in her life."[27]

While her artwork continued to garner more and more attention and support (Christian Dior exhibited Fini in his gallery before becoming a fashion designer), she was also making a name for herself as a doyenne of Parisian nightlife. Dressing up in costumes of her own design was a way of embodying her artistic vision. To hear her tell it, she didn't really even enjoy parties; she was antisocial at heart, but loved the process of transforming herself into a living artwork. She would make a dramatic late entrance and a quiet early exit. Her over-the-top concoctions had press photographers clamoring to capture what Fini wore to the latest costume ball. And sometimes all she sported were knee-high boots, a feather cape, and a mask. "I wear masks in order to be someone else," she said, "and my masks on my living, moving face, are Immobility. I like that...Death on my face. Or perhaps, an ideal life. A life without movement. Movement is a sequence of innumerable deaths."[28]

Among Fini's inner circle, which included Jean Genet, Leonora Carrington, and Federico Fellini (she designed costumes for *8½*), was the philosopher Georges Bataille. He may have been specifically writing about Fini's work when he said, "The domain of eroticism open[s] to us through a conscious refusal to limit ourselves within our individual personalities. Eroticism opens the way to death. Death opens the way to the denial of our individual lives."[29] In other words, when we are erotically engaged with others (and, of course, not all eroticism is sexual and not all sex is erotic), there is a blinding synthesis that takes place, in which our private identity falls away; we aren't sure where we end and they begin. This is simultaneously a death of our separate self and a birth of something new. Bataille wrote, "The whole business of eroticism is to destroy the self-contained character of the participators as they are in their normal lives."[30]

The enticing dread of erotic oblivion is described in Charles Baudelaire's poem "Les aveugles," from which Fini took inspiration. My humble attempt at a translation reads:

Contemplate them, my soul; they make the flesh creep!
Like mannequins; vaguely bizarre;
Uncanny somnambulists, writhing in a dreamless sleep
Tenebrous eyes, know not where they are.

The two androgynous bodies are drawn together in an electromagnetic field of eroticism—or are they collapsing into each other with their dying breaths? Perhaps they are beyond life and death, like gods from the ancient Egyptian pantheon: Geb and Nut, earth and sky in perpetual copulation. These characters seem carved and polished from some dense material, incapable of motion, yet frozen in mid-gesture, redolant of a Zen poem, *Song of the Jewel Mirror Samadhi*, which reads:

When the wooden man begins to sing,
The stone woman gets up dancing...[31]

Through awareness practice we see that the very identity which, in the past, we had viciously fought to defend is fundamentally unreal. The self is a wooden man, a stone woman. Sure, we have personalities, but they are too mercurial to provide us with a solid reference point in the first place. Buddha family's all-encompassing space allows us to both see through the illusion of a continuous self and afford us absolute freedom to play, explore, and express our un-selves: the wooden man begins to sing, the stone woman—or in Leonor Fini's case, the masked woman—gets up dancing.

Pindell

(1943–present)

Columbus
Howardena Pindell

2020 | COURTESY OF THE ARTIST AND GARTH GREENAN GALLERY

O f all our afflictive emotions, what makes working with ignorance the trickiest is that it is, by nature, incredibly difficult to see. In contemplating this energy, I have realized that the word *Buddha* in the Buddha family's name tends to throw me off track a bit, leading me to equate ignorance with a ditzy fogginess, like the lady in *The Gang's All Here* who holds her cat to her ear thinking she's answering the phone. A pretty ignorant view of ignorance, one might say. Sure, ignorance can show up as looking for the glasses you've got perched on your head, but, more often than not, it appears as racism, misogyny, homophobia, transphobia, xenophobia, and so on. This kind of ignorance, I don't have to tell you, leads to pillage, rape, murder, and every kind of warfare. With the Buddha family at the center of the mandala, we are reminded of the extreme pendulum swing from wisdom to insanity that is possible at the heart of all we do and all we are. This extreme contrast imbues the Buddha family in particular with the greatest capacity for wisdom and insanity. Because when we fracture ourselves away from all-encompassing space, we do go insane in one way or another. The work of artist Howardena Pindell asks us to look at the repercussions of this insanity in the hopes of short-circuiting what we don't know and don't want to look at.

Pindell's precocious artistic talent was spotted by her third-grade teacher, who encouraged her parents to nurture it. They signed her up for weekend art classes and took her to visit the Philadelphia Museum of Art. Her talents would earn her an undergraduate degree from Boston's prestigious Museum School (at a time when they had a quota of one Black student per year) and a master's from Yale. In 1967, she moved to New York City with dreams of making it in the art world, little realizing that her eclectic training, which included classical figuration, Abstract Expressionism, and Pop Art, would make her a bit of an anomaly. "I was used to, at times, getting it from both sides. Early on, the African American community rejected abstraction and the white

community rejected you no matter what you did."[32] In 1967, she was hired by MoMA, where she worked for twelve years, rising in the ranks to become the first Black woman curator in the museum's history. In 1979, she left the museum to accept a professorship at Stony Brook University. It was there, on her way to an event, that Pindell was in a near-fatal car crash, which left her with broken bones and short-term memory loss. "The driver was an ex-nun, so we called it an act of God."[33] This accident catalyzed her into making what she called "issues-based" work: "I remember thinking, if I could have died so quickly, I would never have expressed my opinion. That started me looking at my life again and thinking about what I felt about the world."[34]

Pindell's work is not propagandistic. She is an activist. She is not manipulating emotions that arise in response to the facts and histories she's presenting, nor is she embellishing historical events in the hopes of ginning up emotional energy to direct to her own ends. Pindell's brush with death jolted her into expressing the insight that awareness is powerful and education is liberating.

Columbus, commissioned for her retrospective *Rope/Fire/Water* at The Shed in New York City, is a multimedia work consisting of a large wall banner, which is made from one hundred hands cut out of rice paper and inlaid with black acrylic. At first, it seems as though it is a solid black banner, but as we get closer, a dark gray text materializes, rippling across the void to describe the atrocities committed by Christopher Columbus and others. If ignorance has a message for us, it is written in black across its black veil.

The harrowing text reads:

ANCIENT EGYPTIANS CUT OFF ONE HAND OF DEAD ENEMY
SOLDIERS TO COUNT THE ENEMY'S WAR DEAD

LYNCHING OF FIRST NATIONS PEOPLE, TAKING BODY PARTS AS
TROPHIES
WEALTHY, PROMINENT FAMILIES PROFITED FROM THE PLUNDER...
AND LAUNDERED IT THROUGH CULTURE.

COLUMBUS
BAHAMAS, HISPANOLA (HAITI) AND DOMINICAN REPUBLIC

THOUSANDS OF INDIGENOUS PEOPLE SENT TO SPAIN TO BE SOLD
AMPUTATED HANDS OF THE TAINO AND ARAWAK PEOPLE IF THEY
DID NOT BRING HIM GOLD. TRAINED DOGS TO EAT HUMAN FLESH
GRILLED INDIGENOUS PEOPLE ALIVE DISMEMBERED INFANTS
FEEDING THEM TO THE DOGS

CHARGED FOR KILLING AND TORTURING THE INDIGENOUS
POPULATION
COLUMBUS WAS PARDONED FOR HIS CRIMES
BECAUSE HE BROUGHT BACK WEALTH (GOLD)

RUBBER BARONS THROUGHOUT THE WORLD
INCLUDING THE BELGIAN CONGO,
PLUNDERED NATURAL RESOURCES, ENSLAVING, TORTURING,
RAPING, MURDERING AND DISMEMBERING, CUTTING OFF THE
HANDS OF THE INDIGENOUS POPULATION IF THEY RESISTED

On the floor at the base of the banner lies a pile of black severed silicone hands, some of which were molded from the artist's own hands. Adeze Wilford, The Shed's assistant curator, commented, "As we were layering the hands together in the gallery when we were installing the show, I was able to very easily say, 'Oh, that's Howardena's hand. I recognize that hand.' And that is such a jarring thing to experience..."[35] Even without a personal connection to her, Pindell's work ejects us out of abstraction into the corporeal, only for us to fall back into abstraction again. History's phantom limbs cannot hold our weight.

At the heart of Pindell's creative practice is a tenuous balancing act. She makes joyful abstract work to temper the mercilessness of the historical record, which it is her mission to set straight.

Pindell confronts us with challenging work like *Columbus*, and our reflexes might be to recoil. We might think, "Well that's not me!" and turn away in offense at being ambushed by violent and debased content. *Certain things simply aren't discussed in mixed company!* Or, rejecting the violence of the privileged oppressors critiqued in the work, we might immediately spring into action, crafting clever placards and cornering politicians in elevators until we get some answers. While civic action may be precisely what the moment calls for, it is hopefully not in lieu of rigorous self-interrogation. When we reflexively object ("Well, that's not me!"), an appropriate follow-up might be "At least, not yet," or "Not this time." All-encompassing space affords us the mental acreage to both see and feel the impact of our prejudice, without dignifying it with a response. We can hear crazy out without giving it the mic.

Human minds relentlessly produce thoughts, yet thoughts cannot help us to know what a human mind is, and they cannot explain why circumstances arise that cause some people to stumble across heretofore unknown inner wells of painterly talent, or a taste for a fascistic style of crowd control, or to even find themselves murdering another human being with their neighbors and thinking, "Well, they had it coming."

Many of us remember moments from our childhood in which we learned about mythical heroes of history. Somehow the innocence of the time in which we learned about these historical giants becomes conflated with the heroes themselves. When we later learn that, rather than merely being an intrepid explorer who was a bit hapless with directions, Christopher Columbus was actually a homicidal sex fiend, well, some of us take offense at this new information, as if it were a personal indictment of our childhood. And so, rather than reckoning with the shortcomings (to put it mildly) of our forebears, perhaps even integrating them as cautionary myths, we instead become tetchy and defensive, refusing to acknowledge the bloody trail on the linoleum that leads inexorably back through time. Some of us might even become suspicious of the compassionate updaters of the historic record, considering them to be spoilsports who are perversely attempting to vandalize innocence, hope, and Mamie Eisenhower's homemade apple pie. I mean, why not just say Ben Franklin was a dirty old skirt chaser while you're at it?!

Resistance to confronting horror and unpleasantness isn't relegated to the culturally conservative, of course. Many progressively minded people might be willing to abstractly acknowledge that Christopher Columbus is less-than-ideal material for hero worship, but they certainly don't want to be bothered with the gory details. Some feel that to in any way contemplate the bloodshed and depravity through which humankind has made a name for itself is somehow inserting negativity into their minds. Like those New Agey friends many of us have who won't even watch horror movies for fear that they will be "putting those images" into their minds. Some popular Buddhist teachers share this belief, although I do recall hearing about one lama[36] who said that watching horror movies was actually good training in preparation for dying. If we can experience a film's thrills and chills while understanding that it is not real, then we might also be able to see the frightening content of the mind at the time of death as fundamentally unreal, and thereby avoid getting spooked into an unfortunate rebirth. I don't know.

The shocking acts for which human beings are infamous know no limit. Kindly folks who cry at their grandfather's funeral and attend christenings and help children set up lemonade stands have, in the same week, also run other human beings to ground, tied them to trees, and murdered them. We all know this. Of course, ignorance has no easy antidote, and pointing it out in others is a favorite pastime of those of us actively avoiding examining our own. As Sokuzan has said, we should respect other people's confusion (as well as our own). This does not mean that we agree with or condone the confusion, but rather we acknowledge that the ignorance that is showing up in a particular person or group is dependently arisen; it is the result of a tangle of countless threads, ranging from gut bacteria to societal conditioning, whose first causes cannot be found.

It seems that the best chance we have of disrupting our compulsion to act out of ignorance is to train our own minds through the sitting practice of meditation. This is what meditation practice (and Buddha family wisdom) is all about. Through a dedicated meditation practice, we may begin to catch glimpses of our ignorance out of the corner of the mind's eye, little potsherds of prejudice. Our instinct is usually to smash those fragments into tinier bits or bury them out of sight like dragon's teeth. Worse, realizing that these first two approaches are fruitless, but still mistaking the potsherds as some evidence about who we really are, we may throw up our hands and say, "Fine! I really am terrible, and I'm tired of hiding it!" And then we find ourselves reaching for the rope, the torch, the water cannon. We can't get rid of our prejudice, but we can see that the apparent self in which the prejudice arises is unreal. But we have to be willing to be horrified, we have to be willing to look.

With her unflinching—dare I say, even meditative?—gaze, Howardena Pindell encourages us to stay just a moment past what's bearable, out where compassion awaits us. As the Japanese filmmaker Akira Kurosawa once said, "To be an artist means never to avert one's eyes."

af Klint

(1862–1944)

Group IX/SUW, The Swan, No. 1
Hilma af Klint

1915 | MODERNA MUSEET MALMÖ

Swedish artist Hilma af Klint was not immune to the disquietude of the creative act, and she looked to a spiritual path for the courage an artistic life required. Not only did she find her spiritual practices a support for her creative pursuits, but she also found that the creative act itself could become an expression of spirituality in a very direct way. While Agnes Martin waited for inspiration to arrive, af Klint courted it through séances. Using her skills as an artist and as a spiritualist, af Klint became the medium through which her spiritual guides communicated, as well as the medium with which they expressed themselves. By embodying both the container and its content, af Klint became the all-encompassing space she was working with—a very Buddha thing to do.

Af Klint was born into a well-to-do Swedish naval family. Her father was a naval officer, her grandfather designed nautical charts, and so on, back for generations. As a female, she was not pressured to enter the family line, and the family nurtured her natural artistic talents. Among the second generation of young women admitted into the Royal Swedish Academy of Fine Arts in Stockholm, she quickly received commissions for portraits and technical drawings.

As a very young woman, af Klint attended lectures at the Theosophical Society and studied the writings of Madame Helena Petrovna Blavatsky. Madame Blavatsky's Theosophical movement aimed to "form a nucleus of the Universal Brotherhood of Humanity, without distinction of race, creed, sex, caste or colour." While Blavatsky has subsequently been decried by many as a charlatan and a con artist, at its height the Theosophical Society attracted notable figures such as Thomas Edison, W.B. Yeats, and Mahatma Gandhi, and provided a space where women could hold seats of power. Theosophy was largely stewarded by women, and can now be understood as an integral part of the early feminist movement.

Theosophy arose in the foment of spiritualism and acted as a kind of counterpoint to an increasingly materialistic world sent into overdrive by the technological revolution. Each year, new world-shattering discoveries were being made, from the gamma ray to the X-ray to radio waves to radioactivity. A previously invisible world was being made manifest by technological innovations and their effects. Some felt validated in their beliefs that there were realms which, while unseen by the human eye, directly influenced humanity and with which contact and collaboration were possible. For others, these innovations inspired a kind of smug confidence that anything that could be known would be known by scientific methods alone. At best, this latter group regarded the Theosophists as kooks whose fear of progress had them groping back into the past for primeval comforts. At worst, they regarded them as little more than music hall hucksters looking to make an easy buck off superstitious rubes.

Even in contemporary times, we see a continuation of this dynamic. Scientific rationalists twist their napkins in their laps whenever astrology is mentioned, as if the public's interest in this ancient art is tantamount to a resurgence of an unironic celebration of Flag Day. And while, of course, there are always cynical manipulators of human irrationality, what is more to the point is the way in which our patriarchal culture considers linear, evidence-based rationality as the only source of truth in the first place. Meanwhile, intuitive (read: *feminine*) wisdom is dismissed as hysterical and dangerous. Authentic wisdom doesn't require proof or evidence because it doesn't come from anywhere and doesn't rely on anything. In Tibetan Buddhism, the feminine principle of intuitive wisdom works in tandem with the masculine principle of "skillful means." (See traditional Yab-Yum sculptures for depictions of this inseparable union.)

The Theosophical Society itself might not have been a paragon of spiritual rigor, but it was riffing off, and in some cases resuscitating, real ancient teachings systematically blotted out for millennia by Christian fanatics. Love it or hate it, Theosophy is largely responsible for introducing Eastern wisdom to the West. So, rather than dismissing it as superstitious backsliding in the face of reason, intuitive spirituality might be seen as co-emergent with scientific innovation. This could even have been taken as "evidence" that all new technology contains both the intuitive and the rational and that the two categories aren't mutually exclusive.

For thousands of years, literacy has bred a strong sense of individualism in Western cultures, which has inspired all manner of innovation. But because speed begets speed, before we've even had time to synthesize or acclimate to the latest media environment, something new has been invented and we're on to the next thing, like a wound that is never given the chance to heal. The unexpected consequence of electric media such as the telegraph or the Internet is that, while they are meant to make the life of the individual more convenient, given their speed, they brutally confront us with the unflattering fact of our interdependence. Seeing this sends ego into a tailspin, which, from the perspective of the spiritual path, is good news, but from the perspective of the self-centered mind, feels like dying. Because Westerners have been trained since birth to retrofit a personality based on limitless choice about meaningless things, we need meditation and ritual to help us see through our titanic self-delusion, the House that Rationality Built. This does not require a belief in anything. According to Buddhist philosophy, beliefs are not only beside the point, they require exhausting maintenance, and in the long run become obstacles to our awakening.

Séances were a common practice at the end of the nineteenth century. People yearning to contact lost loved ones would turn to mediums who claimed to be porous gateways to the etheric realms. Madame Blavatsky herself was somewhat reserved on the subject of séances, not because she didn't believe some communication was taking place, but because she felt people didn't understand what they were actually communicating *with*.[37] She doubted it was the soul of the departed, but rather believed it was some lingering remnant of the personality they were contacting. In any case, myriad techniques were used to reach beyond the veil, from Morse code–like rapping, to the conjuring up of voices as if by radio wave, to the photographing of spirit visitors. The modes of communication intriguingly paralleled the latest technological innovations.

In the documentary *Beyond the Visible: Hilma af Klint*, the scientific historian Ernst Peter Fischer observes that in the vast range of phenomena that compose the universe, only a negligible amount is actually visible to the human eye. He goes on to say, "If I, as an artist, want to portray the world as it is, I must not portray it as it looks. Because it isn't like that! So if I want to show the world as it is, I must invent it."

Cognitive psychologist Donald Hoffman takes this a step further, claiming that we *do* invent the world every day. It isn't simply a case of human beings being incapable of perceiving some aspects of reality, like, say, a certain shade of violet only bees can see, but rather that we actually can't perceive reality at all—and that not being able to might be a sophisticated adaptation of evolution. The metaphor Hoffman uses is the desktop on your computer: one icon represents your email, another your Internet browser, and so on. Well, the email icon is not really the email—even the screen depicting the dizzying list of coupons and petitions is not *really* what your email is either. What is truly occurring is that somewhere deep inside your computer there are processors and chips and fans and who knows what else. If you had to process how it all works just to check your email, then you'd really never get your inbox cleared out. And so we have a helpful interface that enables us to make use of our computers without needing to have attended MIT. Hoffman goes on to say that "reality" operates in much the same way. The brain can't process all of the incredibly complex goings on that comprise reality, so we create the mental interface shorthand of "cat" and "almond milk" and "sub-atomic particle" in order to be able to function. What we call "reality" is a secondary effect of consciousness.

Feel free to go lie down for a little while, but my point is, to dismiss someone as being "kooky" for trying to connect with "the unseen realm" is just slightly disingenuous when we consider, from this particular point of view, that everything we've ever come in contact with is not only unseen but fundamentally unseeable.

Harkening back to his Tetrad, briefly examined in the introduction, Marshall McLuhan hypothesizes that every tool we make "extends" some part of our body-mind complex (the wheel is an extension of the foot, a lasso is an extension of the arms). This tool, he goes on to say, triggers a trauma response in us as if the body part being extended was actually being amputated. So ghostly visitation is a pretty spot-on metaphor for the psychic shock of experiencing the public annihilation of the private self by the instanta-neous unification of the globe by the telegraph.

Basic meditation techniques show us how to see in a new way. We train our minds to become aware of the way in which we grab at our thoughts with the same intensity as we might grab a shotgun or an apple. We laugh at chil-dren for their imaginary friends, and yet we spend the bulk of our lives doing the same thing under the pretext of "planning for the future." Meditation practice at the very least helps us to begin to see the ways in which we are constantly adding on to that which we receive through all-encompassing space—agreeing, disagreeing, looking away.

In contrast to our self-centered fixations, this glimpse of all-encompassing space can be bewitching. After spending years with our heads up our ass, the first glimpse of daylight can seem like touching enlightenment. And perhaps we have, but enlightenment is not an experience. We can go further. To stop at the first glimmer of awareness is ignorance.

The night after I first saw her canvases, I dreamt myself into one of them, ensnared in the dotted ellipses that intersect the vertiginous golden pods ready to burst with esoteric seedlings. My clothing, soaked in lavender egg tempera, dragged me below its surface, beyond the reflection of the swan.

In the alchemical process of the soul's purification, this experience is depicted as a White Swan. Alchemy scholar Adam McLean describes the swan as a bird that is rarely seen in flight, but rather floating serenely on the surface of a lake or a river.[38] The water symbolizes the threshold between the material world and the transcendent, consciousness and unconsciousness. The White Swan represents albedo, or the reflection of the etheric realm. In scientific terms, albedo is the measure of an object's reflective properties, like an aster-oid or a snowbank or the screen in a movie theater. They may seem like light sources but are just reflective surfaces. As is written in *The Song of the Jewel Mirror Samadhi*:

Filling a silver bowl with snow,
Hiding a heron in the moonlight—
Taken as similar, they're not the same;
When you mix them, you know where they are...[39]

The untimely death of af Klint's younger sister Hermina infused more urgency into her spiritual pursuits. With four friends, she formed a group called De Fem, or The Five, and over a period of ten years the women regularly held séances. Af Klint eventually became the group's primary medium, communicating via a "Psychograph," or dial planchette (a precursor to the Ouija board). They were visited by High Masters with the names of Ananda, Amaliel, Gregor, and Clemens. The group often experimented with automatic drawing, allowing the spirits to move through their bodies, guiding their pencils. But things were about to get kicked up to a whole new scale. On January 1, 1906, De Fem were contacted by the Master Amaliel through af Klint, presenting them with a commission to create paintings for a great temple. Af Klint immediately accepted, but the other four women were wary that sustained, direct contact with the spirit world might drive them insane. A reasonable concern, but af Klint was not deterred. She threw herself into the project alone, completing 193 paintings in a year. The resulting work is a mind-stopping array of vibrant abstract images, ranging from swooning, surging organic forms to luminous, mystical geometry. The central series, called *The Ten Largest*, depicts the stages of human life from childhood to old age, and the paintings are each approximately seven-by-ten feet.

When I attended the af Klint retrospective at the Guggenheim, I heard several people comment that they'd never seen anything like it. I, on the other hand, had. I felt compelled to go back to the show a second time because during my first visit I could barely take in the work for all of my own personal associations with the astrological glyphs, vibrant colors, and sacred geometry. My father was a member of a spiritual group (my grandmother called them a cult, but they frankly didn't have the organizational skills for that sort of thing), called the Builders of the Adytum, or B.O.T.A. for short. They were an offshoot of the Theosophical Society, combining elements of astrology, alchemy, the tarot, and kabbalah. They held weekly ceremonies in the cafeteria of an Episcopal church in Denver. On some weekends, my father couldn't find a babysitter for my brother and me, so along we went. We helped set up the ritual space, unloading props from the custodial closet: the Egyptian-revival pillars with detachable tops, the robes, the large piece of canvas that unrolled to reveal a black-and-white checkered floor, used to cover the less-prepossessing linoleum floor. We weren't allowed to observe the ceremony, which was considered too sacred to be witnessed by the uninitiated, or maybe too embarrassing to enact in front of two young boys. I never found out exactly what happened behind the closed accordion door, but, in any case, my suspicions were confirmed: the world is unutterably strange. It's no wonder I got into the theater business and enjoy a bit of dress-up even now.

Hoping for encouragement and collaboration, af Klint shared some of this work with Rudolf Steiner, founder of the Anthroposophical Society. Steiner appreciated some of the work, but overall pooh-poohed it, echoing her friends' concern regarding its mediumistic transmission. He suggested that she rely on inner inspiration instead.

After her encounter with Steiner, four years passed before af Klint painted again. When she did, it was more in line with what he suggested; she was still receiving communication from the High Masters, but the paintings arose in her mind fully formed, and she would then execute them, rather than being physically manipulated by the masters. She worked on two stunning series in 1915, including *The Swan*. The thirteen paintings start figuratively, depicting two swans, one white, one black, in a mirror-like embrace, and from there, abstract further and further. Buddha energy throws back in our faces our own attempts to solidify reality with our preconceptions, without asking us to exclude our preconceptions. If we want to portray the world as it is, we must not portray it as it looks.

The progression of the paintings in sequence feels almost as if we're looking at frames from an unspooling film reel. (Af Klint's studio of twenty years was in the same building as the first movie house in Stockholm.) As a woman who was interested in the latest technological innovations of the day, perhaps she would have attended this Dream Palace, where frozen images are set in motion through light glancing off a white screen into the darkness.

In more recent times, the Art Establishment has engaged in much hand-wringing over how to incorporate af Klint into the accepted narrative of art history. Sure, she had basically invented abstract art as we know it, five years before Kandinsky or Mondrian, but she hadn't exhibited much in her lifetime, and then there was the whole "guided by the spirit world" thing. Could she even be said to have created the paintings?

Painter Nuala Clarke (see page 247) suggests that the real problem lies in the rigid categories into which art historians try to corral artists. "[Af Klint's paintings] do present as abstractions," Clarke says, "but she wasn't trying to do what a lot of the abstractionists were doing. [Hers] are diagrams of entities and states and methods and techniques. They're pictorial, but they're not pictures. I think we're missing a category. And I think what's happening now is that a new category is emerging." This new category, says Clarke, liberates the artist from the misogynistic categories of "decorative craftsperson" or "entertainer," and reestablishes them in the realm of the sacred and of healing. "Art has a wider, bigger meaning. You know, medicine can be an art. [Af Klint's work] is more in that realm."[40]

Whether these High Masters are to be taken literally (af Klint certainly did so), or merely as an Archemedian point by which she could freely engage all-encompassing space, is neither here nor there. The paintings speak for themselves. She knew they were for the future. In her will, she entrusted this staggering body of work into the care of her nephew, stipulating that the paintings must never be sold and must not be shown until twenty years after her death. These wishes were faithfully followed, further adding to the perplexity of where to place her within the canon. One way both the academic and art worlds gauge where an artist belongs is by whom they are sold to and for how much. If she is not for sale, what to do?

The Guggenheim presented the divine commission for the first time in the United States in 2018, realizing her vision for her paintings: to adorn a round, white temple with a spiral staircase. In her case, the medium really *was* the message. And just as these images were received by af Klint from an unseen realm, we now receive them from Hilma af Klint, herself gone beyond. Like true wisdom, her transcendent images communicate intimately while remaining unknowable.

Beware the ire of the calm.

MURIEL SPARK

Whatever may be their use in civilized societies, mirrors are essential to all violent and heroic action.

VIRGINIA WOOLF, *A ROOM OF ONE'S OWN*

In the early 2000s, I developed a mildly unhealthy obsession with *Trading Spaces*, a program in which homeowners help a design team redecorate the house of a neighbor. One of my favorite episodes featured designer Hildi Santo-Tomas, who was known for wreaking severe editorial chic upon unsuspecting suburban moms. In the episode I'm probably half remembering, she encased the arms of a sofa in sharp-cornered wooden boxes. Upon the big reveal, the horrified homeowners said, "But we have children!" to which Hildi suggested that the kiddies might have to "learn the hard way."

Vajra energy is the hard way. Not for nothing, the Tantric Buddhist path is called the Vajrayana, or "diamond vehicle." On the Mohs Hardness Scale (a scientific chart that measures the hardness of minerals, not the erogenous proclivities of the Three Stooges), diamond is a 10 to talc's 1. Virtually indestructible, diamond is the hardest mineral on earth, capable of cutting through anything, including your bullshit. Sharpening it to a finer point, *vajra* means "diamond thunderbolt," and certainly calls to mind the array of ill-tempered deities, from Indra to Athena, Zeus to Marduk, all of whom wielded this unruly, irresistible force. This is appropriate because, whether on point or irrational, Vajra is the energy of anger.

A vajra is a ceremonial weapon. It consists of two pronged domes joined by a central sphere or diamond. The two domes mirror each other, representing the inseparability of wisdom and compassion, confusion and enlightenment.

Vajra's season is early winter. Its time of day is dawn. The cutting coolness of the frosty morning air cuts through the fog of sleep. The geographical terrain that evokes Vajra energy is high, craggy mountain peaks with vast, panoramic views. The wider perspective afforded us by such a lofty vantage point is said to pacify (the first of the Four Karmas) inflamed situations.

I imagine the Alps—not the ones Julie Andrews twirled through but the ones Mary Shelley wrote *Frankenstein* in: imposing, stark, scraping at the sky, taunting lightning down to strike the surface of Lake Geneva.

Shelley's monster is a Vajra character. Reanimated by the spark of life, he is none too happy about existing. He is frightened, disoriented, and in need of care. There is a basic commitment we have to each other: to love and shepherd each other through the relentless catastrophe of being alive. Because Victor Frankenstein never gave birth to anything, he is incapable of being the dark mother. (Badass Rosemary actually picked up her baby.) Instead, horrified by what he's done, he abdicates responsibility to his creation. Abandonment breeds fear, which fosters rage and ultimately violence.

This is not to say that there isn't plenty to be mad about. Consider the amount of time we spend fretting over how to correctly recycle the milk carton; meanwhile, oil companies have actually found a way to set the ocean on fire. And our calls for racial equality are met with the consolation prize of placing a person of color at the head of ICE in the name of diversity. It *is* enough to make you blow your stack. But it might just be the clear-seeing rage of the Vajra family that saves us. Becoming the energy of the fierce mother is required of us now that the whole world is Frankenstein's monster, and we its collective mad creator. Vajra energy gives us the strength to pick up the baby.

Taeuber-Arp

(1889–1943)

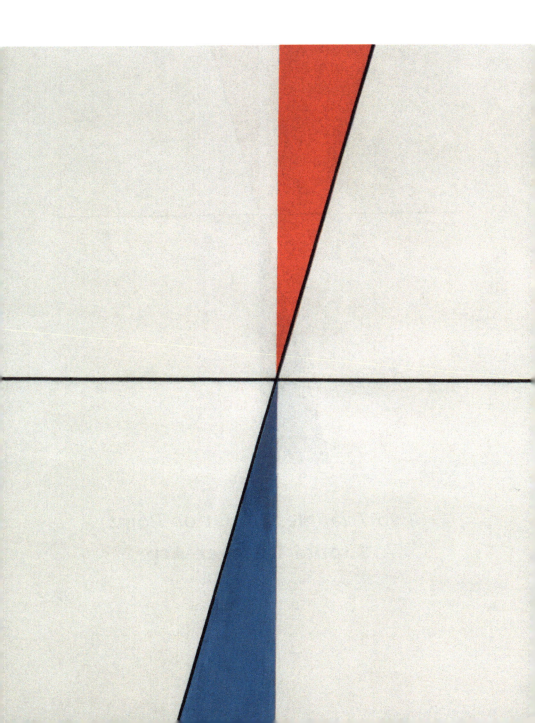

Two Triangles (Point on Point)
Sophie Taeuber-Arp

1931 | PHILADELPHIA MUSEUM OF ART

I n 1916 (one hundred years after *Frankenstein* was first published), the young Swiss artist Sophie Taeuber-Arp began creating creatures of her own; some were marionettes, some were disguises she'd made to enable the artistic double life she'd been forced to lead. By day, Taeuber-Arp had a very respectable and stable job as a professor of textile design and technique at the Zurich School of Arts and Crafts. By night she was dancing at the Cabaret Voltaire, the flashpoint of an iconoclastic art movement known as Dada. Her employers did not approve of her involvement with the Dadaists, and so she put her design skills to use making masks so that she could continue to dance incognito. Going out under cover of darkness in elaborate costumes to combat oppressive institutions, she was basically an art superhero.

Dada was a reactionary art movement that arose in opposition to the atrocities of World War I. Artists from across Europe who saw the unfolding war as a pointless catastrophe, fueled by cocky one-upmanship and petty diplomatic ties labyrinthine enough to trap a minotaur, fled to Switzerland to avoid conscription. Attempting to hold a mirror up to the collateral chaos caused by governmental malfeasance, Dadaists created art that was radically nonsensical—or, put another way, art that could be described in two words: *fuck* and *you*. Fomented in rage, Dada was one big middle finger to the status quo. As the filmmaker Terry Gilliam (a bit of a Dadaist in his own right) described it, "If we're in an absurd situation, a complete nightmare...well, let's create nightmares and throw it back at society and see if we can shake it up."[41]

Marshall McLuhan referred to this as creating an "anti-environment." "Without an anti-environment," he said, "all environments are invisible. The role of the artist is to create anti-environments as a means of perception and adjustment."[42] In other words, the latest technology and political hullabaloo that is constantly swirling around us creates an environment in which we all live, but complete immersion renders it as invisible to us as water is to fish.

Artists, however, seem to be more attuned to their world, able to create work that expresses the effects of these environments, thereby making these environments visible and allowing us to navigate them with greater awareness.

Dada's disruptive streak took its cues from the anarchist philosophy of the day. By peeling back the surface layer of chest-beating nationalism, Dada exposed the underlying horse shit values of bourgeois society that prioritized personal gain, status, and narcotizing comforts at the expense of others. Marcel Duchamp, a contemporary of Taeuber-Arp, scandalized the aesthetic gatekeepers of the day with his "readymades" (the most famous of which is a urinal that he signed with "R. Mutt"). But in her own way, Taeuber-Arp enacted a stealth subversion no less radical by continuing to create arresting work in media typically discounted condescendingly as the "applied arts"—textile design, or decorative objects—which, being functional, were considered to be "lesser-than" what were deemed high art objects, which, in their lack of practical use, it was said, inspired debate or contemplation. The misogyny here is hidden in plain sight, as it was women who were typically "allowed" to work in textile mills while being kept out of the art Académies. Practitioners of the "applied arts" were basically getting a patrician pat on the head on their way to the kitchen to get another tray of burgers for the guys. Though Taeuber-Arp was by no means a hothead, the hypocrisy of cordoning off avenues of creative expression could not have gone unnoticed. But by remixing, repurposing, and reimagining the media she had at her disposal, she was stepping into the station of McLuhan's Tetrad known as "obsolescing." Through her art practice she made obsolete antiquated ways of looking at and being in the world.

In 1918, Taeuber-Arp co-signed the *Dada Manifesto* (there's nothing more Vajra than a manifesto; the flag at the summit, the line in the sand!) concocted by her friend Tristan Tzara, who wrote, "I'm writing this manifesto to show that you can perform contrary actions at the same time, in one single, fresh breath; I am against action; as for continual contradiction, and affirmation too, I am neither for nor against them, and I won't explain myself because I hate common sense."[43]

Not the clearest communication of policy, it is the perfect description of meditation practice. Contrary to outward appearances, when we sit down to practice meditation, we are engaged in an action (*meditate* is a verb, after all). As we meditate, we settle into the stillness of the body, and what quickly becomes apparent by contrast is the incredible amount of movement taking place in the mind and in the immediate environment. Rather than being considered a distraction to our meditation, this contrasting movement is a representative of the very present moment we all seem to be looking for, fresh as a single breath. Meditation is an *anti-environment* in its own right.

In "Dada Performance,"[44] Charles Cramer and Kim Grant write, "Dada was anti-war, anti-authority, anti-nationalist, anti-convention, anti-reason, anti-bourgeois, anti-capitalist, and anti-art." Tiny lightning bolts pierce these conceptual membranes with every anti, anti, anti! At first glance it may seem contradictory that a movement founded on so many "antis" should result in so much creativity. And yet the results speak for themselves. The spirit of this manifesto reminded me of another manifesto of sorts: *The Heart Sutra*. This consternating Buddhist teaching (which took place atop Vulture Peak Mountain, another craggy summit) states, "In emptiness there is no form, no sensation, no perception, no memory, and no consciousness; no eye, no ear, no nose, no tongue, no body, and no mind; no shape, no sound, no smell, no taste, no feeling, and no thought..."[45]

This teaching does not mean that nothing exists, but rather that in any given moment we never have the full picture, and we shouldn't settle for the short-term comfort that our preconceptions provide us. We can cultivate our willingness to take a closer look and still not come to any conclusions. Concepts like "nose" or "nation" can be useful shorthand in getting through the business of the day, but ultimately they cannot be said to really exist in the way that they appear. Everything is dependently arisen, meaning that anything that seems to be "something" is really made up of component parts of other so-called somethings, and therefore cannot be said to exist as a discrete entity.

So to say that one is anti-nationalism or anti-bourgeois or anti-authority is to really say that, seeing as those things can't possibly exist in the way we think they do, we must train our mind to see our addiction to these concepts—concepts that conspire to cover up our true, wakeful nature. And how do we do this? By simply seeing the way in which we grasp them. We don't have to let go of something that isn't real; we just need to see how we grasp at it. The immateriality of what we're grasping at is self-liberating, because when we see what isn't there, we simultaneously become aware of space. And then we have a good laugh.

The Buddha's determination to sit beneath the Bodhi Tree until he achieved perfect, complete enlightenment was a manifesto made physical, one we mirror every time we practice meditation. We sit down to meditate to take a stand against "common sense," which taunts us with promises that "one day in the future" we will get better, be better, have more, stop this, start that, and so on and on and on, as we chase our tails in eternal circles. Instead, we are given the opportunity to see clearly that what we yearn for is not separate from what we reject.

As Sokuzan says, "What you're looking for you're looking at." This is the true nature of Vajra energy: mirror-like wisdom. The outside world with its parades and pandas and Priuses is still relatively there, but our responses to those are our own. All phenomena are reflections of our own minds. The enlightened mind is said to be like a mirror, free of obscurations, simply reflecting back reality as it is while remaining itself unchanged. No greasy fingerprints smudging up the glass so that we look like Liz Taylor in a White Diamonds commercial.

To say that one is "anti-art" is to see the way one erroneously tries to relegate "art-making" to the studio. As the painter Robert Henri once said, "The object isn't to make art, it's to be in that wonderful state which makes art inevitable." Meditation practice naturally cultivates qualities such as receptivity, appreciation, and wonder, which not only inspire us to make art but also imbue mundane activities with artistry.

Even today, specialists in specific artistic disciplines get very territorial about their little fiefdoms and attempt to fortify the illusory boundaries between them. Artist Laurie Anderson (see page 113) wryly suggests to young artists that, if pressed, they refer to themselves as multimedia artists.[46] Sure, it's a meaningless distinction, but it will get people off your back and allow you to do what you want. I wonder if Taeuber-Arp felt any pressure to stay in her lane? Her body of work would suggest otherwise. Just as we see no national boundaries from an airplane, she saw no boundaries in art. Maybe it was her early training as a weaver that enabled her to so deftly incorporate many seemingly disparate threads into her creative practice. Or maybe it went something like this: the geometry of her imagination informed her loom work, the mechanics of which propelled her choreography, which shaped her sculpture and painting. Even in the simple, precise gesture of *Two Triangles (Point on Point)*, which looks exactly like a vajra, she is synthesized as a painter, sculptor, textile designer, and dancer (this could almost be an abstracted Vitruvian Man) all at once. Who knows where else she might have been taken by her insuppressible creative energy had she not tragically died by accidental asphyxiation in her sleep due to a faulty gas stove. She was fifty-three.

The only documentary I could find about the artist online was in French with no subtitles.[47] In using YouTube's automatic translation function I wound up getting an AI-generated poetry slam, which I think Sophie Taeuber-Arp would have gladly danced to. It read:

He says it was a dance filled with art prick
is filled with flickering sun
and shards and razor sharp lines flew in
Shards on his body every gesture was deconstructed
years into precise particles clear and he
madness from the prospect of lighting the ambient atmosphere
Promotes the emergence of witty humor and ironic glosses

As the Dadaists taught us, incoherence is illuminating.

Guy-Blaché

(1873–1968)

Film Still: *Two Little Rangers*
Alice Guy-Blaché

1912 | EYE FILM INSTITUTE NETHERLANDS

Vajra manifested as a sense faculty is the eye. Film is the ultimate Vajra medium, leading the eye around by the nose. Its blueprint, the screenplay, is riddled with instructions to CUT TO, CUT TO, CUT TO. In sparse bursts of language, the screenplay directs the director to guide the camera here and there: zooming in, panning wide, dollying back. Film is a medium of pacification, utilizing wide angles to get a bigger perspective, pushing in to gain intimate access to the details of a flower, a face. Until the days of digital, film editors still used razor blades to cut through celluloid in order to splice it together with other frames and sequences. And in the early days of cinema, film editors were often women. As with the "applied arts" rationale, film editing was considered a technical job, and therefore within a woman's capabilities.

In 1896, the latest thing was about to be unveiled in Paris by the Lumière brothers. A select group was invited to the Society for the Development of the National Industry, including representatives from Lumière's competitor, the Gaumont Company. As the lights went down in the room, images jittered to life on the white screen. The fairly self-explanatory title of the film was *Workers Leaving the Lumière Factory in Lyon*. It was a marvelous achievement, a stunning breakthrough, lustrously beautiful, and unutterably dull. Or, at least so thought Gaumont's secretary, Alice Guy-Blaché. She had worked for Gaumont for several years and had become an expert at using their stable of cameras and in the latest marketing techniques. She felt that while the Lumières achieved a huge breakthrough, they had missed a real opportunity. Their filmmaking style, known as "actuality," depicted mundane, daily activities. Guy-Blaché was inspired to create real magic by applying the new technology to narrative storytelling. Gaumont liked the idea and gave her permission to experiment with the company equipment. The resulting film, *The*

Cabbage Fairy (1896), is now thought to be the first narrative film in history and the first film made by a woman (that we know of).

Guy-Blaché went on to write, direct, edit, and produce hundreds of films for Gaumont before relocating to the United States with her husband, Herbert Blaché, in Fort Lee, New Jersey. Fort Lee was the pre-Hollywood hub of filmmaking in the United States and the early home to many studios, such as Fox, Universal, and MGM. Guy-Blaché and her husband founded Solax, a movie studio that more than held its own in the field.

Many of their films subverted gender norms by casting women in the lead roles of adventure stories. In the frame fragments depicted here from her 1912 western *Two Little Rangers*, it is actress Blanche Cornwall who comes to the rescue of the imperiled male figure dangling from the rocks below. In this serrated Vajra landscape, her precarious vantage point provides her with the panoramic perspective that gives rise to clear seeing and spontaneous compassionate action.

Guy-Blaché's cutting-edge approach to cinematic storytelling would go on to inspire the likes of Sergei Eisenstein and Alfred Hitchcock.[48] Inside Solax, she hung a sign as a reminder to her actors, which read, "BE NATURAL." Her actors came from vaudeville, where they were used to playing to the back of the house, telegraphing emotion by provocatively flaring their nostrils or fluttering their eyebrows. Some filmmakers, not yet savvy about the ramifications of the new medium, encouraged goggle-eyed emoting from their actors to fill the space left by the absence of sound. But Guy-Blaché understood film to be a medium of intimacy. There's no need for broad gestures when the eye of even a rudimentary camera catches everything. Solax's staple actress, Blanche Cornwall, described going to the nickelodeons near the studio, where she could watch her old film performances with an audience. She would make mental notes of where she was acting too broadly so that she could return to set and "rub off the corners" of her performance for her new scene.[49] So the admonition to BE NATURAL asks the actor to trust that their innate humanity is already enough to be captivating. When I studied acting with Suzanne Shepherd, she instructed us that the craft was to "live truthfully under imaginary circumstances." When we asked her by what metric we should adjust our performance in a theater versus in front of a camera, she said, "Intimacy."

Chögyam Trungpa once gave a two-word lecture to his students: "Be genuine." This is a teaching that is equal parts encouraging and consternating. When I first heard it, I felt relieved; I already *am* myself, so there's nothing for me to really do or fix. And yet...I would then, like Jude Law in *I Heart Huckabees*, devolve into the incantation: *How am I not myself? How am I not myself? How am I not myself? How am I not myself?*

In my own meditation practice, I have seen the way I tend to jump on what arises in my mind. This could be a memory, a random image; it could be the sound of traffic out my window or my cat strolling by. I almost immediately start contributing my little punditry on top of the news feed. I like it, I don't like it, I look away. Passion. Aggression. Ignorance. The Three Poisons.

Both my acting and my meditation teachers gave me the same instruction: Be generous; receive anything your scene partner gives you, receive anything that arises in your mind. Don't meddle with the performance of your partner by giving them notes, don't meddle with the process of your mind by adding commentary. Meddling gives us a short-term sense of security and control; we can see how the thing we don't like seems to go away when we shove at it, not realizing that it is the act of shoving itself that keeps the merry-go-round spinning. Our meddling is the very fuel that keeps the machinery of suffering humming along.

Quite often, the way we feel does not jibe with how we feel we *ought* to feel based on the results we think we deserve after all we've been through, and blah blah blah. Put in Vajra terms, this is horse shit. There is a pop psychology sentiment that is fairly commonplace now: you are not your feelings. While on one hand this is true, on the other hand, you could just as accurately say that you ARE your feelings for as long as they last. When you *are* your feelings, what is seen through with Vajra clarity is that there is no individual person who is experiencing the feelings, and therefore the feelings needn't be the jet fuel that sets your collection of bones and organs flailing about. When we feel anger, for example (since we're discussing Vajra), we could just BE GENUINE— just *be* that feeling. By irrigating energy away from our punditry *about* the feeling, and into awareness *of* the feeling, we become the very textures, colors, and tones of the emotional experience, without concretizing it into a fixed identity. Nothing lasts.

According to Sokuzan (who was present for the "Be Genuine" talk), "Being genuine might ruin your reputation." We might look completely foolish when we give up trying to be someone else. And yet being genuine doesn't mean that we should just "express ourselves" like unattended fire hoses in a GOTTA BE ME sort of way. Being genuine might actually feel phony because we're not reflexively acting on our feelings. Your head might feel full of rage, and you could experience it fully without ever actually verbalizing it. That is a full expression of emotion. Meditation practice sharpens the Vajra awareness, which sees what we have coming to us, while providing a wide enough berth to accommodate it. On the other hand, we may well find that we *have* to express something or other—and the way we'll know is that it has just happened spontaneously, genuinely, with no preamble and no postscript.

When living from the leading edge of awareness, we find there is no map, no criteria to follow, and no policy to adhere to. Being genuine always feels precarious, like looking over the edge of a precipice, which is how I imagine Alice Guy-Blaché must have felt as she pushed both herself and this new art form forward. Our proximity, if not to outright danger, then at least to the edge of our comfort zone, can cause us to fall apart. It can also have the opposite effect. The giddiness of Vajra clarity prioritizes awareness, causing fripperies to fall away as our attention crystallizes into a precision instrument, like a razor.

Lipi

(1969–present)

My Mother's Dressing Table
Tayeba Begum Lipi

2013 | COURTESY OF THE ARTIST AND SUNDARAM TAGORE GALLERY

Vajra people teeter on the cutting edge. Their capacity for clear seeing is nonpareil, but, wielded heedlessly, their penetrating intellect cuts everyone—themselves included—to ribbons. Tayeba Begum Lipi's work vibrates with this energy—so much so that she uses razor blades, not in the construction of her work but as the medium itself. Creating blouses, handbags, high-heeled shoes, bathtubs, and beds completely out of razor blades, Lipi's objects evoke the spaces in which women are meant to find refuge in a man's world, while reminding us that without true equality there is nowhere to rest. A room of one's own is little comfort if it's made of razors.

Looking closely at the structure of her work, I was struck by a coincidence in the shape of the blade itself. Lipi uses old-school razor blades that have a negative zig-zag space at their center where the shaver handle can be attached. Oddly, the shape of that negative space is identical to the silhouette of a ceremonial vajra.

Throughout this series, Lipi subverts the notion that the functionality of the "applied arts" renders them incapable of stimulating the intellect in the way "fine arts" can. By transmuting a utilitarian tool into a luxury item, she renders the utility useless and the luxury dysfunctional and therefore beautiful. This is the intellectual power of Vajra energy: with just a few flicks of the wrist, the instruction manual is transformed into a decorative garland of snowflakes.

"I did not even think about why I was choosing it," Lipi said of the razor blade in an interview. "I was only looking for a sharp, violent, ready-made object that could express my reaction to the vulnerable political situation in both Bangladesh and Pakistan. At some point, I questioned why I was attracted to this object, and then I found my answer in a childhood memory."[50] This memory is of being a little girl in rural Bangladesh, helping the local midwives disinfect razor blades by boiling them in water. Still, to this day,

101

razor blades are the only tools available in many rural parts of Bangladesh in case an emergency cesarean section needs to be performed. It is truly adding injury to insult when what is demanded by the female body is deemed unnatural, while what is necessary is forbidden.

My favorite piece, *My Mother's Dressing Table*, is a masterwork of cognitive dissonance, riding the razor's edge between the beautiful and the brutally punitive. I can imagine the artist's mother—an archetypal mother—taking her seat at *her* table to enact the sacred ritual of beautification, if not beatification.

When I was growing up, my aunt Susan introduced me to the Golden Age of Hollywood. I would spend hours poring over her collection of photography books displaying glamorously coiffed ladies performing their toilette. I was fascinated by the way even a Plain Jane could contour, rouge, tease, and tweeze herself into a glittering demi-goddess. But as my friend, the writer Maeve Higgins, once quipped, "When does tweezing become self-harm?" Don't get me wrong, I love dress-up and glamor as much as the next person—I made "fashion over comfort" both a manifesto and a mantra when I was a teenager—but you don't have to exfoliate that much to unearth the mean-spiritedness in most beauty regimens, and that can't really be a coincidence, now, can it? After all, it's not a wild extrapolation to start off at Botox and wind up at rhinoplasty. This is foremost in Lipi's razor blade series: the suffering implicit in the sparkle.

While *Dressing Table* is as resplendent as an altar, it is bare of the usual offerings; no flowers, fruit, or incense here. Not so much as a lip liner. Perhaps this is because, in this case, the deity and the sacrifice are whoever gazes into the mirror. Am I the only one getting Narcissus vibes? Narcissus, of course, was a mythological Greek cutie who saw his own reflection in a pool of water and was so turned on by himself that he couldn't move, and he wound up wasting away. The message being…what? Don't be so into yourself? This is a misreading of the myth, according to Marshall McLuhan. McLuhan makes the important distinction that Narcissus *does not recognize himself* in the reflection—he thinks it's somebody else, and that is what traps him in a self-centered feedback loop. McLuhan calls this "Narcissus Narcosis" and uses it as a central metaphor for his Tetrad theory positing that all tools extend some part of the human body. In the case of razor blades, you could say they extend our fingernails; a mirror extends our vision. But if used thoughtlessly or too speedily, the tool "reverses"[51] on itself and does the opposite of what it was intended to do: a razor can cut your fingers off, a mirror can deceive you. And yet even these experiences help us to wake up.

With the rise of the Me Too movement, countries around the world are feeling the ramifications of an eons-old fuck-up: namely, the moronic notion that men are somehow superior to women. The very fact that women take umbrage at this miscalculation and can clearly articulate why it is a total cock-up is evidence enough of patriarchy's fatal flaw (to use a writing analogy). This message is implicit in Lipi's work: buried under the seeming softness of femininity is the potential for real violence. As she describes it, societal suppression has turned women into an unused matchstick: when struck, women's disregarded anger and intellect can explode and annihilate everything in its path (more on destroying in the Karma chapter). This capacity for violence, of course, lies within us all. "Maybe it's hidden somewhere," says Lipi, "but it can come out at any time."[52]

Tayeba Begum Lipi's penetrating vision helps to counteract the incredible amount of time wasted and the incredible amount of pain caused because somewhere along the way men took a very wrong turn and would not go back to ask for directions. Vajra energy, which has no compunction about meanness but loathes stupidity, gleefully whets its diamond razor blade on misogyny's thick skull.

de Saint Phalle

(1930–2002)

Tirs
Niki de Saint Phalle

1962 | PHOTOGRAPH BY GIANCARLO BOTTI

To read rage and violence into the art of Niki de Saint Phalle isn't exactly knocking down any doors. Her work is riddled with monsters both mundane (pythons, politicians) and mythic (dragons, King Kong). *Tirs*, or "Shooting Paintings," act as killing fields in which she is judge, jury, executioner, and executed. To witness the spectacle of a gun-toting wayward fashion model shooting art in an alley begs the patrician question, How did a nice gal like you wind up in a place like this?

In 1994, de Saint Phalle published her illustrated autobiography *Mon Secret*, in which she describes her "Summer of Serpents." She was eleven years old, walking through the countryside, when she came across two snakes entwined on a rock, which both terrified and entranced her. The incident not only instilled a lifelong ophidiophobia in her, but the snake would become a personal emblem of a horrifying event that took place a few days later: she was raped by her father. Her beloved protector became her assailant, revealing once and for all the horrible hypocrisy of the world. The unthinkable fact, ragged as steel wool, swallowed up by merciful serpents.

De Saint Phalle was born into an ancient, aristocratic family, which, by some accounts, can be traced back to the founding of France in 987 CE. From her father's side of the family, she is said to be related to Gilles de Rais, the comrade-in-arms to Joan of Arc, who was later tried and executed for murdering over 150 children. He's credited as being history's first serial killer, though that can hardly be true. Over the centuries, the historical Gilles de Rais had merged with the fabled Bluebeard. While Gilles de Rais allegedly killed children and Bluebeard his wives, still, the fairy tale conveys the *feeling* of the murderer, if not the facts.[53]

Blue (Vajra's color) is a funny color for a beard. Ancient Germans used to dye their gray hair with woad—the original blueheads. Ancient Romans disliked blue, associating it with violence and barbarism, since the Celts and

Germans painted their bodies blue in order to appear fiercer in battle.[54] It wasn't until the twelfth century that blue started appearing more regularly in Christian art, eventually becoming the Virgin Mary's go-to fashion choice. Because of its association with the Holy Mother, blue came to symbolize grief and compassion. Many of the wrathful deities that populate the nontheistic pantheon of Tibetan Buddhism have blue skin, symbolizing wrathful compassion, the transmutation of righteous anger into compassionate action.

One Tibetan legend tells the tale of Palden Lhamo, whose husband, the king of Lanka, was hell-bent on eradicating all Buddhists. The only hope of stopping him was to end his lineage, which, awkwardly, meant killing her own son. When her husband was away on a hunting trip, she killed their son, ate his flesh, and drank his blood from his own skull. She then turned his skin into a saddle and rode away to safety. Upon discovering his wife's treachery, the king shot a poison arrow at her, which landed in the rump of her getaway mule. She removed the arrow and there an eye grew, which kept a lookout over all the lands. Today, Palden Lhamo is known as the protector of Tibet and all the Dalai Lamas. You could say that by abdicating her most essential duty as a wife and mother, she made space for a greater truth to take root and flourish. And yet, while she is a wrathful deity, she can't really be too mad about not receiving a Mother's Day card.

During a cringe-worthy French TV program from February 1965, in which the interviewer can't seem to wrap his head around the fact that de Saint Phalle is *not* in a kitchen but is making art, she deftly skewers him by explaining her work in this way: "Here, the character which inspired me is Gilles de Rais. First, he was an ancestor of mine, and second, I admire him because he really saw things through to the end. He is a true criminal, not a petty one. He went all out so I'm impressed. Among all my ancestors, he is the one. There is him and there is me, all the rest don't count."[55]

De Saint Phalle was groomed from an early age to be a wife and mother, one of the Ladies Who Lunch, hosting charity functions and quietly lobotomizing themselves on vodka stingers. One of her earliest memories was of her mother counting linens, a sight that made her blood run cold. She vowed never to be trapped by dreary domesticity. "I decided to become a heroine," she said. "Who would I be? George Sand? Joan of Arc? Napoleon in drag?

What did it matter who I would be? The main thing was it had to be difficult, grandiose, exciting."[56]

By the age of eighteen, de Saint Phalle was pursuing an acting career and working regularly as a model, appearing on the covers of *Life*, *Elle*, and *Vogue* magazines. In order to get out of her parents' house, she eloped with Harry Mathews, a young man she'd known since childhood. Within the year, she became pregnant, sidelining her burgeoning career. De Saint Phalle quickly began to realize that, despite its bohemian trappings, her life was slowly being subsumed by domesticity; she was counting the linens. She and Harry began engaging in competitive affairs, which escalated one night with de Saint Phalle attacking his mistress. He then discovered his wife wasn't just holding grudges, she was hoarding scissors, razors, and knives under their bed. Taking this as a real threat, Harry had her committed to a mental hospital in Nice. The doctors speculated that, given her condition, it would take about five years to cure her—an optimistic prognosis considering that what ailed her was the fact that society had no use for her ambition, talent, or intelligence as it pertained to anything outside the home. In an attempt to help her accept her lot in life, the doctors subjected her to ten rounds of electroshock therapy. To their surprise, it was art that had the most transformative effect on her, though perhaps not in the way they had intended. At the hospital, de Saint Phalle threw herself into painting the way one might throw oneself into a lifeboat from a sinking ship. She was out of the hospital in six weeks, determined to be an artist. The week following her release from the hospital, she received a letter from her father that said, "I'm sure you remember when you were eleven and I tried to make you my mistress."[57] I'm not sure if this was meant to be an olive branch, but it could have hardly been comforting in her fragile state.

Back home, de Saint Phalle split her time between modeling gigs, painting, and home life. Eight years on, however, she'd had a second child and felt that as a wife and mother she would never truly be able to devote herself to art-making. So, in 1960, she moved out, leaving the child-rearing to her husband. Needless to say, this was quite a radical move, especially considering that in France, up until 1965 a woman had to gain permission from her husband to get a job. "If I didn't want to be a second-class citizen," she said, "I would have to go out into the world and fight to impose myself as an artist."[58]

She took a studio in L'Impasse Ronsin, a ramshackle warren of workshops in Montparnasse, where she ate, talked, and created alongside other artists such as Constantin Brancusi, Marcel Duchamp, and Jean Tinguely (whom she would later marry). It was there that she began experimenting with blending painting, sculpture, and performance into what would become her *Tirs* (you can find clips online). *Tir* is French for "shoot"—it sounds like the English word *tear* (as in crying), which itself looks like the English word *tear* (as in ripping). All of these meanings had been considered and intended by de Saint Phalle, who was a polyglot.

With no wifely demands hindering her work, de Saint Phalle was surprised by the volcano of repressed fury that was unleashed. She referred to her art in this period as "voodoo" and "an exorcism."[59] In other words, an externalized ritual designed to effect inner change. Indeed, her shooting paintings had all the elements of a ceremony: first the sacrifice must be prepared, the white board (always white) festooned with assemblage, sacs of paint hidden in each object, perhaps some raw eggs, a food offering. All of these painted white. A pure offering.

Then there was the donning of her jumpsuit, as pristine as pontifical vestments, accented dramatically by black boots, cuffs, and collar. Reverently holding her .22 long rifle, she brings it to her shoulder, her eye, her finger assuming the position. Taking the painting in her sights she pulls the trigger:

> I shot against daddy. Against all men. Big men, tall men, fat men. Men...I shot against myself. I shot against men. I shot because it was fun and it made me feel great. Because I was fascinated watching the painting bleed and die...Instead of becoming a terrorist I became a terrorist in art...Sacrifice. Ready, aim, fire! Red, yellow, blue. The painting is crying. The painting is dead. I have killed the painting. It is reborn. War with no victims.[60]

The violence in the canvases' fractures and eruptions are self-evident. The pressure de Saint Phalle was under personally and socially was so intense, who wouldn't have experienced tectonic rumbling? There was her father's abuse, her ambivalent feelings about motherhood, wanting to be taken seriously as an artist when her primary value was her fertility and her appearance—not to mention the Cuban Missile Crisis, the Algerian War of Independence, and the Vietnam War.

A fragment of a poem de Saint Phalle wrote says, "...Hell is a monster. I am the monster. Hell is hunger. I am the devouring mother..."[61] In order to make art, she felt she had to strike out on her own, strike out serpent-like at a fabricated object so that the invisible shackles she was trying to liberate herself from could be seen. Perhaps she feared, as a mother, that in creating art she was killing her children, that she was Gilles de Rais. She later wrote, "I felt that I had done such a terrible thing in leaving my family that I buried myself 100% in my work for the rest of my life to make up for it. I needed to prove that what I had done had not been in vain and had been worthwhile..."[62]

It's easy to turn another person's life into a fairy tale, to mix both the fraught and frothy episodes into an elixir from which we extract pat moralities. While the traditional reading of Bluebeard warns of the perils of curiosity in a young woman, a more contemporary reading could be that nobody deserves the trauma they have coming to them—or time alone doesn't heal all wounds. Perhaps by placing us outside the event, art can pacify trauma through the ritual of making, which buys the mind the few extra seconds it needs to catch up to the nervous system.

It is the precision of Vajra energy that creates ritualized forms. By observing these forms, we create space in which we can observe the tumult of the mind. However, the instruction is to *observe* a form, not to *obey* it. The ritual itself is a jumping-off point, not a conclusion. When we use ritual as a means of wresting imaginary control from somewhere or other, we miss the meaning of the form. Or, put another way, when we become addicted to the ritual, we miss the metaphor (Joseph Campbell described this as seeing steak on the menu and then eating the menu).

After two years, Niki de Saint Phalle abandoned the *Tirs*, concerned they were becoming too addictive. In gratifying her rage through the act of shooting, she was fortifying the very negativity she was trying to expunge. The thrill of metaphorical violence started to backslide into the thrill of actual violence—the ego's fail-safe technique of reifying itself: looky what I broke! She was able to walk away once they had served their purpose: the transmutation of anger into art through Vajra awareness. "In my work," she said,

"I am condemned to reveal every joy, desire, sorrow, and pain. Transformed, they become other form, other color, other texture. It is all my life. Nothing is secret."[63]

Anderson

(1947–present)

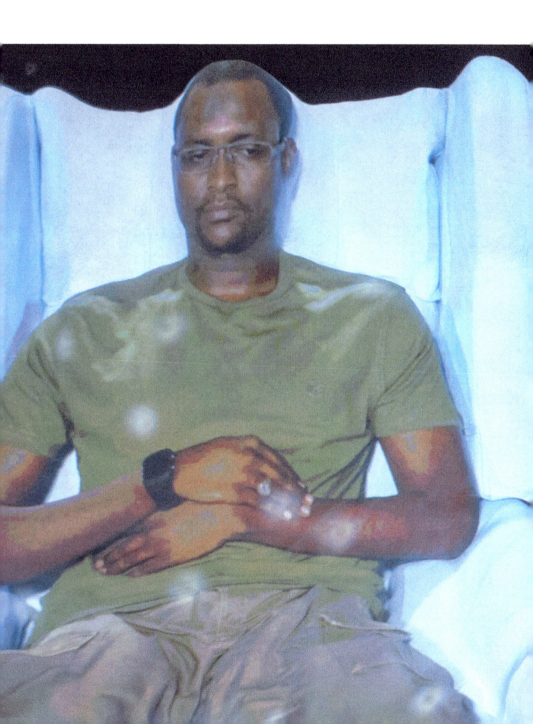

Habeas Corpus
Laurie Anderson

2015 | PHOTOGRAPH BY STEPHANIE BERGER

Vajra is the Buddha family of the intellect, concerning itself with matters of invention, advocacy, gadgetry, philosophy, and linguistics—the conceptual realm. All present in the work of Laurie Anderson, who has invented several iterations of electric violin, designed virtual reality experiences, and acted as the first (and last) artist in residence at NASA.

Anderson came up in the pre-Reagan art world of 1970s New York City, when housing was cheap and expression was free because nobody thought for a minute they would actually make a living off their artwork anyway. But lightning struck for Anderson when her self-released single *O Superman (For Massenet)* became an unexpected hit in the U.K. in 1981. This led to an eight-album deal with Warner Music, world tours, and commissions for work in every conceivable medium. But whether she is sculpting, painting, composing, or even collaborating with William S. Burroughs (she turned his epigram "Language is a virus from outer space" into a fabulously asymmetrical dance song) Laurie Anderson still sees a consistent through line in her work. "At the root of all these works are stories," she writes. "They are the engines. Stories and words are what I love most."[64]

In her 2015 film *Heart of a Dog*, Anderson cites the Austrian philosopher Ludwig Wittgenstein: "His books are full of cryptic sentences about logic and about how language has the power to actually create the world."[65] She quotes Wittgenstein's koan-like seventh proposition, "What we cannot speak about, we must pass over in silence," which Anderson interprets as "If you can't talk about it, it simply doesn't exist."[66] In a later interview she elaborates:

> That's an insane thing to say, first of all. I mean, think of the number of things you just can't put into words, and your silent eyes looking around at everything...Words come into your eyes in a very different way [than] through your ears. And in a way they stream in, and it's

115

more sly somehow, and it's not as emotional as hearing...It comes through the eyes and you're more weirdly analytical and...very dream-like. You're not sure you saw that—did you see it? If it doesn't get articulated you're not even sure sometimes that you saw it.[67]

This is an instructive observation for understanding Vajra energy, which manifests through the eyes as the visual sense field. Of the five senses, vision is the most abstracted and least intimate; hearing, taste, smell, and touch all seem to be happening in or on our bodies, whereas the images we receive through the eyes appear to be coming at us from "out there." This experience of "out there" becomes very convincing evidence of duality. From there, our concepts about what it is we're perceiving quickly rush in and suddenly we're forming language to articulate, codify, and control the external phenomena. The apparently solid, discreet visual objects we perceive, more often than not weren't informed of our unassailable authority, and as a result do not give a hoot about what we expect of them. This, in turn, gives rise to an emotion we call anger, and which itself feels as solid as a cudgel. The "solid" anger then strikes out at the "solid" object, making contact: DO WHAT I SAY!

"Language is so powerful," Anderson says. "It will make you remember [things] in a certain way. Or it will make you realize that you're having an experience that you weren't so sure you were having."[68] And if the old words, which were crafted to corral the outside world to our specifications, then reveal themselves to be ineffectual, well, then new words are created or repurposed from the old ones. There they hang in the air, like Calder mobiles, casting long, strange shadows that morph too quickly to be collectively interpreted. In his novel *Nineteen Eighty-Four*, George Orwell illustrated the Vajra-like ability to exert control by forcing language into conceptual contortions via Newspeak, with words like *pornosec*, *doubleplusungood*, and *thoughtcrime*.

In 1998, Anderson created a work called *Dal Vivo* (Life) at the Fondazione Prada Milan, where she orchestrated a virtual prison break by telepresencing a bank robber named Santino from San Vittore prison onto a life-size sculpture in the gallery. Apparently, his girlfriend came to stand by the sculpture every day of the exhibit, even though Santino could neither hear nor see anyone in the gallery. Anderson described this project as "the combination of an

Egyptian tomb, a time warp, and a meditation chamber."[69] It was a project she had long wanted to remount in the United States, which has the highest number of incarcerated people in the world. In 2015, when she was commissioned to create an installation for New York City's Park Avenue Armory, she had her opportunity. While the technology required to realize the project had become more sophisticated, we were now in post-9/11 America, and despite meeting with several wardens, Anderson and her team were told in no uncertain terms by the Department of Homeland Security that "this will never happen in the United States of America."[70] This temporarily derailed the project, sending Anderson down a creative off-ramp into a project that would involve working with live ponies—not completely unrelated, it turns out, as her sister Lisa, a horse trainer, said, "If ponies were people they would all be in jail. They're mean and they're also smart. Like psychopaths."[71]

Luckily, Anderson and the original project were rescued by a London-based NGO called Reprieve, which, according to its website, "defend[s] marginalised people who are facing human rights abuses, often at the hands of powerful governments." The people at Reprieve were working with a former Guantanamo Bay detainee who might be interested in participating in the project. She flew to West Africa to meet her soon-to-be collaborator, Mohammed el Gharani. Together they went on a guided tour of one of the prisons where enslaved African people were held before being forced onto ships and sent along the Gold Coast, to the Middle Passage, and on to the Caribbean. The same path el Gharani suffered centuries later. "I was acutely aware of his physical presence," Anderson wrote. "His back had been broken. He was still missing teeth. His head had been smashed. I couldn't forget that it was my country that had done this."[72] Anderson was the first American el Gharani had met who was not his captor.

Mohammed el Gharani is a Saudi-born Chadian citizen who worked on a farm in Saudi Arabia with his family, tending goats. When he was thirteen, he traveled to Pakistan to study at his uncle's computer school. One evening, while he was worshipping at a mosque, he was kidnapped in a raid by the Northern Alliance. He was then taken to Bagram, where he was sold for $5,000 to the U.S. government, which was in search of evil-doers. According to the U.S. government, el Garani had been part of an Al Qaeda terrorist cell in London in 1998. (How he managed to make it to London from a Saudi goat farm at age eleven, and then gain admittance to this terrorist cell, the U.S. government never deigned to say.)

After being sold to the U.S. government by the Northern Alliance, el Gharani was taken to Guantanamo Bay, although it would be six months before he even found out where he was. He was fourteen years old, the youngest detainee in Guantanamo's sordid history. During the nearly eight years he was imprisoned, he was frequently held in solitary confinement, humiliated, and tortured.

One of the most surreal episodes el Gharani recounted to Anderson was an incident involving a fellow detainee who told a guard he had dreamt that a submarine had come and rescued all of the prisoners. The guard interpreted his dream as a literal threat, and that night the sky above Guantanamo was ablaze with searchlights as boats and planes scanned the horizon for the prisoner's dream submarine.

El Gharani was twenty-one when he was released. There were no charges, and therefore no possibility of those charges being dismissed. Like all former Guantanamo detainees, el Gharani is barred from ever reentering the United States, and therefore made a perfect candidate for telepresence in Anderson's piece.

In an interview with journalist Laura Flanders, Anderson contextualized the project:

> The first thing [the U.S. Government] did in order to be able to do what they wanted to do, was to declare Guantanamo detainees "nonpersons." Nobody actually gave them the right to actually say "I'll call you a non-person"—I'm not sure how they got that right, but they are non-persons. One of the directives in founding Guantanamo was to find a "Legal Outer Space." So that's what Guantanamo became. It was a non-place...where our laws don't apply. None of them. So, we could do what we wanted. There were also...questions I would ask [like], "Were doctors present when Mohammed was being tortured?" That question can only be answered by [saying] "There were 'behavioral-science consultancy teams' involved in the treatment

of detainees at Guantanamo Bay"...People were committing suicide until, suddenly—Wow!—the suicide rates dropped! However, suicide was simultaneously redefined as "manipulative self-injurious behavior." Now, there were lots of people who died of manipulative self-injurious behavior, but no suicides! Bingo! So, language is operating in a very, very heavy way...Why is this combination of pornography and violence happening? Why are we doing this?[73]

The imbroglio Anderson describes with its mutating language, clinical cruelty, and righteous anger, encapsulates the dizzying ellipse Vajra energy can travel between viciousness and valor.

In their first phone call together, el Gharani told Anderson he hoped this project would help his brothers still locked up in Guantanamo. She reminded him that this was an art project and there was no guarantee that it would help his brothers. "Whatever happens, what are you hoping will come out of this?" she asked. "An apology," he said.[74] Whether Anderson had the heart to inform him this was an even more unlikely outcome, I don't know. But the project, *Habeas Corpus*, was underway.

According to the Cambridge English Dictionary, *habeas corpus* is "a legal order that states that a person in prison must appear before and be judged by a court of law before he or she can be forced by law to stay in prison." Derived from medieval Latin, it literally translates as "you shall have the body." And so the resonances begin: Mohammed el Gharani is a non-person who was never afforded due process of law, with no bodily rights, who is physically barred from entering the U.S. and yet is here—a discarnate angel.

I had the privilege of attending *Habeas Corpus*. Inside the main exhibition area, a former drill hall, the only source of illumination was a mirror-ball the size of one of Saturn's smaller moons. From it refracted countless beams of light in the darkness, evoking both cosmic and legal outer space. At the far end of the hall stood the seventeen-foot-tall biomorphic sculpture, an abstracted Lincoln Memorial onto which the livestream image of el Gharani was projected. Unlike the *Dal Vivo* piece, however, el Gharani could see us. We brought our bodies before him like a judge, begging to be freed from the prison of crimes we'd paid to have committed against him. We waved into the camera, futilely mouthing "I'm sorry. I'm so, so sorry."

Is an apology admissible if it cannot be heard?

Too much of a good thing is wonderful.

LIBERACE

The strongest guard is placed at the gateway to nothing. Maybe because the condition of emptiness is too shameful to be divulged.

F. SCOTT FITZGERALD, *TENDER IS THE NIGHT*

Years ago, when I was a young actor trying to make it in the big city, I worked as a maître d' at Nobu, a trendy Japanese restaurant in Tribeca, famous for its blackened miso cod and rock shrimp tempura with creamy-spicy sauce. While it had become a tourist trap for people who had seen every episode of *Sex and the City* and never recovered, it remained a hotspot for celebrities as well. One of our jobs as front-of-house staff was to coordinate with the teams of film stars to make sure they were "taken care of," which to me always sounded a bit like a gangland threat (we also served our share of mobsters, or at least beefy guys who made their money in waste management and offered big handshakes).

In any case, one evening we'd gotten word that Tom Cruise, Katie Holmes, and their daughter Suri would be hosting a dinner for mystery guests. The Cruise security detail came in early to make note of all the entrances and exits. Tom, Katie, and Suri would enter through the staff entrance to be whisked to the back room to sit at "Bob's Table" (as in De Niro), where their very important guests would later join them. I asked who I should be looking out for and was summarily informed to mind my own business. "You'll know them when you see them."

Later, just as the security guards had foretold, the Cruise family showed up and were discreetly ushered into the back of the restaurant. The mystery guests, however, had yet to appear. While the normal stream of diners were greeted and seated, I maintained a hospitality hyper-vigilance, eyes peeled for the special guests whom I would know when I saw them, and feeling more and more like I was living in a seafood-themed John le Carré novel. Who could be more high-profile than Tom Cruise and Katie Holmes?! It couldn't be Kanye (surprisingly shy). It couldn't be Patrick Stewart, because he makes his own reservations! Kofi Annan? Madonna?!

Just as my hyper-vigilance began to boil over into a mania, a woman with a child about Suri's age walked in and said in hushed tones, "I'm here for the Cruise party." I sprang into action and escorted them to the back room. But as we approached the table, things lurched into slow motion: I saw that all of the chairs were taken and that the mystery guests were Ben Stiller, Christine Taylor, and *their* kid (no offense, but *that* was what all of the hullabaloo was over?). The Cruise security detail rushed at me shouting, "Don't encourage them! Don't encourage them!" I turned in horror to the woman behind me, who hissed, "If you think you can shove me in a back corner with a bunch of strangers just because I've got a kid, too, you've got another thing coming!" It turned out she was there for the *Cruz* party. Come for the status, stay for the rock shrimp.

Are you on the list?

Who are you wearing?

Don't you know who I think I am?

Would you like whipped cream on that?

Ratna ("jewel" in Sanskrit) is all about status, pride, and the frail ineffectualness that conspicuous consumption tries to mask.

Ratna's time of day is high noon, when the sun's nuclear power pummels the earth, accelerating growth and decomposition alike. It is also the natural bounty of the autumn harvest, Ratna's season.

Ratna is Big Mac energy with extra Special Sauce. It's the Ghost of Christmas Present lobbing éclair heels at Central Park's raccoons on their overflowing trash can thrones. Its terrain is the forest floor sprouting mushrooms from a decomposing carcass. It's Thanksgiving dinner and Barbara Cartland's hot-pink walk-in wardrobe. It's too much too soon and you can't afford *not* to have it, no matter how high the price.

Ratna at its best experiences the entire world as the Wish-Fulfilling Jewel, a symbol of the potentiality of infinite enrichment. The wish granted is the wisdom that you have never actually lacked anything in your entire life; there is nothing to gain and nothing to lose. To paraphrase Byron Katie, if your partner falls in love with someone else, you joyfully help them pack.

My main practice is *shikantaza*. This is a Japanese word that loosely translates as "Just Precisely This," or "Just Sitting." The instruction is to face a wall and sit on the floor or in a chair in an upright, relaxed position. The hands are either nested in the lap left-over-right with the thumbs touching, or they're resting palms-down on the thighs. The eyes remain open in a soft, downcast gaze, blinking as you normally would. That's it. Although it is a very simple practice, there is also something very Ratna about shikantaza, in that it allows us to embody generosity by giving everything our attention without discrimination and receiving everything that arises without commenting. Just precisely this.

In meditation practice, we become aware of the beautiful cut-crystal bowl of awareness. But then we swiftly lose confidence in it. I mean, what is the point, really, of a crystal bowl if there's nothing in it? So we fill it with wax fruit or hard grandma-candy or car keys. Philosopher Georges Bataille equated this unbridled impulse to fill space by hoarding wealth with the hope of attaining "sovereignty"—the freedom "to be and do nothing." And so we continue to tarry away, stockpiling our little nuts or NTFS (see page 227) or whatever, for some future liberation. However, this creates a dynamic in which we're like the cast of *The Discreet Charm of the Bourgeoisie*, wandering from meal to meal, but never getting to dine. André Gregory, in *My Dinner with André*, perfectly sums up the Ratna predicament:

> My mother knew a woman, Lady Hatfield, who was one of the richest women in the world and she died of starvation because all she would eat was chicken...her body was starving, but she didn't know it because she was quite happy eating her chicken, and so she finally died. See, I honestly believe that we're all like Lady Hatfield now. We're having a lovely, comfortable time with our electric blankets and our chicken and meanwhile we're starving because we're so cut off from contact with reality that we're not getting any real sustenance...[75]

Rather than reprioritizing our own values so that we may be truly enriched, most of the rest of us keep our heads down, dipping the stale fantasy of tomorrow's fortune in the bitter tears of today, hoping for nourishment.

de Garis Davies

(1881–1965)

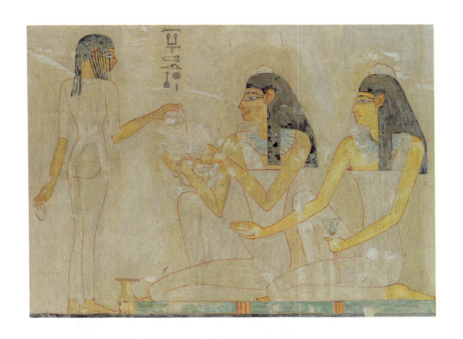

Women at a Banquet
Nina de Garis Davies

1925 CE | ORIGINAL CA. 1479–1425 BCE, METROPOLITAN MUSEUM OF ART

Ratna energy lolls between splendor and decay. To my mind, no culture better exemplifies this dance than ancient Egypt. With its juxtaposition of tombs and temples, arid desert and verdant Nile Delta, Egypt has inspired two-bit adventurers and big-time crooks to search the sand for treasure—a little bit of forever.

Joseph Campbell once wryly observed that anyone who sets eyes on an ancient Egyptian temple can't help but have a past-life experience as a high priestess. Maybe it's the stunning graphic simplicity of the hieroglyphs, or the technicolor wall paintings, or the jaw-dropping architectural feats. Maybe it's their fabulous dress sense and their appreciation for a smoky eye. Or maybe it's the mummies, simultaneously comforting and inflaming our fear of death. Whatever the inspiration, you have to give props to a culture whose funerary arrangements can out-dazzle a Liza Minnelli wedding. Even a modern facsimile like *Women at a Banquet* by Nina de Garis Davies manages to conjure the magic and majesty of ancient Egypt. The impulse to preserve, replicate, and display the ephemera of history is a particularly Ratna one. Whether what is being displayed is authentic or not is beside the point. Ratna likes what it likes but is not a connoisseur. What is important is that we have it and can show it off. Museums themselves are born of this Ratna impulse, as are cabinets of curiosities, roadside attractions, and Madame Tussauds.

The image here is a detail of a wall relief from TT100 (Theban Tomb 100), which belonged to Rekhmire, the vizier to pharaohs Thutmose III and Amenhotep II. A vizier was like a prime minister, with duties ranging from overseeing the state archives to acting as head of the judiciary. After the pharaoh, he was the most powerful person in Egypt. One hopes for Vizier Rekhmire's sake that the judgment of Osiris was made favorably, before earthly opinion of him began to tank, which, if the apparently deliberate ancient vandalism of his tomb walls are any indication, tank it did. Hieroglyphs and portraits have been chiseled off, some covered over in red paint. It's not known what Rekhmire might have done to fall out of public favor after nearly fifty years in power. Up today, down tomorrow. This dynamic evokes the Buddhist teaching on the Eight Worldly Dharmas: praise and blame, pleasure and pain, loss and gain, infamy and fame—pairs of seeming opposites, requiring each other to exist, keeping us teeter-tottering back and forth in a cycle of suffering.

Rekhmire's tomb is one of the oldest known in modern Egyptology (Western documentation of it goes back to the 1830s). The purpose of tomb paintings was not just to show how beloved, powerful, and popular you were in life; they were also propagandistic evidence of the life you deserved to *continue* to have in the life to come. Like an ancient vision board. But what makes the art in this particular tomb so noteworthy and invaluable is its rich depictions of everyday life in ancient Egypt. The image here, which the Metropolitan Museum of Art has titled *Women at a Banquet,* shows a servant girl in a sheer dress pouring drinks from a tiny pitcher for a pair of elegant, seated ladies. The hieroglyphs above their heads read, "For your Ka! Make a happy day!"[76] Their opulent pectoral jewelry and the lumps of aromatic wax that adorn their heads indicate status and the significance of the occasion. Ancient Egyptians celebrated many festivals throughout the year; this one is thought to depict the Beautiful Festival of the Valley. Although dedicated to honoring the dead, it was not a somber affair—on the contrary, it was a multi-day blowout in which, according to the Met's wall text, drinking ran to "excess to achieve an altered state of inebriation, disorientation, and sleepiness that was thought to enable communication with a deity or the dead. For this purpose, drugs might have also been used."[77] In other words, ancient Egyptians got next-level blasted fairly regularly as a part of their cultural heritage, which explains a lot about their talking hippo gods. This kind of in-it-to-win-it, over-the-top celebration is the perfect example of Ratna excess.

The color of Ratna is a rich golden yellow. Its monetary value notwithstanding, gold was an incredibly important material and color to the ancient Egyptians. The flesh of the gods was said to be made of gold, and, according to Egyptologist Richard H. Wilkinson, "Its untarnishing nature provid[ed] a metaphor of eternal life and its brightness an image of the brilliance of the sun."[78] The sun itself is the greatest metaphor for the ceaseless, indiscriminate generosity of enlightened Ratna energy.

As for the artist who originally painted this image, not much can be said. Ancient Egyptians had no concept of art as self-expression, as we do today.[79] And while one lofty Egyptian term for "artist" was "He-who-keeps-alive" (no pressure), painters and sculptors were really considered to be craftspeople along the lines of jewelry- or textile-makers who passed their knowledge down the family line. In the case of wall paintings and sculpture, very precise templates and grid systems were implemented to achieve the correct results. So not a lot of self-expression going on. Evidence of this is how little is known about the individual artists who made the work. It's unknown whether any of them were women, but it is difficult to imagine that in ancient Egypt's five-thousand-year history, no woman ever carried on in the family painting or sculpting business. After all, women were allowed to own property, run their own businesses, choose who they married, and get divorced if they wanted to. Textile-making was not an unusual occupation for a woman, nor was it unheard of to act as brewers, psychics, dentists, and physicians, not to mention, on occasion, pharaohs.

This image, dated 1925, is an egg tempera reproduction of the tomb wall by Nina de Garis Davies. Little is known of her life either, although we do know that after graduating from the Royal College of Art in London, de Garis Davies traveled to Alexandria, Egypt, in 1906, to visit some friends. There she fell in love with the country's monuments, as well as with fellow artist, Norman de Garis (the two merged surnames after marrying), who worked in Egypt as a freelance copyist. These were the days before any sort of reliable color photography, and so the accurate recording of color was left to artists who could travel light and work quickly in rugged conditions. In 1907, Norman de Garis was appointed head of the graphic section of the Metropolitan Museum of Art's Egyptian expedition, and he quickly put de Garis Davies' talents to work. Angling a series of mirrors to reflect light into the tombs, she would use tracing paper to copy the forms from the wall and then transfer them to a heavier paper stock. She then applied color in the same order as the original artisans, painting the background first, then the body, and finally the clothing.[80] Most of the pigments used in ancient Egyptian painting are mineral based, which is why they've lasted as long as they have. Unlike most modern copyists who used watercolor, de Garis Davies preferred egg tempera in the tombs, which she felt more accurately captured the rich tones used by the ancient artists. From 1908 to 1938, de Garis Davies and her husband created approximately 350 facsimiles for the Met, many of which remain in its collection today, all the record we have of a vanishing Egypt.

It must be said that the Egypt they documented was vanishing precisely because of colonial pillaging taking place with dizzying alacrity. We cannot really look at a Western museum's collection of another culture's artifacts without acknowledging their questionable provenance (to put it politely). Egypt has certainly seen more than its fair share of plundering. And I'm not talking about the contemporaneous plunder of royal tombs by the very people who built them. As a person who also lives in a culture in which the bulk of the wealth is hoarded away from public circulation by a sliver of the population, I can get behind a proto-ancient-Egyptian-Robin-Hood character stealing and melting down the golden toe-caps (look it up) of the One Percent so that their own family could eat.

No, I'm talking about the plunder of Egypt by Western empires like France and America and the Great-Granddaddy of them all, Great Britain. There is frankly nothing more Ratna than an imperialist empire that basically says, "We have all of this stuff, but we could actually have a lot more stuff if we made up a lot of convoluted hierarchical theories about why we're so much better than you, so that we can take *your* stuff and then we'd have your stuff, too!" Or, as Egyptologist Toby Wilkinson writes, "From its very inception, Egyptology was thus the handmaid of Imperialism, in a manner that Caesar would have recognized and applauded."[81]

But to return to our egg tempera facsimile of this ancient Egyptian scene, what stopped me in my tracks when I passed it at the Met was the unusual physicality of the women. In ancient Egyptian art, bodies were depicted in a way that made them the most legible: the face and legs are seen in pro-file while the torso and eyeball are facing outward. This bears out with our two seated ladies; there's a kind of presentational, performative quality to them, as if they're cheating out to camera to say, "I just stopped by to tell you how fabulous I am!" But what is really remarkable is the way the servant girl is standing. In a complete break with any other known painting in ancient Egyptian art, the subject has her back turned to us. This reminded me of something I read in Kara Cooney's biography of Pharaoh Hatshepsut, who ruled not long before this painting was made: "The royal women may have been envious of their ladies-in-waiting's freedom to run their own household...Admittedly, these attendants did not have the power and money of the king's daughters, wives, and sisters, but the visibility of this unattainable 'normal' life must have been painful for some of the royal women."[82] The young servant girl may not have access to whatever creature comforts were on offer in 1479 BCE, but she, perhaps, has something far richer: a private life, which she can deny us access to in a way the privileged cannot. As nobodies, we yearn to be somebodies, only to spend our time trying to regain a little slice of what we were so hasty to get rid of. As someone once said of the spiritual path, better not to start.

Haverman

(1693–unknown)

A Vase of Flowers

Margareta Haverman

1716 | METROPOLITAN MUSEUM OF ART

F abulous art nun Sister Wendy Beckett said that, at its prime, Dutch still-life painting was considered "the lowest form, and those who painted it were considered foot soldiers in the army of art, mean of spirit, who only painted things instead of people and events. And yet what hypocrisy, because everybody loved it and we still love it."[83]

Dutch still-life master Jan van Huysum wasn't mean of spirit so much as he was just plain mean. Known as a recalcitrant grump, he refused to take on any pupils. He only employed female family members as assistants because he deemed them incapable of copying his techniques and stealing his ideas, as a male assistant might. And yet, despite his no-student policy, he found himself bending to the pressures of a Danish army captain named Daniël Haverman. Captain Haverman had relocated to Amsterdam from Breda with his family to run a boys' school. The student that he wished van Huysum to take on was his daughter Margareta, who showed great promise as an artist.

Sadly, most details regarding the life of Margareta Haverman are lost to us, and today only two works can definitely be attributed to her. What is clear from her painting *A Vase of Flowers* is that by 1716 Haverman had not only mastered her teacher's techniques but outstripped him. According to van Huysum's biographer, Jan van Gool, this was a pill too bitter to swallow, and on several occasions he attempted to sever ties with Haverman, only to be persuaded to the contrary by her father. Jan van Huysum would eventually get an out, as Haverman became embroiled in a scandal, the details of which remain obscured. According to van Gool, she committed a "bad deed" that "dragged her father to the grave and the whole family to the tomb."[84] Van Huysum relished kicking her to the curb and spreading vicious gossip about her transgressions, commonly thought to be romantic in nature (big surprise).

Shortly after this incident, Haverman married architect Jacques de Mondoteguy. Together they moved to Paris, where, on the strength of her painting, she became the second woman to be accepted into the Académie Royale.[85] Sadly, scandal pursued her again and, a year after her acceptance, she was expelled on the accusation that her submission painting was actually a Jan van Huysum. Suspicion was aroused because she had apparently been unable to create a comparable work within that year. Had van Huysum defamed her, terrified that his reputation might be damaged if it was known that he'd been outshone by a woman? Had she behaved in some dubious manner? Was the Académie biased against her because she was a woman? Luckily, we have her art, which more than speaks for itself.

This is a vase packed to the rafters with flowers and greenery. There's so much going on, one can't help but wonder if Haverman was worried that she wouldn't be allowed to paint flowers ever again and so did a lifetime's worth in one go. I had to contact my gardener friend, Nathan Lambstrom, to help me distinguish what all was even in this floral extravaganza! Nathan singled out carnations, roses, hollyhocks, larkspur, poppy buds, iris, and passionflower, all swirling around to frame the belle of the ball, the virused tulip. Also known as a "broken bulb" tulip, these flowers are beset by a mosaic virus that creates a vibrantly colored feathering on the petals. It was this virus that triggered Dutch tulip fever in the seventeenth century, when obsession inflated the value of these exotic Asian flowers, transforming their bulbs into grubby gems.[86] It is characteristic of the acquisitive Ratna family, whose element is earth, to turn dirt into dollars.

While Dutch still-life painting is lauded for its painstaking detail and realism, this arrangement is impossible on just about every level. Not only would the whole thing topple under its own weight, but these flowers don't all bloom at the same time of year, making this both a gravity- and season-defying arrangement.

If you notice an odd bluish hue to the image, giving it a desaturated, 1980s look, that isn't a printing error. This is because in the early eighteenth century there was no stable green paint, so Haverman mixed Prussian blue with yellow lake.[87] Derived from the secretions of lac insects rather than mineral based, "lake" pigments are not light-stable and tend to fade over time. Here, the result is that the greens have turned to blues. In contrast, however, the peach bottom-center still remains quite radiant—this is because she was experimenting with a brand-new pigment called Naples yellow, which has proved far more resilient. Gerrit Albertson, the conservationist at the Metropolitan Museum of Art who worked to restore the painting, says that the innovative use of cutting-edge materials proves that "[Haverman] wasn't following her teacher—she wasn't just copying his work, she was really doing her best to create a composition on her own terms."[88]

The gregarious bounty of this picture perfectly captures Ratna's fecund energy, its tendrils practically pulling us into the canvas. This bouquet has been arranged not by the human hand but by the human eyeball, and a leering one at that. Haverman ogled with the best of them, exploring every fold of every petal with a licentiousness that would make even Georgia O'Keeffe blush. Peeking voyeuristically through the curtains of greenery, we can see that the vase of the title is decorated with a dimpled Cupid's rump and a puckering Bacchus in profile—erotic love and intoxication are the container for these throbbing buds. Even the grapes have broken a sweat. This floral hurly-burly taunts our sense of taste and smell, which are Ratna's realm. Scent pollinates the olfactory bulb, a tulip buried in the brain causing memory and emotion to flower from the amygdala and hippocampus.

In true Ratna form, the picture isn't just visually full, it is also overflowing with symbolic meaning. The Dutch Protestants of the day considered overtly religious painting to be idolatrous, so still-lives did a lot of heavy lifting to compensate.[89] Here's a brief Dutch still-life cheat sheet:[90]

1. **BUTTERFLIES:** The soul and salvation.
2. **BEES:** The brittleness of life and how we must continue to toil despite not knowing what destiny has in store for us.
3. **FLIES:** Associated with decomposition, and therefore a memento mori.
4. **PEACHES:** Good trade; the human heart, and good health.
5. **GRAPES:** Earthly pleasure.
6. **ROSES AND IRISES:** The Virgin Mary's suffering.
7. **POPPIES:** The Passion of Christ.
8. **SNAILS:** Immaculate conception and the Virgin Birth. Apparently seventeenth- and eighteenth-century people hadn't yet figured out how snails reproduce, and thought they propagated by asexual reproduction. Amen.

So maybe this is a painting about sex and pleasure giving rise to life, in which we have the opportunity for true spiritual awakening. Or maybe, as Sister Wendy suggests, still-life artists painted what they did mostly because they liked how it looked. Artists are aesthetic creatures, after all, and Ratna energy, whether it manifests as art or as the natural world, lifts us out of the mindset of glum functionality and into the realm of beauty and aesthetic delight. It's okay for us to actually enjoy the pleasures of our senses; it's just that, as humans, we have a tendency to get very transactional: we want to know how much stuff will cost us and what the takeaway will be. But at the risk of sounding a bit like a nun trying to solve a problem like Maria, one might just as well ask, What is the takeaway of the first snowfall of the season? What is the purpose of a harvest moon? I don't know what bumblebee bats are *for* exactly, but they are cute as hell and having the times of their lives.

If we must transactionalize things, perhaps we could invest more time in receiving what is offered to us, rather than trying to get more of what we don't have. We often equate generosity with giving to the less fortunate, but Ratna reminds us that receiving is as much a part of generosity as giving is; they are fundamentally not separate. While we might very well feel justifiable concern for someone who actually had a floral orgy like Margareta Haverman's in their home, as a painting its gifts are relentless.

Minter

(1948–present)

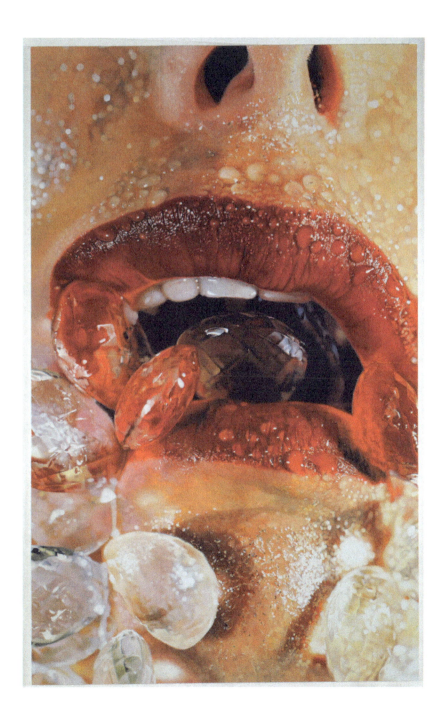

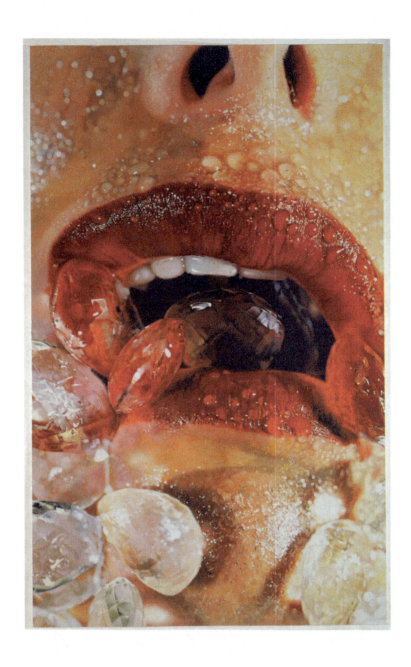

Crystal Swallow

Marilyn Minter

2006 | COURTESY OF THE ARTIST AND SALON 94

Critic George W.S. Trow envisioned a grid that integrated public and private life. But over time, through disuse, the middle distance of American culture collapsed, leaving only the polar extremes: the grid of the two hundred million and the grid of intimacy. He wrote, "A product consumed by a man alone in a room exists in the grid of one, alone and in the grid of two hundred million. To the man alone, it is a comfort. But just for a minute."[91]

Advertisers spend enormous sums to act like spies, peering through the keyholes of our hearts, hoping to create glossy hieroglyphs resonating at the same frequency as our wallet clasps and our genitals. Often, they get it right. We just want to fulfill our innermost wish to be happy; they just want us to shop. Surely some mutually beneficial arrangement can be made.

Companies try their best to operate by the chivalric code of the vampire, draining our lifeblood only if we invite them in by signing the byzantine terms and conditions—which we lonely hearts eagerly do. We are grateful for the willing ear of corporate personhood. After triplicating our EKGs, they then whisper back sweet algorithmic nothings into our ears.

Marilyn Minter's canvases dance between intimacy and alienation. Hers is the world of the overlooked, described in the language of advertising. Whether it's the soft skin where the nose meets the lip or the transgressive desires of the human heart, Minter conveys the intensity of her attention by blowing up intimacy to billboard size. Marshall McLuhan's Tetrad describes technology as the extension or amplifying of some part of the human body or psyche, and in the early 2000s Minter realized the apogee of this vision when her already enormous pictures (some are as large as nine-by-fifteen feet) appeared on billboards and Times Square jumbotrons. Her gigantic mouths and high-heeled shoes stomped and oozed throughout the city as if the 50-Foot Woman had channeled her understandable rage into art rather than mere wanton havoc. If you relocated the *Vogue* offices to Three Mile Island, you might get something akin to the work of Marilyn Minter.

In a conversation with Madonna at the Brooklyn Museum,[92] Minter discussed how the streets of New York have always informed her work. In the 1980s, seeing Keith Haring's graffiti or how he opened his Pop Shop to sell posters and hats as an extension of his work inspired her to "make things that anyone could have."[93] While I'm not currently in a position to "have" a Minter of my own (Jay-Z and Beyoncé own a few pieces), she has enriched public space with her work in a way that many artists haven't, partly due to her ability to play with the palette of advertising. The language of "Just can't get enough. Just can't get satiated. There's just not enough in the world," as she puts it,[94] is a perfect articulation of Ratna energy, which, left unchecked, can devolve into glutting, gorging, and hoarding.

The symbol of Ratna is the Wish-Fulfilling Jewel, also known as the *Cintāmaṇi*. This might, at first, seem a peculiar image for the spiritual path, but despite its reputation for being a no-fun tradition of renunciation, Buddhism can really bring the bling. With the belief that perfect, supreme enlightenment may be realized right now, this instant, through the senses, Tibetan Buddhism employs a mind-stopping array of color, texture, and fragrance in its artwork and rituals. Some refer to it as the "Catholicism of Buddhism," with all of its smells and bells.

One of my favorite characters from the Buddhist nontheistic pantheon is Jambhala, a wealth deity. He is a corpulent figure who looks a bit like Orson Welles from his Paul Masson period, immediately recognizable by his trademark accessories, which he'd sooner *die* than leave home without: a pet mongoose and the Wish-Fulfilling Jewel. Again, amassing wealth might seem at odds with the tenets of Buddhism, but the thinking is that if you're living in squalor and aren't sleeping well and don't know where your next meal is coming from, it is very hard to study the Dharma. This is where Jambhala steps in. According to the myth, there are serpent-like water spirits called *nagas* who love to swallow jewels, hoarding them in their bellies, in a perpetual game of keepaway with humanity. To retrieve the jewels for the benefit of humankind, Jambhala sends his pet mongoose out to gobble up the *nagas*. Serpent meat digested, the mongoose is then left with a bellyful of jewels, which Jambhala retrieves by squeezing it like a set of bagpipes. In pleasanter versions of the story, the mongoose just barfs out the jewels (see the Rubin Museum's hilarious thirteenth-century *Black Jambhala*, which depicts a mongoose burning the candle at both ends, so to speak). The bounty reclaimed, Jambhala then bestows these riches upon us. Yay! (As Donald Hoffman said of reality, "it should not be taken literally, but it should be taken seriously.")

The Wish-Fulfilling Jewel is a talisman for equanimity. It immediately grants your heart's desire the moment it is born—not in a bullshitty *The Secret* kind of way, where you hold your thoughts ransom for some big future pay-off—but because, when you do not separate yourself from the world, you know that there isn't anything you don't belong to. You belong to the whole world and it belongs to you. The Wish-Fulfilling Jewel is the whole world, just as it is right now.

What you're looking for, you're looking at, as Sokuzan says.

Perhaps no other industry has hoarded the jewels of our desires more egregiously than the beauty industry. "[Fashion photography is] the biggest inspiration," Minter has said of her work. "Because it is a desiring machine... It's a love/hate thing because you're never going to look that good; no one ever is...I think I'm trying to make a picture out of that constant failure: armpits with hair growing out of them, sweat running into the eyes, eyelashes that clump together because of too much mascara."[95]

When I was a teenager in Boulder, Colorado, my friends and I pored over fashion magazines. *Vogue* and *W* were not just our prayer book and hymnal, they conjured a Phantom City in which we felt we'd arrived and where we could rest from the tribulations of living in a town where, for most people, formal wear comprised shoes with toe cubbies and tie-dyed T-shirts advertising brewery-sponsored river-rafting events. We adored the featured supermodels, such as Nadja Auermann, Naomi Campbell, and Shalom Harlow. We wanted to *be* them. The images were a comfort and refuge. *But just for a minute.*

After finally making it to the real New York, the Phantom City of the magazines began to collapse like a house of perfume samples. The flimsiness of the illusions peddled in the magazines became embarrassingly apparent. All along, there had been a breach of contract between our high school desires and the magazine publishers. We were meant to invest five bucks and our teenage yearning for access to a world of acceptance and beauty, when instead, the magazines were just providing advertisers access to *us*.

In 2009, Minter had a gig photographing a campaign for MAC Cosmetics. She was meant to be shooting the model's glitter-laden eye, but she made the most of the setup and piggybacked a shoot of her own. Every time they would break for the model to get her eye makeup redone, Minter would snap some pictures of the model licking a pane of glass, which was shellacked with neon goo and candy. She also had the videographer shoot the model using her tongue to paint the glass with the fluorescent slime. This became the video *Green Pink Caviar*, which appeared both in Times Square and in Madonna's *Sticky & Sweet* tour. "Now, MAC was furious that I did this," she told a group at New York's School of Visual Arts. "But then when MoMA bought it and put it in their lobby, they were fine."[96]

Hearing this touched my teenage heart. By cannibalizing the flashy motifs of big business, Marilyn Minter manages to repatriate our desires to us in all their sloppy, glittery dignity. Her work is an offering in the vocabulary of transactionality, but freely given. A true Ratna transmutation.

Vigée Le Brun

(1755–1842)

Portrait of Madame du Barry

Élisabeth Louise Vigée Le Brun

1781 | PHILADELPHIA MUSEUM OF ART

Both the painter and the subject of this portrait were working women, though not quite in the same line. Élisabeth Louise Vigée Le Brun showed artistic promise as a child and, encouraged by her family, was a professional portrait painter by the age of fourteen. By nineteen, she had enough of a reputation for the government to take notice, and they shut down her studio for operating without a license. Her father, who passed away when she was twelve, had also been an artist, and his professional connections helped her to secure one of only four slots allocated to women in the Académie Royale.[97] Her studies there were more or less in step with the education male students received, except that she was not allowed to partake in life-drawing classes, where she might catch a glimpse of a naked man, thereby ruining her brain and her reputation.

In contrast, Jeanne Bécu, the illegitimate daughter of a seamstress and a monk, would make her fortune *because* of naked men. Sophisticated, kind, and stunningly beautiful, Jeanne Bécu had to make her own way in the world, taking an array of jobs, from hairdresser's assistant to lady's companion. In 1763, however, she really hit her stride. She met a casino owner and pimp called Jean-Baptiste Vicomte du Barry, who took her as a mistress and began training her for a life as a high-class prostitute. Assuming her pimp's name, Madame du Barry began taking an ever-ascending caliber of lovers in the upper echelons of the French aristocracy. These assignations eventually led to an introduction to Lebel, the *valet de chambre* of King Louis XV. Madame du Barry and the king got on like a house on fire. What began as a fling escalated into something more serious. She was witty and fun, and unlike her predecessor, Madame de Pompadour, she had no head for business or political ambitions. She just wanted to look hot and be comfortable while raking in shitloads of money (to borrow from Liz Phair).

A prostitute daring to mingle in their midst drove Versailles completely insane. The aristocracy made her the brunt of nasty poems and took some comfort in the fact that, no matter how high-class the call girl, there was only so far she could go within the impenetrable hierarchy of French society. In order to officially become the king's *maîtresse-en-titre*, she would not only have to be a married woman of noble blood, she would also need a sponsor to formally introduce her to the king at court, which everyone resolutely refused to do. Well, where there's a will there's a way, especially if you're a horny old king, so Louis XV arranged to have Jeanne Bécu married to the brother of her pimp (who also forged documents, making her both a noblewoman and three years younger). She was then officially a du Barry. The problem of the introduction at court was solved by the king promising to pay off Maréchal de Mirepoix's gambling debts if she would act as sponsor. She agreed. After the passing of his beloved Pompadour and not-quite-as-beloved Queen Marie Leszczyńska, Louis XV was now footloose and fancy-free, and wasn't about to let a bunch of stodgy courtiers cramp his style, no matter how jewel-encrusted they were. Madame du Barry triumphantly grabbed the big brass ring, becoming *maîtresse-en-titre*, a position she maintained for four fabulous years, until Louis XV's death from smallpox in 1774.[98] His body wasn't even cold in the ground (it was so badly riddled with disease that his corpse had to be covered in quicklime) before Queen Marie Antoinette had Madame du Barry exiled to the nunnery Abbey du Pont-aux-Dames. Marie Antoinette had always resented the low-born du Barry for outshining her at court and couldn't wait to sweep her under the convent rug.[99]

Meanwhile in Paris, Vigée Le Brun was doing quite well for herself. She had married art dealer Jean-Baptiste-Pierre Le Brun, who helped her to secure top-tier portrait clients. This came in handy because she had to keep working to cover his gambling debts, a common albatross in eighteenth-century France. In 1791, she painted the first (pictured here) of what would be three portraits of Madame du Barry, who by this time had been freed from the convent and allowed to reclaim the home and pension that Louis XV had left to her. In her memoirs, Vigée Le Brun describes Madame du Barry as "tall without being too much so; she had a certain roundness, her throat being rather pronounced but very beautiful; her face was still attractive, her features were regular and graceful; her hair was ashy, and curly like a child's. But her complexion was beginning to fade. She received me with much courtesy, and seemed to me very well behaved, but I found her more spontaneous in mind than in manner: her glance was that of a coquette, for her long eyes were never quite open, and her pronunciation had something childish which no longer suited her age."[100]

Though this is certainly a lovely painting, Madame du Barry's getup always struck me as an odd choice for a formal portrait. Vigée Le Brun describes her as wearing a "dressing gown," but the hat looks more like something out of *Hello, Dolly!* than loungewear. Was she making a comment on the fact that, for Madame du Barry, going to bed and "going out" were not two different things? Not quite. This kind of dress, known as *chemise à la reine*, was gaining popularity among the ladies of the French aristocracy. Madame du Barry eschewed the gaudy lifestyle expected of the *maîtresse-en-titre*, preferring now these less constrained, flowing cotton dresses, which she wore year-round.[101] And yet reading this style of dress as "intimate wear" isn't wrong. Ladies' undergarments from this period were made of similarly gauzy cotton, and it was precisely this association that infuriated the general public: *as if it weren't bad enough that you're all eating rabbit out of silver tureens while we starve, now you're not even going to bother to do your job and get dressed properly?* To put a finer point on it, the nobility was spending enormous amounts of money to look like poor shepherdesses. And adding insult to injury, by popularizing cotton among the aristocracy, Madame du Barry and her ilk were accused of imperiling the country's silk trade. As a visiting American, Gouverneur Morris, wrote in his diary of 1789, "Royalty has here endeavored at great expense to conceal itself from its own eye. But the attempt is in vain."[102]

So was this painting a poorly timed humble-brag? Madame du Barry, who by all accounts was a kindly woman and generous with the local poor, could hardly have been considered spiteful. Perhaps the worst she could be accused of is going soft—being out of the game so long that she could not see the trouble that was brewing all around her. Even today there are many nice, liberal people who deeply wish for the happiness of others but don't really want to be inconvenienced by their suffering. They don't want others to be unhappy, but what they don't want *more* is to be bothered. In this way, ego slyly masquerades as beneficent, without giving up the feather in its enormous straw hat.

By 1789, the heat of revolution had brought Paris to a boil. The Bastille had been stormed, the royal family arrested, and Vigée Le Brun knew that, being Marie Antoinette's favorite portraitist, it was just a matter of time before they came for her too. She escaped to Italy with her daughter under the pretense of artistic self-improvement. She remained in exile for twelve years, continuing to work as a painter as she traveled through Italy, Austria, Russia, and Germany.

Madame du Barry, on the other hand, proved unable to read the room. While she was on a trip to England in the winter of 1792, her banker implored her to stay until things cooled down in France. Ignoring his advice, she returned, only to find that she had been betrayed by both her cook and the man that Louis XV had "gifted" to her, Louis-Benoit Zamor. In her absence they had joined the Jacobin Club and reported her to the Committee of Public Safety for her lavish lifestyle. Du Barry was completely broadsided by Zamor's disloyalty—surprised to discover, it seems, that people do not like to be gifted to others, no matter what the occasion or how friendly the owners happen to be.

Even as she was put on trial and sentenced to public execution by guillotine, Madame du Barry really seemed to believe that someone would come rescue her, that at the last minute her Prince Charming would swoop in and have a word with the judge. At some point, people would realize who she was, that she had been like them, that she represented what anyone could attain. But in the roiling passions of revolution, status and loyalty are always in flux, and by this point, anyone who could have saved her was dead or hiding. She even tried ingratiating herself to the tribunal by revealing where she had buried her jewels around her house, to no avail. Still, she didn't seem to really know what was happening to her until she was taken to the scaffold, where, rather than taking a page from the playbook of the nobles who had gone before her, she panicked, screaming at the crowd, "You are going to hurt me! Why?!" Her last words were, apparently, "One more moment, Mr. Executioner, I beg you!"[103] Her wild display of emotion reportedly moved the crowd to tears, proving

Joni Mitchell correct in her assessment that "the three great stimulants" for a weary populace have always been "artifice, brutality, and innocence."[104]

Élisabeth Louise Vigée Le Brun later wrote that du Barry's end "always confirmed my belief that if the victims of that period of execrable memory had not had the noble pride of dying with fortitude the Terror would have ceased long before it did."[105] Time heals all wounds, though, I suppose, and in true Gallic style, the French repatriated Madame du Barry in the way they do many of their past bêtes noires: by naming a cooking style after her. To prepare a dish "du Barry" implies cauliflower (representative of her powdered wigs) and a creamy white sauce, which is meant to evoke her porcelain complexion...but I'll let you draw your own conclusions on that point. Aside from being high in caloric content, this is cuisine inspired by the physical attributes of another human being, which certainly takes the revolutionary rallying cry "Eat the Rich!" to a mad extreme. Ratna would have it no other way.

Stoller

(1981–present)

Untitled (floral bust)

Jessica Stoller

2019 | COURTESY OF THE ARTIST

Jessica Stoller's mordantly funny, morbidly fascinating porcelain sculptures remind me of an exchange between Patsy and Edina from the comedy series *Absolutely Fabulous*.

EDINA: God, I hate Morgan Fairchild.

PATSY: I hate Jane bloody Fonda.

EDINA: I hope all their old skin comes back to haunt them.

PATSY: I bought that bloody woman's tapes. I paid for those plastic domes on her chest. I want them when she dies.

EDINA: You know, there must be a moment, about a week after death, when all those women finally achieve the figure they desire.

PATSY: Skeleton-thin with plastic bumps.

EDINA: The flesh will rot away, but the bumps will still be there. Little coffins full of bones and bumps.[106]

With its screaming colors and nutty designs, which include an elephant-headed candelabra and a perfume-burner-cum-egg-steamer, eighteenth-century French porcelain was always considered witty, a baton that Stoller grabs and sprints away with.

Porcelain has always been a symbol of prestige. The Chinese managed to jealously guard their secret recipe for over a thousand years, creating a colossal porcelain industry, which wealthy Europeans kept humming along. It wasn't until the early eighteenth century that the porcelain code was finally cracked. When the Saxons finally identified kaolin as the secret to making hard-paste porcelain, they quickly established the factory at Meissen, becoming the gold standard for European porcelain production. Noting the exorbitant amount of money the French were shelling out for Asian and European porcelain, Louis XV's mistress Madame de Pompadour suggested that France hop into the porcelain game. Louis XV liked the idea and established a factory at Sèvres, overseen by Madame de Pompadour. The king was so pleased with the results that he would host an annual party in his apartments at Versailles to show off the latest Sèvres designs. His guests understood that they were expected to buy.[107] Louis XV invented the Tupperware party.

In an interview with art critic Jane Ursula Harris, Stoller describes her work as exploring "ornamentation, the female body, notions of the grotesque, ceramic history/art history, memento mori motifs, etc. Keep in mind," she adds, "the work has been developing over years and my process is slow—clay makes you contend."[108]

Clay makes you contend. The medium dictates the terms by which it will deign to execute your vision. As far as media go, you could hardly find a fussier one than porcelain. First, the actual sculpture is created, by coiling, slab building, throwing on a wheel, or some combination of the three. Then the various components are assembled and kiln fired. Stoller prefers to use china paints in her work, which "allow for a great deal of specificity, subtlety, and detail, which is not achievable with standard glazes."[109] The piece must be refired after each application of pigment, so the color capable of withstanding the highest temperature is applied first, and so on down the line. And if there are any firing cracks, or you screw up at any point in the process, you have to start again from scratch. "I often think I have a masochistic impulse for making what I make in clay," she says. "Despite all my strategies to build evenly, dry the piece slowly, etcetera, you hand it over to the kiln and relinquish control."[110]

The innate challenges of working with porcelain obviously factor into its value. It is estimated that to fill Catherine the Great's order of an eight-hundred-piece porcelain dinner set, three thousand pieces had to be made to accommodate porcelain's finicky process. And yet the very fact that Catherine the Great could purchase one Sèvres ice cream cooler (a Ratna image if there ever was one), at a cost equivalent to a Sèvres factory worker's lifetime earnings,[111] has sparked ideologies and revolutions alike.

Many a Ratna head has rolled for its flagrantly conspicuous consumption. Yet for all of its swagger and bling, Ratna's true wisdom is called equanimity, or equality. And what greater equalizer is there than death, which comes for us all? The second of the Four Reminders that turn the mind toward the

Dharma states, "The world and its inhabitants are impermanent, in particular, the life of beings is like a bubble, death comes without warning, this body will be a corpse..."[112]

Through this lens, Jessica Stoller's comment, "Clay makes you contend," takes on a deeper resonance. Money and access might buy us the illusion of immortality by negotiating adipose tissue and laugh lines away, but with each microdermabrasion and chemical peel we creep ever closer to the skull beneath the skin. Or, put another way, fifty might be the new thirty, but eighty is still pretty much the same eighty.

Sherwood

(1977–present)

Feral Cakes

Dana Sherwood

2017 | COURTESY OF THE ARTIST AND DENNY DIMIN GALLERY

Awareness meditation practices provide an arena in which we witness the theatrics of the mind. Over time, through a dedicated practice, we discover the jewel of our true nature in the rubbish heap that is our identity. From delusional superiority, we may step down into seeing the equality of all things, which inspires us to become generous guests and consummate hosts to whatever accepts the invitation of our awareness.

Dana Sherwood's body of work exemplifies the Ratna quality of equanimity by elevating hosting to an art form. She describes her art as "ritualized feedings [performed] for animals who live among or at the borders of human populations." Giving Betty Crocker and Martha Stewart a run for their money, Sherwood creates ostentatiously elaborate confections that are the epitome of Ratna splendiferousness. Applying her research into what animals native to her project locations might actually like to eat, Sherwood has gone on to create Spam castles crowned with rococo snail shells, meat cakes bedazzled with powdered donut gems, and spiraling, hotdog-stuffed jellies atop cake towers. These offerings, served at twilight, quiver in the liminal space between the glamorous and the grotesque. She then leaves her banquets outdoors, sometimes just overnight, sometimes over a span of several days, and films the proceedings, whatever they may be, with infrared trail cameras (silent, battery-operated cameras used by hunters and scientists to observe animal behavior[113]) so that her physical presence doesn't interfere. She also paints film stills as companion pieces to the feasts—some taken directly from the footage, and some imagined, yearned for. "When you invite the chaos of nature as a collaborator," says Sherwood, "there is no telling what's going to happen."[114]

Buddhism describes four immutable qualities of mind known as the Four Immeasurables: loving-kindness, compassion, sympathetic joy, and equanimity. While these qualities are said to be innate to all of us (yes, even Harvey

Weinstein), obviously not everyone got the memo (like Harvey Weinstein); even those of us who did get the memo might feel the need to "exercise" these qualities in order to strengthen them. One could probably even imagine scenarios in which one might amp up a kind gesture, listen deeply, or cheer on another person's success. Equanimity, however, is not something we can do; it is something we are. In order to find balance, we first need to see how imbalanced we are. Seeing that we're imbalanced without reflexively rushing to tip the opposite scale is equanimity. From the bleachers, the highwire artist looks all out of whack standing on one foot and holding a chair in her teeth, and yet her balance comes from an acute awareness of her precarious position. Luckily, we don't have to join the circus to discover equanimity. Through the sitting practice of meditation, which, admittedly, often feels like a circus, we have the opportunity to strengthen our awareness, which reveals equanimity.

A fancy that often strikes me when I sit in meditation is that I am a nature show documentarian. In the same way that they set up their cameras and tripods in Serengeti National Park, in hopes of capturing some hot cheetah action, I sit in open awareness with a willingness to see what emerges from the underbrush. Whether the action is sexy, violent, or dull, the camera is rolling. None of my business. Just include everything. Zen teacher Thich Nhat Hanh described equanimity as "inclusion." Anything that arises in my mind stream is included with no preference, taking the attitude of a good host.

One of Sherwood's smorgasbords, *Feral Cakes*, took place after nightfall in a backyard in Florida in 2017. In the video, we see the artist putting the finishing touches on her table, topping up a teacup here, reaffixing a fallen snail shell there, making sure everything is just so before the guests arrive. The guests, in this case, are whatever nocturnal animals happen by. As might be expected, the raccoons are the first to arrive at the party and the last to leave. Their glowing marble eyes bob into view through the spiny fronds in the yard. A fox shyly sniffs around the perimeter, but it doesn't seem worth the risk to this quintessential wallflower. Raccoons come forward, happily setting themselves up on the tabletop, knocking things over, frightening themselves, and then jumping back in to dampen their paws in the teacups. As they dig in, a sweet, dopey-looking possum sneaks up to grab a donut or two. A feral cat hisses at a nonplussed raccoon as it tries to steal a nibble. The raccoons appear to enjoy making a mess as much as they enjoy eating, a bit like wobbly rock stars trashing their room at the Four Seasons just because they can.

Artists point out our collective, inherited hypocrisies. To do so is a fierce gesture of generosity, as the emphasizing of neurosis often requires embodying it (which in turn confuses increasingly literal-minded audiences). "We love nature and we want it to flourish and be accessible in our daily lives," says Sherwood, "but the moment it starts to encroach on our territory, and subvert our perceived control, we reject it and try to dominate it." I could not think of a better description of meditation practice. We deeply wish to be free from suffering and at peace with our minds, but when thoughts get wild or unwieldy, we panic and begin to perceive them as problems to solve. As spiritual guide Byron Katie writes, "No one has ever been able to control his thinking, although people may tell the story of how they have. I don't let go of my thoughts—I meet them with understanding. Then they let go of me."[115]

When we realize that meditation is about awareness, we become free to give up absurd projects like trying to "turn our brains off" or, God forbid, "unplugging," as if our minds were insolent air conditioners. Simply put, we don't need to be somebody else in order to wake up, and any pursuit to the contrary is an unbearable waste of time. Not only that, but it is also mean, and often with surprisingly avoidable ramifications. Just as mountain lions wind up in our yards as a result of their natural habitat being engulfed by our homes and highways, suppressed anger or sexual desire can erupt at inappropriate moments in our lives.

In "Eating in the Dark (Raised By Raccoons)," Sherwood writes, "I have spent many hours observing animals in the wild and in domesticity; they have been my greatest teachers and offered some of the parenting I did not receive early on. More than anything, they taught me to accept chaos and embrace the loss of control."[116] Her poignant words reminded me of the traditional Buddhist contemplation that every being has been your mother, or, from another point of view, everyone is your child.

Normally, the degree of care Sherwood invests in her feasts would be saved for a special occasion, a sacred ritual. But from the point of view of the intended guests, while the occurrence might be unusual, there's nothing really special about it—which is the message of equanimity: when nothing is special, everything is sacred.

Although she acknowledges the fickleness of her chosen collaborators, Sherwood is not immune to some disappointment when they do not deign to participate. In documentary footage from her project *The Wild and the Tame* (2015), she says, "The extravaganza that I put out last night in hopes of a second evening of fox filming was completely dashed this morning when I went out and found that none of the food had been slightly touched."[117] In another area frequented by deer, she left stacks of pancakes heaped with fresh fruit and syrup. But when the deer happen upon the trespassing flapjacks, they jump and skitter off in fright. Despite her diligent attempts at hospitality, which spanned several days, the deer refused to eat. Some animals partake, some don't, and either way, Sherwood gets no thanks for her generous efforts. Maybe that's how Mother Nature feels. And we human beings, with our arrogant sense of entitlement, have taken and taken from Her with impunity, fostered by various religions' deranged notion that nature is wicked and impure, here simply for us to use. A similar attitude with similar justification has been directed at women as well, of course, and so when we can find the same roots in both the unfolding climate catastrophe and in misogyny in general, it seems worthwhile to ask, Are these not, in reality, the same issue?

Our world doesn't ask for much and expresses its gratitude by not annihilating us with relentless fires and flooding (themselves an expression of equanimity). The greatest gesture of appreciation one can make to the natural world is to have a deep understanding that we don't have a relationship with it, we *are* the natural world. And so, with all of her delicacies' intricacies, Dana Sherwood's ritualistic offerings are made as much to herself as they are to the fox or the possum. *Feral Cakes* evokes the beautifully cryptic Buddhist teaching that states that in a pure expression of generosity there is no giver, there is no receiver, and there is no gift.

Padma

To whom shall I give all that now flows through me, from my warm, my porous body? I will gather my flowers and present them—Oh! to whom?

VIRGINIA WOOLF, *THE WAVES*

Maybe the greatest strength is a great desire.

PINA BAUSCH

I was thirteen when, like Tennyson's Lady of Shalott, the curse had come upon me. While the Lady's curse was brought on by abandoning her weaving to ogle Lancelot out her window, mine was the result of stumbling across a lobby card of Keanu Reeves at my local movie theater. Nevertheless, the curse was the same: craving.

Craving is the crux of the human predicament: we crave a reality other than the one we happen to be in. This is the pith of the Buddha's first teaching: we suffer because we want something else to happen. Laughably simple. *So* simple that when we hear this, it feels like our intelligence is being insulted. And yet, there you have it.

I don't think I even registered that the movie was called *Point Break*. All I saw was Keanu, soaking wet in his black T-shirt, his head turned forlornly back over his shoulder. He looked through a curtain of bangs and straight into my soul, as if to say, "I waited as long as I could, my darling, but it's no use!" I felt as though a trapdoor had opened in me, sending my entrails plummeting into a fogbank of melancholy. Though I didn't have the words to describe it at the time, now I would say I felt more lonely than horny; it would be many years until I realized how, like Torvill and Dean, those two impulses twirl together through the mind.

Padma is pious longing and carnal lust. Padma is walking on his favorite patch of moorland, where you just so happen to bump into him, while coincidentally wearing his favorite cologne and reading his favorite William Gibson novel. It must be fate! Padma is the consumption you hope to catch on his favorite patch of moorland when he reveals that he's always been in love with you, but he values the friendship too much to demean it with fumbling clammy hands—and then he marries a spin instructor on a whim.

166

Padma sometimes appears as the love that dare not speak its name—not because of some societal taboo but because it hurts better that way. Or Padma might appear as the love that won't be ignored, like Glenn Close in *Fatal Attraction*. Whatever the case, when the magnifying eye of Padma isn't superglued to a self (which is doing the looking with a particular agenda) but is still astutely attuned to its environment, something interesting happens. Frantic grasping becomes discreet connoisseurship. The thrill at noticing something is beautiful or rare is still present, but that thrill is seen as arising from one's *own* mind and not some fact about the inevitable need to possess some separate other. Awareness of space reveals passion to be discriminating awareness; one can see both the preciousness of this unique object of affection while acknowledging the desire for it as a dependently arisen aftershock—not some irrefutable evidence justifying one's grabbiness.

Padma energy pines, looking back over its shoulder at missed opportunity, a past moment of glory. As Marshall McLuhan once described it, "We look at the present through a rearview mirror. We march backwards into the future."[118] However, when asked to expand on this theme in an interview on Australian television, he said:

> Having accused a lot of people of living in the rearview mirror, and having meant by that that they were out of date, that they were nineteenth-century minds, I then took another look...and I discovered somewhat to my surprise that when you look in the rearview mirror, you do not see what has gone past, you see what is coming. The rearview mirror is the foreseeable future. It is not the past at all... In terms of media, of course, the thing that is occupying the foreground in terms of the rearview mirror is nostalgia...This is a rather mysterious thing: the costumes worn by the young—the fashionable costumes—are really very old hat and nostalgic...[T]he costumes worn by the young today are a kind of...clown costume. And paradoxically, the clown is a person with a grievance.[119]

(Maybe the unconsciously hilarious Joan Crawford was invoking McLuhan in her book *My Way of Life*, in which she rather pompously wrote, "All my nostalgia is for tomorrow. Not for any yesterdays.")

For hundreds of years, nostalgia was considered to be, at best, a mental illness and, at worst, demonic possession. The word *nostalgia*, first used by the Swiss doctor Johannes Hofer in 1688, means a "sickness" for "escape," or for a "return to some place" like home. Many believed nostalgia to be a uniquely Swiss affliction attributed to a maladjustment to lower altitudes, exacerbated by a lifetime of exposure to clanging cowbells. Scientific research in the twenty-first century, however, suggests that nostalgia is actually beneficial to the brain. In a *New York Times* article, Clay Routledge says, "Nostalgia serves a crucial existential function. It brings to mind cherished experiences that assure us we are valued people who have meaningful lives. Some of our research shows that people who regularly engage in nostalgia are better at coping with concerns about death."[120]

Padma is that Bette Davis movie in which she gets a makeover transforming her from a frump into a stunner who can't be with the guy but raises his daughter anyway. And it's also that other Bette Davis movie in which her honest love of a good man helps him to realize that the only thing he wants more than to go on loving her for the rest of his days is to be...a priest?

Priests, by the way, often have Padma problems. Surrounded by erotic depictions of fruitional compassion (see Bernini's Saint "Is-she-or-isn't-she?" Teresa of Avila sculpture), they are asked to suppress their personal eroticism in order to realize some kind of universal compassion. Good luck with that. Not that Buddhist monks aren't all horned up with nowhere to go, but they do at least have the *doha*. Overtaken by the Padma energy of appreciation and yearning for a teacher or a flower or the glory of the sense faculties, they stand up and spontaneously utter an improvised poem or *doha*—an early precursor to the *Def Poetry Jam*.

Padma is that beautiful yearning that is said to be the hallmark of human beings, the beautiful impulse that leads to Keats and Audre Lorde and gang-bang videos and Amway seminars and coronavirus vaccines and Danielle Steel novels...and loses sleep over all of them equally.

Ōi

(ca. 1800–1866)

Night Scene in Yoshiwara
Katsushika Ōi

CA. 1844–54 | ŌTA MEMORIAL MUSEUM OF ART

At its most bewitched, bothered, and bewildered, Padma energy is called passion. Also: desire, craving, grasping, or attachment. Whatever you name it, the emotion sets us ablaze, spurring us on to find something to consume in the hopes of quelling it. But passion is, by its nature, unsatisfactory and unsatisfiable. To use a sciency term, Padma energy is the *dopaminergic* impulse, which keeps us striving, innovating, and checking into no-tell motels. Daniel Z. Lieberman and Michael E. Long could be describing Padma energy in their book about dopamine, *The Molecule of More*. To quote another doctor (Frank-N-Furter), Padma passion makes us quiver with anti-ci...pation!

In the waning years of the Edo period (1603–1867), there was no more accomplished painter of geisha and courtesans than Katsushika Ōi.[121] Known for her inventive use of pattern and color in her depictions of women, Ōi had many admirers of her work, not least of whom was her own father, perhaps the most famous Japanese artist of all time, Katsushika Hokusai (the iconic woodblock image *The Great Wave off Kanagawa* was his). Hokusai said of his daughter Ōi, "When it comes to paintings of beautiful women, I can't compete with her—she's quite talented and expert in the technical aspects of painting."[122]

She herself could not have been further from the Japanese ideal of femininity, and, from all reports, did not give a damn. In a culture that valued demure women, Ōi was brash and outspoken. She married a fellow artist, Tsutsumi Tōmei, but they divorced in under three years, reportedly because she relentlessly mocked his artistic abilities. After her mother's death, Ōi moved back in with her father, where she stayed, working as his North Star Studio manager and assistant for the rest of his life. Her birth name was likely Ei or Oei, but on the rare occasions that she actually signed her work (only about ten works can be confidently attributed to her) she used the nickname her father gave her, "Ōi," which loosely translates to mean, "HEY YOU!" She drank and smoked a pipe, couldn't sew, got takeout for every meal, and never cleaned up. She and Hokusai would just work and work until their living arrangements became uninhabitable disaster zones. Then they would pack up and move somewhere new.

The style of art at which Ōi so excelled was called *ukiyo-e*, or "Floating World pictures." I don't speak Japanese, and so tracking the etymology of this word is a little complex, but my friend and Buddhist teacher Maho Kawachi kindly took the time to walk me through the implications of its meaning.

The Japanese word that describes Padma's insatiable yearning is *uki yo* (憂き世), which translates to mean "melancholic" or "world of sorrow and hardships." Uki yo is the ache felt at the fleeting beauty of the cherry blossoms, which are so brilliant and so alive, but only last a few weeks in the springtime (Padma's season). Uki yo was felt brutally in the conflagrations, tsunamis, and earthquakes that regularly devastated the city of Edo (now Tokyo). This shimmering world we live in is constantly coalescing and then dissipating again like a mirage. *Ukiyo* (浮世), a homonym for *uki yo* (憂き世), translates to mean "Floating World" and describes the decadent pleasure-seeking that marked life in Edo-era Japan. So uki yo is really a description of *samsara*, the closed feedback loop of birth, old age, sickness, and death we become trapped in when we abandon reality for what we *think* should be happening, whereas *ukiyo*, or the Floating World, is an attitude toward uki yo. It is precisely because things only last for a little bit that you give yourself to them fully. You give it all you've got for as long as it lasts. YOLO, as the children say.

The Buddha lays life's suffering at the doorstep of this feedback loop of incessant grasping. This is often misinterpreted to mean that if you are a sommelier, or you cry when your grandma dies, or you hope to have sex with Donny Osmond, you are "attached" and therefore "unenlightened." I'm not an expert by any means, but I will go out on a limb and say this is likely a problem of semantic discord more than a moral failing. The Buddhist nun Venerable Robina Courtin says, "The clichéd idea is that somehow we're supposed to give up *samsara*, which is where we can have sex, drugs, and rock 'n' roll, and then enter into boring old *nirvana*, a place a bit like heaven."[123] Basically, the Buddha wants you to have as much sex, drugs, and rock 'n' roll as you can get, but don't expect lasting happiness from a world whose chief characteristic is impermanence.

Japan during the Edo period was extremely culturally conservative. In *Images from the Floating World*, Richard Lane writes, "Quite boldly then, much of the best *ukiyo-e* took as its subjects the courtesans and actors, classes which were considered parasitic outcasts by the feudal government, but which were actually the idols of the masses and the bourgeoisie alike."[124] The results of living in this way are a mixed bag, of course, and ukiyo-e, favored depictions of courtesans, actors, and geisha—the characters who mostly populated Yoshiwara in what we today would call the red-light district (also a perfect metaphor for Padma, whose erotically inflamed energy is blood red). In Yoshiwara there was a kind of egalitarian pursuit of pleasure; all were welcome, though you got what you paid for, ranging from a quick roll on the tatami to a transcendent audience with the embodied muse, the geisha.

Elementally, Padma is fire, which, uncontained, consumes anything in its path indiscriminately, like the blazes that repeatedly destroyed the Yoshiwara district throughout the eighteenth and nineteenth centuries. And yet, of course, when fire is controlled and directed, it has incredibly positive effects. Discriminating awareness wisdom shows up as "I'm going to burn up these logs here, but not the whole house." Padma's discriminating awareness wisdom works in counterpoint to Ratna's equanimity. While equanimity emphasizes the equality of all things, discriminating awareness says, "Fair enough, but have you seen the feathers on this hummingbird? No, not that one, *this* one." Discriminating awareness is the capacity to get granular, to really get to know what makes something unique. This is the realm of the perfectly attentive lover, but also the aesthete, and the epicure.

Padma's time of day is sunset. In the waning light, starched nine-to-fivers scurry to little out-of-the-way spots where they cozy up for backroom deals and amorous assignations. Aspects of themselves that seemed shameful at noon don't look so bad in candlelight. Even the sun slips into something more comfortable as the children of the night begin to make their sweet music. This is the hour of the geisha.

To my mind, no one more fully embodies the qualities of discriminating awareness better than the geisha, one of the most popular subjects of ukiyo-e.

Geisha means "art person," not just because they were masters of many art forms, such as singing, dancing, ikebana, joke-telling, tea service, and playing multiple musical instruments, but because as masters they themselves were works of art. Whereas a courtesan might also have been talented and charming, she was employed as a sex worker, not as an entertainer. As scholars Stephen and Ethel Longstreet write, "The geisha, while not a professional courtesan, was a sexually free person, whose moral values were those of any girl who was out to earn her keep in a male society and seldom turned away from a good cash offer when she found it."[125] All the same, they were able to choose whether or not they took a client to bed, and, in any case, were legally forbidden from infringing upon the courtesans' union in Yoshiwara.

While the ability to tell a geisha from a courtesan would have been challenging even for many of their contemporaries, it was highly unlikely that your Average Joe carousing in the streets of the pleasure district would even spot a geisha, much less be entertained by one. A certain level of connoisseurship was required to be served by these human works of art. You had to know a guy who knew a guy who could vouch for you. You had to be *worthy* of being served.

With a flick of her fan, the flash of the unpainted nape of her neck, or a strum on her shamisen, the geisha was able to conjure an erotic, Padma-charged atmosphere in which a perpetual state of becoming was an end in itself. What arises in the space of anticipation is a bittersweet melancholy—the kind that can lead to weeping, fucking, flower-arranging, or committing suicide by flinging yourself into the sea while in the ecstatic embrace of your forbidden love (a popular Edo-era theme). A poem by a geisha says, "When the autumn rain falls, My heart aches for somebody."[126] This is yearning in the abstract—the dopaminergic urge, which is only spoiled by attainment.

Most ukiyo-e artists were men and, as such, focused on the glamor and eroticism of the geisha and courtesans that bejeweled the seedy back streets and teahouses of Yoshiwara. Even this painting, with its warm, inviting light and resplendent colors, seduces us. But taking a closer look, a very different story begins to unfold.

Night Scene in Yoshiwara is a painting of a brothel called Izumiya. The young women on display in the barred shop window are not geisha; these are courtesans waiting to be hired for the night. Someone with the keen eye of discriminating awareness would be able to tell the difference between a courtesan and a geisha. While both wore white pancake makeup made from rice powder (and sometimes lead), their mouths stained red with a safflower lip paint, courtesans were distinguishable from geisha in that they tended to wear more elaborate wig decorations and brighter colors, and, whereas geisha had dressers to tie their obis in the back for them, courtesans tied their sashes in the front for easier access. Sex work was legal in Yoshiwara, provided that the prostitute herself did not benefit directly—most of these young women were sold into slavery by their own families and would send their wages back home.

Ōi has chosen to depict in a wash of light what we might normally consider shadowy or transgressive, while the ordinary world of earthquakes and letdowns lurks in the shadows. The composition compels us to crane our necks to get a glimpse of these illicit beauties and their admirers, involving us in the same activity as its subjects: looking. The passersby are looking in, the courtesans are looking out, but no one clearly sees each other.

In the central foreground, a little girl is illuminated by lanterns, perhaps as a reminder that not long ago these women were children themselves, and that one day she could be one of them. Just above the girl, a shadow haunts the bars of the brothel: the silhouette of a courtesan chatting with a potential customer on the street. She is an unknowable figure floating between the Floating World and the workaday, a blank surface onto which the customer's abstract desire can, literally, get fleshed out. She's so close, but we cannot see her on our own. For that we need Ōi, whose own discriminating awareness pierces through the miasma of desire, revealing an actual human being who is neither the cause of, nor responsible for, our lust.

What befell Katsushika Ōi is unknown. After her father died, she walked out of her house and was never seen again. Some say she became a devout Buddhist nun. Others say she temporarily moved in with her brother and his family until they tried to make her cook and clean, at which point she promptly moved out again. Given a choice between safe domestic drudgery and the uncertainty of an untethered life, Padma will always take its chances with the horizon.

Mantooth

(1924–present)

*The Human Talking
and Listening Machine*
Henrietta Mantooth

2018 | PHOTOGRAPH BY ERICA LANSNER

Padma embodied is the sense faculty of hearing. When we endeavor to truly listen, there is an implicit willingness to receive whatever is arising in the silence. This does not mean that we like what we hear or that our minds aren't flooded with a zillion zingers and comebacks, but deep listening does mean unhooking those impulses from our vocal cords and, more often than not, zipping it. The willingness to be with our uncomfortable reactions to what another person is saying, without immediately rushing in to fill the space, is an act of compassion.

Compassion is our capacity to be with (*com*) pain (*passion*). While I haven't run any sort of verifiable scientific experiment in this regard, there does seem to be some corollary between the degree to which we refuse to be with our own pain and our avoidance of other people's suffering. I mean, if we've worked very hard at soldiering on in the face of loss or disappointment, and then we see someone else blubbering over a similar situation, we can actually become quite irritated with them. Or, when faced with an afflicted individual, we might be tempted to give them advice, or to try to fix them so that they won't be in pain anymore, and we won't have to be distressed looking at their mascara-streaked face. Well, needless to say, this is not what is meant by compassion.

Performance artist and painter Henrietta Mantooth embodies the discipline of compassionate listening in much of her work. Compassionate listening is the practice of really receiving what another is saying—not only the content but the whole environment: their body language, the timbre of their vocalizations, the temperature of the room, and so on. You don't have to stare them down or reflect back to them the content of what they're saying in some kind of theatricalized attentiveness—just listen. Just receive.

I am lucky enough to call Henrietta a friend, so I was able to ask her about a recent work called *The Human Talking and Listening Machine*.

KT: When were you born?

HM: December 7th, 1924. It's now Pearl Harbor Day, but I turned seventeen the day Pearl Harbor was attacked. I was born in Missouri, but when I was fourteen my mother married again and took my sister and me and her new husband from Kansas City to California on a Greyhound bus. That was one of the most important events of my life because I got out of the quicksand of my Missouri family and their problems. I found the first letter that I wrote to my father at that time: Dear Daddy, I love California! We go to school with Negroes and Japanese and real figs grow in the backyard! I was thrilled because I grew up in such a segregated city. And there was some segregation of my own life because my father was Jewish. My mother was Scotch-Irish-Cherokee and my father's family never accepted us as real grandchildren, and my mother's family did accept us, but still—they accepted my father because he was so nice, but he was still a Jew.

KT: And that is subject matter that has continued to inform your work.

HM: Absolutely. When we were still in Missouri it was the Great Depression. In fact, I was on the sidewalk playing hopscotch when I heard Franklin Roosevelt say, "There's nothing to fear but fear itself." I still question that.

KT: Your parents divorced and then your mother moved with you and your sister to California?

HM: What happened was that my father had a relationship with another woman for many years. In fact, something that has affected me so much is how my mother always said on the phone, or to this or that person visiting, "Everything was all right until Henrietta was born."

I know she didn't mean it against me. But I took it very personally, and she added details such as, "I was torn and had never been able to be repaired." And Momma would say about my sister, who was three at the time, "and Marge has never been the same." Of course, no kid's ever the same when the second one is born, right? And she said, "Alex (my father) started going out." So those three things I thought I had to repair in my life. Years later, I belonged to a yoga breathing group and when the guru came from India once, we had a big meeting. He went around to everybody so that each of us could all ask him a question. It was almost the end of the line when he got to me, and I told him what I had heard my mother say so often early in my life: "Everything was all right until Henrietta was born." And I was a grown-up! Old even, then. And he said, "Well, you know, she didn't mean it that way." And I always knew she didn't mean it that way, I knew it was like her saying, "Everything was all right till we moved to Chicago." Something like that. For her it was just marking the time, though it was not very sensitive of her. I grew up thinking I had to make up for the damage I caused being born.

KT: When do you remember first connecting with making art?

HM: Art-making was a big part of my childhood because in the summer we used to go to a little house we had in the country...until it was foreclosed. It was a small, brown shingled house on two acres, and as soon as we were out of school, my mother would pack up all our furniture, call the transport company and move everything out of the apartment to the country so we wouldn't have to pay rent in the city. This cottage was near the town of Independence, Missouri, and my parents went every day to Kansas City to work. Gypsies used to park on the oiled road in front of our house, which was about a half-acre back. My mother and father were away all day and my mother warned us of things that might happen, you know, "If a tramp comes, give him a glass of water, but don't let him in the house" and "Don't go near the gypsies." But in this little country place, my mother let us make a mud hole to the side of the front door, quite a big mud hole, and there we spent the summer. All we had was a box of Crayolas and a little container of Prang watercolors from school. We'd pick berries—there was a mulberry bush with wonderful dark red berries—we'd use them to paint. Also, washtub bluing. Everything was on these Big Chief paper tablets that we had for school, so our paper dolls all had lines through them. Nobody said anything about our "art"; no one criticized. They didn't even look at what we were doing, as long as we were safe. They never even asked questions or put up anything on the refrigerator. We only had an icebox that you put in big squares of ice. You know, I learned in school that the center of civilization were these two rivers, the Tigris and Euphrates. Did you ever learn that?

KT: The cradle of civilization.

HM: Okay, so that was my cradle of civilization. That was my Tigris and Euphrates, that mud hole. To this day, I consider it the center of the earth, creatively. I had a tin can with water, and I still remember that feeling of carrying that tin can, and pouring out the water and having a stick and turning it around in the dirt to get just the right consistency. We also had a little iron stove, a tiny little thing that we pretended to make cookies and stuff on, mud pies. And, years ago, when my sister was in her eighties and I was a little less, she said, "Oh, I wonder what happened to that little stove?" Because foreclosure is just a word you read in the newspaper, but it means everything disappears. And as a kid, you don't know what happened to belongings. We knew bills hadn't been paid; we knew that much. But that loss. I still paint a lot of houses. Once I did a portrait of my mother and she's carrying a big purse that is in the shape of that house. All these things affect your sensibilities, right? They're woven into your life.

KT: Fast-forwarding a little bit, you went to junior college?

HM: Yes, because I didn't have money to go to any of the big colleges. I lived in Long Beach, California. I really left home when I was sixteen. When I was in high school, my mother's new husband, who used to take a walk every afternoon, didn't come back one day. Finally we looked in the closet, and we saw his luggage was gone. My sister had gone back to Missouri because she wanted to be with my father. And one day—I was still in my last year of high school—Momma said, "We're going back to Kansas City to look for Mister Poole (that was the husband), and without thinking I said, "Momma, leave me here." I was about six weeks from graduating high school. So she said, "Where will you stay?" and I said, "Well, I'll stay with Mrs. Stalcup." She was the next-door neighbor who had a girl about my age.

KT: Did your mother ever find Mr. Poole?

HM: (laughing) No, she didn't!

KT: You not only studied journalism, you were a journalist.

HM: Yes, that's how I made my living for quite a long time. I started being freelance. When I graduated from the Missouri School of Journalism I came to New York, and it was just when the Second World War was ending and so all the male journalists were coming back. A female journalist didn't have much of a chance. I had a friend who was always wanting me to come to Venezuela, so he sent me a ticket and I went. And there I got a really good job, which was talking to farm families out in the country and writing up their stories. I did it for five years. And during the years that I was there, the Venezuelans had their first-ever democratically elected president. Before that it was always a dictatorship. The party was called Acción Democrática. Five years later, the military staged a coup and threw out the government. Some believed it was with the help of the U.S. because Venezuela was an oil-rich country. Anyway, I was in despair.

I was in my second year of night school at the University of Caracas, studying Spanish. As students we protested, and the military junta immediately closed the university. I said to my boss when he came down from New York, "Can't you send me someplace?" He said, "I can send you to Brazil. The person in that job is going away for two months and I need some stories." So I did the job in Brazil for two months and then, when I was supposed to leave because the man that I was covering for was coming back, there was an airline strike and I couldn't go. So I stayed another two or three weeks and I met the man whose place I'd been taking and we eventually married and I moved to Brazil.

KT: Oh wow! I'm curious: did your training as a journalist inform your art practice?

HM: Yes. Absolutely. I still have thousands of clippings of photos and stories that I work from. That's a very strong part of my art. We call it the daily news, but as I look through clippings that I cut out ten years ago, it's still the same problems.

KT: It seems to me that good journalism isn't just about doing good research, but about really listening.

HM: I think that maybe listening is the most important human quality.

KT: And when did you really start painting?

HM: As a kid, I was often the class artist in elementary school. But when I got to high school I lost track of my talent. Then, after I got married, my boss said, "I'm going to give you a job in Brazil, but you have to take two months off to adjust to marriage." And I was so indignant! I said, "What about him?! Doesn't he have to adjust?!" Well, the way I adjusted to marriage is I went three nights a week to a "Drawing from the Model" session in São Paulo, where we lived. That's how I got connected to art again. As soon as I started drawing, all this talent came shooting back. I started painting and looking at these farm families that I'd been interviewing with an artist's eye. I was still interested in their stories, but I wanted to draw and paint their stories. Little by little, I gave up my journalism job and became an artist.

KT: Did you maintain your painting discipline through the birth of your sons?

HM: Oh, yes. My sons were born in Brazil. By that time, I was an artist. I also had the journalism job, but I realized that I couldn't take care of my first son and be an artist and keep a job. So I stopped working. I had some savings and my husband had a good salary. And so I really worked at being an artist and exhibiting my work at museum shows and was accepted at the São Paulo Biennial. But I have to tell you, theater's always been a part of my life, too.

KT: How did you get involved in the theater?

HM: Well, we came back to the States in the late sixties. What year were you born?

KT: 1978.

HM: Okay, so you were somewhere else. We came back to New York in the 1960s, and I started off drawing at the Art Students League. We lived on the Upper West Side and a friend called me and said that she wanted to do a project that would connect visual artists with theater people. There was this theater that had a reception area where she wanted me to do an exhibit. It was at 83rd and Broadway. There was a well-known dress store below called Charivari and upstairs was a little theater, which was an absolutely delightful place. And so I went over there to look, and in those days, guys would just come in off the street and pee at the bottom of the stairs. I went upstairs, and I saw the headshots of the actors pinned to the wall in the reception room. They included people like—I don't know if you know Trish Hawkins and Judd Hirsch and Conchata Ferrell, who later became well known in theater and film. It was the beginning of a theater called Circle Repertory Company. None of those people were very well known in those days. So I said, "Well, I'll do the show, but I've got to clean up this entrance space." So my kids went over with me with their friends and we painted, so it looked nice and clean, and I put up a show. And then I kept hearing the acting workshops going on in the back of the theater, and since I was so enthusiastic the directors said to me, "Look, if you want you can come in and join the workshops." So that's how I got actively involved with Circle Repertory. They had this wonderful playwright, Lanford Wilson. When he was in the hospital, I went to see him in the last days. He couldn't talk, but he could listen, and I told him how much I loved him and loved being in his plays. We were glad that we were able to express our feelings in that difficult time. So anyway, I eventually became part of their acting company and stayed for fifteen years.

You know, I went through this bad stage recently. I had a terrible attack of envy. I have one friend who's become a very famous painter. She sent me a message that she just sold a big painting to a London museum and another one to some other important museum, and I got this attack of envy. Plus, I have a friend in Brazil who also became very famous, and I was looking through some books she had produced—she was a photographer, writer, and videographer—and I realized how much she had produced, and it joined with the attack of envy that I was going through. For about two days I had this terrible attack of envy.

KT: Oh, yeah.

HM: And there's no inoculation. You've got to go through it. So, anyway, I did get through it because I realized that my painter friend had been a painter her whole life and I never did anything my whole life. I was a journalist, and I became a painter, then I became an actor, a writer. I never focused on one thing as a career. I'm glad I did it that way because it's been a hell of an experience and still is.

KT: I really relate to that. I often feel envious when I see people that I came up with in improv or acting class who've done so well. It's not that I don't want them to do well, but I often feel like, well, where did I go wrong? It's not like I didn't have opportunities, but then I realized I never really did one thing. I did a little comedy. I did some improv. I've studied art.

HM: You sang and danced!

KT: I was in a band, I devised theater. I never saw myself as sticking to one thing. I guess I always felt that I was living artfully but that I didn't really have a career.

HM: Exactly. That's the way it is. I'm glad I did it that way. I mean, I hadn't been interested in easel painting for quite a while. I started doing these stage sets. And I think that the best work I've done artistically was the stage sets I invented. I worked with directors who let me do anything I wanted and, you know, I'd paint the stage floor as if it were a huge canvas. Then, when I went back to my studio with all that kind of artistic improv, all my work became bigger. You were at one of those openings where I had people tell their stories on a wall and floor painting.

KT: Yes! Works like *The Human Talking and Listening Machine* are a Venn diagram of all of your disciplines and interests. It is almost like a stage set that you're creating. You create these—I don't know if they're canvas—these sort of mats or painted platforms that everyone is always so timid to be around and you have to really coax people to stand on them. They are these fabulous paintings that are meant to be stood in, to be lived in. So, it's a painting, it has the theatricality of a stage set, but there's also a sincere invitation for those who stand in that space with you to share their authentic human experience, which is sort of journalistic in its way.

HM: Absolutely accurate.

KT: What was the inspiration to make *The Human Talking and Listening Machine*?

HM: There's this organization called Art in Odd Places, and every year they do river-to-river art and performance on 14th Street. They sent me an email to see if I would be interested in participating. I called my collaborator, Niko Lowery—we're a ninety-six/twenty-six connection (that's age-wise)—he came over and we sat in my studio, and in ten minutes, honey, these ideas were formulated. They were there waiting for us. I mean, I knew I wanted to do something about mass incarceration or solitary confinement, and the idea just came to me: The Talking and Listening Machine. It just came to me like a gift. I didn't think it up!

KT: *The Human Talking and Listening Machine* took place over two days on 14th Street in Manhattan. Do you remember what people wanted to talk about?

HM: Oh, yes, I remember. A couple came up. He was from Cuba and she was from Ecuador. So I asked them if, in coming to the States, they had any experience with feeling segregated. He said, "Oh no, I never noticed anything." But she told me that she had applied for some class and she was talking to this registrar and the woman says, "Now, what is your last name?" She said, "Gonzales," and the registrar said, "Oh, I know about you people. You're a lazy bunch."

KT: Oh my god. Was it related to this work where you asked people about their experience with segregation?

HM: Yes...I decided I was going to ask people about segregation a couple of years ago. Three attractive young Black women were walking down Main Street in Catskill, New York, so I went up to them—this was my first experience doing this—I said, "Could I ask you something?" And they said, "Why?" They were kind of suspicious. And I said, "Because there's something I need to know. How has segregation affected your life?" And, you know, I really felt something like love arose at that moment. And they told me things, such as, one said that when she was a child and her best friend was white, she found out that she couldn't go to the child's house because she was Black. And another one said how she first realized that she had to be afraid walking back and forth to school. It's a powerful thing, segregation. To be segregated, to be afraid and to not have opportunities. Well, you can see it's happening all around us and has been happening forever. But it's a subject I still have asked a lot of people about.

Once I was in the elevator and a tall Black guy got in and I said to myself, "I gotta ask him before we get to the ground floor!" I said, "How has segregation affected your life?" He said, "You know, I got over that. Now when I walk down the street, I say to myself, 'You're just as good as anybody.'" And then he said, "But thank you for asking." You get different reactions. The last time I asked, I was in a taxi going to Brooklyn and the driver was Black, so I said, "Can I ask you something? How has segregation affected your life?" He turned around in traffic and said, "You mean it's over?" From then on, I changed the verb tense.

KT: And why do you feel it's powerful for you, a white woman, to instigate this kind of conversation when it seems like so many people who are white and are upset by segregation wouldn't want to bring it up because they wouldn't want to seem rude or make somebody think about something that's unpleasant—you know, the banality of politeness.

HM: Early in life, I noticed that people were discriminated against. In Kansas City, the streetcar went through what we called then the Negro District. I would look out the window and I would see the run-down houses, the rusted-out cars. The clothes on the lines impressed me—they were like maid's uniforms or overalls—and the kids didn't have shoes. School was totally segregated. And I was segregated from my Jewish family. My grandmother's sister came over to visit her and I was there just for the day, and her sister asked, "Who's the little girl?" and my grandmother said, "It's the neighbor girl." And on Sundays my father would drive to see his mother and family, and we'd always want to go with him because we wanted to be with our father. But we couldn't go with him up to the apartment; we had to wait in the car. I don't understand my father to this day. Why didn't he have the guts to say, "My kids are in the car," and at least bring us a piece of cake or something? I had a lot of experiences as a kid, which I see that my grandchildren don't have. They have other experiences, but they've never played in a mudhole. Everybody should have something equivalent to a mudhole.

KT: The Fertile Crescent of your life.

HM: That's right, the Tigris and Euphretes.

Boty

(1938–1966)

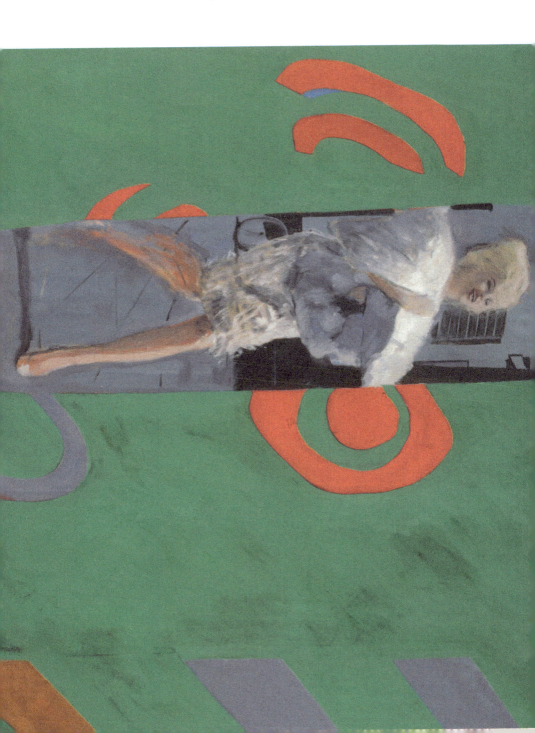

The Only Blonde in the World
Pauline Boty

1963 | TATE

When in Los Angeles, I have the feeling that I'm on the cusp of something huge. Riding around in a car at night, listening to Julee Cruise on the stereo as downtown twinkles in the distance, I'm flooded with that same old rush of teenage melancholy. Being in Los Angeles feels like perpetually being on the way to the greatest party ever... without ever arriving anywhere.

Hollywood, the Dream Factory, whose negative pole magnetizes the positive one in your heart, dragging you from your dirt patch in Oklahoma, or your hatchery in Maine, to the tinsel wonderland of high hopes and a low water table. One of the last conversations I had with my acting manager before she died was about whether I should move out to Los Angeles for better work opportunities. "Puddin'," Dale said (she was from South Carolina and called people she liked sweet names), "The thing about Hollywood is that it will always try to trick you into believing it gave you your talent and that you owe it your life in exchange."

Maybe this is what Pauline Boty saw in Marilyn Monroe, the subject of her 1963 Pop Art masterpiece *The Only Blonde in the World*. At the time of her death, on August 4, 1962, Monroe was arguably the most famous woman in the world; a woman whom everyone wanted but no one knew, perhaps least of all herself; and a woman who perversely felt she could never reimburse Hollywood for the gifts she had given it.

Boty herself was exquisitely beautiful, a Pop bombshell known as the Wimbledon Bardot. However, of all the cinema's bombshells, it was Marilyn Monroe that Boty most related to personally. Like Monroe, she suffered a chaotic childhood. While mental illness forced Monroe's mother to leave her in foster care, Boty was thrust into a parental role when her mother was stricken with tuberculosis. As the only other female in the house, she was expected to cook and clean up after her father and three brothers, even though she was

191

only eleven years old. The absurdity of the situation won out, and, as she later described it, "The whole family became chaotic and we really had a fantastic amount of freedom, in fact we were left completely to ourselves..."[127]

The unconventional circumstances that befell the family instilled in Boty an independent, resourceful streak, which dashed her father's retro-Victorian fantasies of seeing his daughter married off at his earliest possible convenience. Despite her father's objections, her mother encouraged her to attend the Wimbledon School of Art, where she'd won a scholarship in 1954 (the same year Monroe starred in *River of No Return*). At Wimbledon, she worked in stained glass, lithography, painting, and collage, informed by the burgeoning Pop Art sensibility. On the strength of her talent and training, Boty hoped to apply to the Royal College of Art. However, the bald reality was that, as a woman, her odds of being accepted into the painting program were slim. She decided to hedge her bets and applied to the stained-glass program, where she was accepted. Here again we see this completely arbitrary and bizarre distinction between "crafts" and "fine arts." The prejudice, one assumes, is that since they belong in the home, it makes sense that women should know about ceramics and looms and, in the case of stained glass...soldering?

The institutionalized sexism of the college shook Boty's faith in her artistic abilities, although she did continue to pursue her collages and paintings outside of school. Her stained-glass self-portrait, in London's National Portrait Gallery, shows a lead bar bisecting her mouth, as if she were silenced by the art she was authorized to make.

I also can't help but imagine that, its stuffy connotations notwithstanding, the discipline of stained glass may have informed Boty's more renegade collage work. Both disciplines actively display Padma's discriminating awareness wisdom. Faced with fragments of glass, or an array of magazine cutouts, discriminating awareness can see that this green triangle needs to go here, and the lower left-hand corner has too much going on, and this corner could use more red, and so on.

Despite being in different departments, it was at the RCA that she befriended fellow students David Hockney, Derek Boshier, and Peter Blake, with whom she is now credited as co-founder of the British Pop Movement. Boty was also active in the student film society, which screened everything from the classics to the latest in the French New Wave. Derek Boshier recalls, "She talked about her European film stars of course—but the person she most talked about was Marilyn Monroe."[128]

Today, Pop Art like Warhol's *Campbell's Soup Cans* or Lichtenstein's *Comic Book Damsels* are as ubiquitous and quaint as a Monet lily pond. But in their prime, they were controversial for allowing chintzy material like cheeseburgers and nudie magazines to poison the triple-filtered well water of the art establishment. After all, everyone knew what kinds of subject matter merited artistic representation: epic battles, epic landscapes, epic nudes, even epic abstractions—all art-worthy subject matter. But a movie magazine is a ridiculous thing to paint because it's just something anyone at all might read while waiting in line at the grocery store, hardly epic. With Pop Art, the blood-brain barrier of high and low culture had been irrevocably breached. But as Andy Warhol once said, "Pop Art is about liking things." The fact of the matter is, people really love their fashion magazines and their Cokes and their celebrity crushes, and while the object of affection might seem silly or inappropriate, the feeling that arises is real, and that tenderness can be a conduit to the spiritual path. "I really feel that love's terribly important to everybody," Boty said in an interview, "and I don't mean romantic love or anything, I mean, say, love of things or love of, say, flowers, or love of machines, or anything like that, you know, generalized sort of love, I think that's terribly important to people."[129]

Just as we might object, "That can't be art, that's my lunch," we could just as well say, "That can't be the doorway to realization, that's my life."

This dynamic finds expression in the symbol of Padma, the lotus flower. In both Hinduism and Buddhism, the lotus flower represents the spiritual path because this stunning flower grows out of sludgy, slimy muck. If you haven't gotten ahead of the metaphor yet, human beings are the same: we don't achieve enlightenment in spite of the sludge of our confusion, but actually *because* of it. Neurosis and sanity, samsara and nirvana, are not separate things. This is also the pith teaching of the Five Wisdoms: the very negativity we're trying to get rid of is fertilizing our brilliance.

Marshall McLuhan viewed advertisements as the mythological artifacts of our time. He believed that by carefully studying them, we could better identify and integrate our values and vices. Similarly, Pauline Boty described her work as exploring "a kind of nostalgia for the present, for NOW...it's almost like painting mythology, only present-day mythology."[130] Her paintings of stars like Marilyn, Elvis, and Jean-Paul Belmondo have the loose, breathless execution of a palpitating fangirl. She translates into oil paint subject matter that might normally be relegated to a doodle in the back of a biology notebook. This is Padma power on tap. Directed at a mythic star, it manages to pulse and illuminate harmlessly like a plasma ball at the mall, while also possessing the purchasing power to keep the gears of Hollywood greased and humming.

Yet in her own day, until practically this present moment, Boty has been overlooked as a major contributor to Pop Art. Her male contemporaries, on the other hand, have been lauded for being "in on the joke" of Pop Art content, which was largely low-brow housewife stuff: the world of romance novels, cosmetics, fast food, household cleaners, and Hollywood gossip rags. Just as Marilyn Monroe wasn't rated enough to be both the butt of the joke and its architect, Boty was overlooked as a serious artist because, as a woman, it was unfathomable that she could be both the subject and the object of the Pop milieu.[131] In addition to being a painter, Boty was also a working actress, appearing in film, on stage, and on TV. Along with Derek Boshier, she regularly featured as a dancer on the BBC music program *Ready Steady Go!*, further cementing her reputation as a Pop person.

"She had, you know, this glamorous side," Boshier said. "That's what the tabloid press concentrated on and she was portrayed as...'The Wimbledon Bardot.' So, this aspect was not good for her and although she did in some way partake in it, they would take the worst aspects—they talked about her sexuality and sensuality rather than talk about that aspect within her work—so she wouldn't get serious coverage."[132]

In 1962, this reputation was sealed when she, along with four other artists, were featured in Ken Russell's BBC documentary *Pop Goes the Easel*. Boty in particular cuts a very glamorous figure indeed, dances with abandon, horses around at an amusement park, as well as earnestly and intelligently discussing her art practice: "I've always had very vivid dreams and I can always remember them very, very easily. And I've used the kind of atmosphere of the dreams in my collages. I think there are two things about this, and one is that I often take the moment before something has actually happened, when you don't know if it's going to be terrible, or it might be very funny. The other thing is that there's something very extraordinary that is actually happening, and yet everyone around isn't taking any notice of it at all."[133]

Boty was not above parlaying her desirability into conversations about her art. On several occasions she agreed to pose for photographs scantily clad, provided her paintings were in the background. By granting the viewer access to their own carnality through desire for her body, lust is redirected into artistic appreciation. The desire to fuck and the desire to paint ain't so different.

When we're stumbling through the world in a haze of Padma grasping, we either have our tentacles wriggling out into the horizon, or we're looking back at what we lost with a nostalgic melancholy. But what we aren't doing is paying attention to the very extraordinary life that's happening all around us right this instant. If I am obsessing over how to pin Pauline down or bemoaning how I let Pauline get away, the one thing I'm not actually paying any attention to is Pauline. The object of our desire becomes abstracted by the squeeze of our wanting.

Just a few months after the airing of *Pop Goes the Easel*, Marilyn Monroe died of apparent suicide. The world was in shock. How could someone who had everything everyone else seemed to be trying to get—wealth, beauty, fame—still feel so bereft? As Sister Wendy said of Monroe, "If you're a great celebrity, your image is up for grabs. People can do what they want with you. You become a sort of nobody if you're a celebrity."[134] This was a global loss that must have felt very personal to Boty. Over the next year she completed three portraits of Monroe, the last of which is included here. (Not that it's a contest, but it is interesting to note that Warhol's *Marilyn* didn't appear until 1967, giving Boty the jump on Warhol by four years.)

The Only Blonde in the World depicts a tremulous Monroe—quite a contrast to Warhol's flat, impassive *Marilyn*, vacuum packed for mass distribution. Boty's Monroe comes from a promotional still for *Some Like It Hot*. Tabloids reported that Monroe was pregnant at the time of filming and that the very scene Boty painted was one Monroe had been forced to retake again and again, leading to a miscarriage. The great green panels close in on Monroe, who is losing ground in a sea of abstraction. The object of desire is occluded by the desire itself, which has its own agenda. This is the electric zap of Padma energy, sputtering like an old neon sign between desiring this specific blonde and just needing *a* blonde on whom to focus the intensity of desire. By becoming the *only blonde*, she grows mythic, thereby losing her distinguishing features and becoming *any blonde*.

Boty was the only blonde in the world for the actor and writer Clive Goodwin. They were married the same year she completed *The Only Blonde in the World*. In 1967, she became pregnant and discovered at her prenatal exam that she also had cancer. In order to save her own life, she would need to undergo chemotherapy, which would cause her to lose the child. Boty decided to keep the baby. After giving birth to a healthy baby girl, she commenced chemotherapy treatment, but it was too late. She died five months later, on July 1, 1968, at age twenty-eight.

"Even now," the novelist Sabine Durrant wrote twenty-five years later, "grown men with grey hair in dark houses in Notting Hill cry at the sound of Pauline Boty's name."[35]

Wheeler
Waring
(1887–1948)

The Study of a Student
Laura Wheeler Waring

CA. 1940 | PENNSYLVANIA ACADEMY OF THE FINE ARTS

Byron Katie once said, "No two people have ever met." First impressions are always impressions of ourselves, which sometimes coincidentally apply to the other person as well. We are so convinced of our point of view (and why shouldn't we be, given all of the time we spend bathing, nursing, and putting false eyelashes on it?) that we believe we know how to improve the world. If, on top of this, you have a lot of money, look out.

In 1922, a man called William E. Harmon, a white Christian real estate magnate, established his eponymous foundation with the intention of improving the lives of African Americans. While the foundation attempted to enrich Black communities through the promotion of nursing programs and religious education, today it is mostly remembered for its support of the Black artists of the Harlem Renaissance. In 1926, under the direction of Mary Beattie Brady, the Harmon Foundation began awarding cash prizes and arranging art exhibitions in recognition of the groundbreaking Black American artists who might have otherwise remained marginalized and invisible. Some saw this as a much-needed lifeline, while others saw it as just another form of paternalistic meddling. For example, its financial support notwithstanding, the Harmon Foundation suggested that Black people should consider their art avocational.[136] In other words, don't quit your day job, pal.

One of the early recipients of the Harmon Gold Award (and the only woman recipient) was Laura Wheeler Waring. She was born in Hartford, Connecticut, in 1887, to Mary and Reverend Robert Foster Wheeler. Her parents, both artistically inclined, encouraged their daughter's talent: "I remember being taken to the art galleries in Hartford many times and I suppose my delight in them was not only because of the outing it gave me but perhaps I had a love of paintings—the color, the beauty of the galleries. I noticed particularly, I recall, the portraits. I often drew them at home. In fact,

I cannot remember a time that I did not have a great thrill with my paints and pencils."[137]

Not only did Wheeler Waring recreate the portraits she saw in the galleries, she also often bribed her brothers with peppermint candies to sit for portraits of her own.

On graduating from Hartford High School, Wheeler Waring was accepted into the prestigious Pennsylvania Academy of the Fine Arts, where she studied for six years. Throughout her time at PAFA, she taught drawing part-time at the historically Black Cheyney Training School for Teachers (now Cheyney University). After completing her studies, she was awarded the prestigious Cresson Memorial Travel Scholarship in 1914, enabling her to make the Grand Tour through Europe (previous recipients of this award include Singer Sargent, Cassatt, Whistler, and Homer).[138] Wheeler Waring traveled through Europe, visiting the Louvre, where she studied works by Manet, Cézanne, and Degas.

"I thought again and again how little of the beauty of really great pictures is revealed in the reproductions which we see, and how freely and with what ease the great masters paint."[139] Her trip was cut short after two and a half months when World War I inconveniently broke out. American currency was not accepted at the time, so her father had to purchase her return passage to the United States in gold, thought to have been secured through the help of a neighbor, Mark Twain.[140]

Back in the U.S., she resumed teaching at Cheyney, where she continued to work for the next thirty years, establishing the school's art and music programs. Cheyney was a boarding school, often requiring Wheeler Waring to work right through the weekends, leaving her little time to paint.[141]

In the early 1920s, Wheeler Waring began contributing artwork to the magazine *The Crisis*, founded by W.E.B. Du Bois. Through the magazine, Du Bois hoped to create a platform that could not only combat racism but also foster a sense of pride in Black Americans. This, he felt, could be achieved by claiming and integrating the diverse cultural riches of Africa while also celebrating contemporary artists.

Du Bois, who also co-founded the NAACP and was at the forefront of applied sociology, wrote that the "[Negro race] is going to be saved by its exceptional men...Can the masses of the Negro people be in any way more quickly raised than by the effort and example of this aristocracy of talent and character? Was there ever a nation on God's fair earth civilized from the bottom upward? Never; it is, ever was and ever will be from the top downward that culture filters."[142] As the founding editor of *The Crisis* magazine, Du Bois promoted and employed Black women artists to an unparalleled degree, Wheeler Waring foremost among them. Nevertheless, he was shrewd when it came to whom he would include in the publication, claiming some artists were not quite "ready to represent the race."[143] This is a rather chilling comment with the hindsight of history, as we can see how the racist delusion of eugenics had infiltrated the thinking of even one of the founders of the civil rights movement.

Padma's seductive energy can show up in every stratum of society, from cruising someone at a bar, to pitching your TV show idea to a network, or, in the case of eugenics, trying to engineer the apotheosis of the human race. The very notion that there is an "ideal human being" that can be molded out of the dud material of the "low-born," or whatever, is an act of seduction, albeit a perverted one.

Wheeler Waring returned to Europe with friends in 1924, staying for over a year. In France, she studied at the Académie de la Grande Chaumière under the instruction of painter Bernard Boutet de Monvel, whose bold, photorealistic style and elegant use of color she admired. "This was my only period of uninterrupted life as an artist with an environment and associates that were a constant stimulus and inspiration. My savings, however, would not allow me to continue this life indefinitely."[144]

Wheeler Waring felt she had some wind in her sails on her return from Europe, and this momentum only increased in 1927, when she won a Harmon Foundation Gold Award in the amount of $400. She called this success a "stamp of approval on my work."[145] She would return to Europe one last time in 1929. This trip was both a belated honeymoon (she had married Walter Waring in June 1927) and an opportunity to attend an exhibition of her work at the Galerie du Luxembourg on the Boulevard Saint-Germain-des-Prés. This international recognition of her work was an incredible boon for her, though sadly the particulars of the exhibition and the whereabouts of her work from her time in Paris remain opaque.

Today, Wheeler Waring is most remembered for her contributions to the Harmon-commissioned touring exhibition, *Portraits of Outstanding American Citizens of Negro Origin*. This collection of portraits was conceived in 1943 by Harmon Foundation director Mary Beattie Brady and painter Betsy Graves Reyneau. The exhibition was meant to combat prevailing American prejudices about Black people by spotlighting luminaries of the African American community. In order to get the project off the ground, however, Brady and Reyneau, both white women, knew they needed to get a Black artist on board to legitimize the project, as many progressive Black artists were ambivalent about—if not downright suspicious of—the Harmon Foundation. In a 1936 letter regarding the artist Charles Alston, Mary Beattie Brady wrote, "Charles Alston apparently belongs to a rather communistic group here called the Harlem Artists Guild. For some reason they have taken the attitude that we are a patronizing influence and should be avoided...This [is] rather strange inasmuch as we had been of considerable help to Mr. Alston when he was doing W.P.A. work..."[146]

So Brady proposed the project to Wheeler Waring. As Steven Nelson of the National Gallery of Art in Washington, D.C., puts it, "In essence, with... Wheeler [Waring], a well-respected and well-connected African American artist in the mix, Reyneau and Brady could credibly claim that the exhibition was a prime example of not only the representation of Black achievement, but also of interracial cooperation."[147]

Of the initial twenty-three portraits produced for the exhibition, only six were done by Wheeler Waring (she succumbed to a long illness in 1948). Half of her portraits were of women, including the opera singer Marian Anderson, her friend Jessie Redmon Fauset, and fellow painter Alma Thomas (with whom she worked briefly at Cheyney). There is a distinct contrast between the portraits of men and those of women in the exhibition: the men are usually depicted with some attribute suggesting their area of expertise, while the women just sit there. Nelson comments, "Black femininity gets molded into white Victorian mores and morals...Especially when you have an artist like [Wheeler] Waring in the mix, who herself was conservative; her work was conservative, she in her life was conservative—that ethos carries forward well into the twentieth century and comes up against real fears of 'wild Black women.' And so you want them to be accomplished, but not *too* accomplished."[148]

To visually highlight the achievements of these Black women, who included judges, doctors, and scientists, would not only put them on equal footing with the Black men in their company but also show them to be superior to the white men who had come to look at their portraits. Probably not what the foundation had in mind.

To Nelson's point, Wheeler Waring's paintings do tend toward the conservative. They are expertly rendered with a distinct style, but even with the occasional flights of fancy that appear in the backgrounds, the subjects have a slightly stolid air about them, as if they were being pinned down by the burden of their own accomplishments and all they must mean to their race. This makes sense, given that this collection of paintings was meant to do nothing less than Stop Racism. Of course, representation is important. If we are to believe that we ourselves can attain our heart's desires, it is encouraging to know that someone we relate to has gone before us and succeeded. But at the same time, to feel that to be a role model you need to have walked on the moon, or to be a credit to your marginalized group, that you need to even aspire to walking on the moon, well, that's a lot of pressure. It doesn't leave a lot of room to just be yourself.

Portraits of Outstanding American Citizens of Negro Origin toured for ten years to standing-room-only crowds at venues all over the United States. But after the Supreme Court struck down legalized segregation in *Brown v. Board of Education* in 1954, the Harmon Foundation retired the exhibit. They assumed, I suppose, that the ruling signified "mission accomplished" where American race relations were concerned.

The exhibit really did inspire people and perhaps even changed some hearts and minds, but the problem is that the world into which it was trying to help induct Black people—the world of upward class mobility based on merit within a corporate hierarchy—was actually the same world as had been dreamed up by the very people who had oppressed them in the first place. In other words, as the "communistic" painter Charles Alston could see, the Harmon Foundation was trying to help Blacks to fit into a white pyramid scheme, which requires someone to be at the bottom. And if you yourself have suffered at the bottom, then how could you in good conscience "move up" the ladder, knowing that the rungs are actually made of the bodies of other people?

I'm sure that William E. Harmon meant well. Seeing the plight of African Americans in the U.S., Harmon no doubt felt pity and wanted to help them to have more of the outward trappings of respectability and success that he equated with equality. But, as it is said in Buddhist teachings, "Pity is the 'near-enemy' of Compassion." Pity can *look* like compassion, but the very notion of pity is based on the idea that *you* see that X is happening and isn't that terrible for *them*. Compassion, on the other hand, is the realization that you are not separate from any other person. Or as Martin Luther King, Jr., said in his *Letter from Birmingham Jail*, "Injustice anywhere is a threat to justice everywhere. We are caught in an inescapable network of mutuality, tied in a single garment of destiny. Whatever affects one directly, affects all indirectly."

(And don't get me wrong. I'm not suggesting that Wheeler Waring should not have taken Harmon's money. I'm glad she did, and whatever the amount she received, she was underpaid.)

On rare occasions, we may run across someone who perfectly embodies our ideals and we try to scoop them up as quickly as possible. More often than not, however, we spend our time trying to cram others into the Jell-O mold of our preconceptions. Often, we call this "helping." This kind of grasping at another is the essence of confused Padma energy and basically sums up the human condition: If *you* were more like *this*, it would be better for *me*.

What I find so fascinating about the work of Wheeler Waring is that, while her portraits of Very Important People do tend toward the conservative (when asked whether his wife liked Surrealism or Modernist art, Walter Waring replied, "Downright no"[149]), her portraits of "nobodys" are quite free, with the undulating energy of El Greco or contemporary portraitist Lynette Yiadom-Boakye.

To my mind, none are as fresh, spontaneous, and expressive as the picture I've selected for this essay, *The Study of a Student* (compare its color palette to Philip Guston's later work, *Deluge II*). This was painted not long before she received her *Outstanding American Citizens* commission. As a study, it may well have been dashed off without too much thought, a quick impression of a young woman in profile, gazing off into the middle distance, a blue rose pinned in her hair. What is going through her mind? This is the kind of girl you want to tell to smile, to cheer up, honey, it's not that bad. But then, maybe it is.

Art-making itself is a Padma practice. When someone paints a portrait, they're trying to "capture" a likeness, a gesture, a moment. The results, like this work, can be wonderful. But when we tangle with Padma energy, we capture not what is there, but what we *see*—and revealed in that is often a "tell"— something about ourselves that even we aren't aware of bleeds through, like a double-exposed photograph. Here, the tell seems to be in the blue rose. In the work of the German poet Novalis, the blue rose was emblematic of the impossible quest for a pure or perfect love. In the *Twin Peaks* universe of David Lynch (also a graduate of PAFA), a Blue Rose is an FBI case that has some supernatural element. Blue roses don't exist in nature and have come to symbolize the mysterious, the uncanny, the unknowable (a Japanese lab tried to make one, but it turned out purple).

What is troubling this young student? What does she see? Was it something I said? Is she thinking of me? If only she would let me love her. We want to get inside her head, but the way is blocked by the Blue Rose. If anything, the young woman's body language and expression seem to scream LEAVE ME ALONE! But maybe that's just me.

Spartali
Stillman

(1844–1927)

Love's Messenger
Marie Spartali Stillman

1885 | DELAWARE ART MUSEUM

first heard of the Pre-Raphaelites in high school. My best friend, Jennifer Engelmann, bought a wall calendar featuring the artwork of romantically named men: Dante Gabriel Rossetti, John William Waterhouse, Edward Burne-Jones. Men with a penchant for medieval-looking ladies whose ennui was so advanced they could scarcely operate their looms. These were paintings of ill-fated heroines from literature who wildly loved and recklessly lived, often tossing themselves into flower-strewn rivers in weighty velvet gowns without waiting a full hour after lunch.

This was all very enticing to us fledgling goth-curiousers (among other things). We were already menaces with an eyeliner and had mastered the art of pole dancing (not the sexy athletic sort, but the kind where you circumambulate a support pillar in the club as if decorating a maypole with unseen ribbons of dread) to Skinny Puppy or Bauhaus. We were young and rebellious, and only the dead, like Mary Shelley or Lord Byron—or the dead-adjacent, like Robert Smith—could feel our pain. As Sarah Vowell put it on *This American Life*, "If the funny T-shirt slogans and crisp khaki pants of the average American tell the lie that everything's going to be okay, the black lace garbs and ghoulish capes of goth tell the truth—that you suffer, then you die."[150]

I found Jennifer's calendar enormously appealing and relatable. Sure, the subjects in the paintings weren't dressed in black crêpe or being crushed alive by the weight of their own mascara, but they did seem to be drowning in a sea of melancholy, which was close enough. After all, we were miserable at the prospect of being ground through the gears of mainstream culture, and disgusted by the drab banality of a world that celebrated Frisbee over Foucault and Richard Marx over Karl Marx. We were too sensitive for the vulgar abrasiveness of mid-nineties Colorado, and so we looked back to some imagined past port-of-call to drop anchor. This, it turned out, we had in common with the Pre-Raphaelites—also looking back to find a way forward.

209

The Pre-Raphaelite Brotherhood, as they christened themselves, was founded in 1848 by seven British art school students, the most renowned of whom are William Holman Hunt, John Everett Millais, and Dante Gabriel Rossetti. Marx's *Communist Manifesto* had just been published, social hierarchies were getting a shakeup throughout Europe, and the Pre-Raphaelites wanted to sluice some of that revolutionary spirit into the British art world. The Pre-Raphaelite Brotherhood bridled at what they felt were formulaic art-making rules foisted on them by the Royal Academy of Art. They knocked titans of British Art like Sir "Sloshua"[51] (Joshua) Reynolds, who had continued to rinse and repeat the stylistic techniques practiced by Raphael and his followers since the Renaissance. So the idea of being a "Pre-Raphaelite" was not a strike against Raphael in particular but against the stodgy fidelity to Renaissance compositional techniques, which, in the intervening centuries, had calcified into dogma. To find the painting of the future, these young Victorians looked into the past for some pristine time before the followers of Raphael had gummed up the works for everybody else. Their beef with the institution inspired them in a MAGA (Make Art Great Again) pursuit, which led them to medieval frescoes and the early Renaissance. Rather than always arranging their subject matter in a pyramid and lighting the principal figure, medieval art favored a more free-wheeling, panoramic approach, with lots of everyday folks canoodling in various architectural nooks and crannies.

To say that something was a shock to the Victorian sensibility probably seems a pretty low threshold to cross, but nevertheless, the PRBs (not to be confused with a PBR, though you can probably picture a guy with a bun and a Pabst Blue Ribbon explaining Betty Friedan to you), as the Pre-Raphaelite Brotherhood called themselves, did shock. They created formally radical religious paintings that asked questions like, "What would happen if we depicted the Holy Family like ordinary folks with wrinkles and tan lines and dirty feet?" or "What would it feel like if an angel really visited you in your bedchamber and told you he was going to touch you with a flower, thereby impregnating you with the Messiah?" These young painters were hungry for notoriety, and they got a bellyful. Journalists relished pillorying them, claiming their hyper-realistic depictions of biblical scenes rendered them sacrilegious. Even Charles Dickens elbowed into the fray, writing, "Wherever it is possible to express ugliness of feature, limb, or attitude you have it expressed."[152] But for all the heat they got, they had their supporters as well, including the art critic John Ruskin, who was just glad they weren't painting "the eternal brown cows in ditches, and white sails in squalls" that overwhelmed English canvases. Ruskin's opinion was so revered that his vote of confidence in the movement caused an about-face in public opinion. Overnight, the PRBs went from personae non gratae to superstars.

More than their biblical paintings or their pathologically detailed floral landscapes (Padma terrain is the lush, manicured garden), today the Pre-Raphaelites are mostly remembered for their opulently technicolor depictions of bedroom-eyed damsels—the very ones featured in Jennifer's calendar. It wasn't just the compositional style that the PRBs retrieved from medieval times: the women came out in all farthingales, tippets, and ruffs. This can be viewed not only as a dark premonition of the Society for Creative Anachronism that was to come, but also the formidable power of Padma energy to magnetize even the past into the present. This evokes Marshall McLuhan's Tetrad, and the aspect of the principle he called "retrieving," pointing out the power of technologies to reveal aspects of the past that never actually went anywhere (see the downfall of Western civilization for reference). This romantic magnetizing power is on full display in the work of the PRBs.

After all, it was in the medieval period that the troubadours strummed through Europe on their lutes, singing exquisite love ballads to unavailable women. Just catching a glimpse of their Faire Laydee from a balcony in the moonlight was enough to set off a paroxism of poetry and the inevitable romantic heartburn. These idealists popularized love poems and the idea of love as self-expression. In *The Power of Myth*, Joseph Campbell distinguishes the two main concepts of love in this period: Eros (erotic love) and Agape (love-thy-neighbor compassion). Both of these iterations of love are, of course, powerful, but they are impersonal. If it's closing time at the bar and you haven't gotten laid in six months, you're probably not going to be too particular about who you take home. And if your neighbor is in crisis and there's something you can do to help, you do it because help is needed. You don't review their resumé first to make sure they're worthy of helping. But his new kind of love was called Amor, which Campbell points out is "Roma" spelled backwards. The very notion of Amor is in direct opposition to the Roman Catholic Church, whose prerogative it was to marry you off to whomever might prove to be the most lucrative or politically expeditious.

The notion of marrying for love where "the eyes are the scouts of the heart" (as the troubadour Giraut de Bornelh put it) was not only blasphemy, it was adultery. You were cheating on Jesus! For the Pre-Raphaelites this romantic bravery must also have symbolized the rebellion of the heart against institutional oppression. The ideal of a personal love born through the eyes has since completely dominated our view of relationships in the West.

Nothing calls out both the compassionate concern and the frenzied clinging of Padma energy like romantic love. When one falls head over heels for someone, any little detail about them is vital nourishment. In order to communicate how nonchalantly crazy one is for the person, one remembers that poinsettias are their favorite flower because they remind them of Christmas (their favorite holiday), and that they have a thing for cabernet sauvignon, Schaupenhauer, and Captain Beefheart (don't let *that* one get away). The fact that you remember all this stuff might strike them as thoughtful or just plain creepy. Discriminating awareness wisdom trembles on the brink of grasping, always.

In reality, most of the women the troubadours swooned over were married, and the likelihood that an intimate exchange would occur was slim-to-none, and also beside the point. One does wonder, then, what the psychological significance was for the PRBs in dressing their girlfriends as abstract, untouchable love goddesses? Perhaps it was in reaction to the fact that the mechanization of the Industrial Revolution was rapidly expanding the workforce to include women, unravelling outmoded gender roles. Perhaps this was an attempt to return to the good old days when everyone agreed women should be seen as bewitching muses but not heard.

What else could be the significance of this cosplay? In the same way that Jennifer and I were putting on the clothing of Victorian undertakers in order to understand and express something about ourselves in the world *now*, so too did the Pre-Raphaelites play with the costumes of a bygone era in order to understand and express something about themselves as Victorians.

Living life as misunderstood teens, Jennifer and I certainly had our share of grievances and seemed to be nostalgic for a time that never quite existed. And yet in yearning for it, we found a sense of community and play. If we were mocked by our fellow classmates for getting up like sad clowns, we took comfort in knowing other oddballs had gone before us and enjoyed great success. People like my art-rock hero Kate Bush, or Jennifer's god, Robert Smith. In his book *Gothic: Four Hundred Years of Excess, Horror, Evil, and Ruin*, Richard Davenport-Hines writes, "Goths reject the bourgeois sense of human identity as a serious business, stable, abiding and continuous, requiring the assertion of one true cohesive inner self as proof of health and good citizenry. Instead, goths celebrate human identity as an improvised performance, discontinuous and incessantly re-devised by stylized acts..."[153]

What Davenport-Hines is describing here is a sense of humor. Not only is a sense of humor essential in art-making, it is also an indication of profound spiritual realization. Now, I'm not advocating that we should all be interminably guffawing and sneaking whoopie cushions onto each other's chairs, but a sense of humor does provide an illuminating contrast to the state we more commonly find ourselves in—namely a kind of brittle mental rigor mortis. We become dogmatically committed to our prejudices and preferences and wind up missing our lives. We add insult to injury by being dead but still holding down a nine-to-five job. Not only does this rigidity make it extremely difficult (if not impossible) to engage in the creative daydreaming and exploration that might lead to a song or a ceramic ashtray, but if we don't watch our asses that same creative energy can be co-opted by the paranoid mind and deployed into all sorts of conspiratorial theorizing. Anything that doesn't match our preconceptions could be characterized as a conspiracy. And yet as we contort ourselves into non-Euclidean shapes to justify our own insanity, it is we who are conspiring against reality, not the other way around. I don't blame anyone for subscribing to seditious counterplots, but honestly, you'd probably be better off taking up bagpipe lessons in the long run. Sure, people still won't want to listen to you, but at least you'll have a skill and a better shot at earning cab fare home after a long day of carrying on in the town square.

We see the burden of mirthlessness all around us today. The ever-growing intensity with which our instinctive narcissistic tendencies have been pumped with fiberoptic steroids in the electric age has amplified our grievances, causing them to come volleying back at us, which we then take for corroborating sources rather than the echoes they truly are. Or as Marshall McLuhan said, "A point of view can be a dangerous luxury when substituted for insight and understanding."

In this state, nostalgia becomes rigid, weaponized, as in the case of the MAGA crowd who dream of returning to some magical before-time where things were wonderful (McLuhan's retrieving again). That particular time clearly never existed, or else you wouldn't have multitudes of downtrodden people fighting tooth and nail to keep from being dragged back into a time that was deeply un-wonderful, to put it mildly. The difference between MAGA nostalgia and Goth nostalgia is that while neither of the periods to which they glance backward may have ever actually existed, with the exception of some vampiric subsets, Goths don't actually need you to join them in order to feel their lives are worthwhile. They don't want to force you to agree to some bygone dress code or legislation—they don't want you to join them at all. They want you to leave them alone because you're annoying.

Positive nostalgia, I would say, is really a form of deep appreciation. When I have gone on longer meditation retreats, morning practice sessions are often spent chanting the names of the lineage holders who passed the teachings and techniques down to this present moment, it is said, since the time of the Buddha. This isn't done to daydream about how wonderful it would have been to be a medieval Tibetan (it would not have been wonderful); instead, it is a way of expressing appreciation to what I am sure was a motley crew for keeping the Dharma alive. And in expressing appreciation, we realize that we are not looking back at all; the appreciation of nostalgia helps us realize that the lineage is right here all the time. That which we appreciate *is* now. So McLuhan was right: the rear-view mirror of nostalgia points at what is to come, because it shows us what we value, what is filling our minds.

The past that the Pre-Raphaelites were invoking and predicting wasn't a particularly jolly one. Several women in the PRB orbit suffered fates as tragic as the ladies they depicted in their canvases. The painter Joanna Boyce Wells died tragically from a postpartum infection, and Elizabeth Siddal, Rossetti's wife and muse, died of a laudanum overdose after delivering a stillborn child.

Heartbroken, Rossetti buried Siddal along with all of the love poems he'd written to her...only to have her exhumed seven years later to get the poems back. Writing is hard.

Marie Spartali Stillman, on the other hand, led a life that was relatively free of sonnet-worthy catastrophe. Despite being dismissed as an amateur, she managed to paint steadily for fifty years, leaving behind over 150 paintings, making her one of the most prolific of the Pre-Raphaelites.

The daughter of a wealthy Greek businessman, she met many of the art-world luminaries of her day. The Spartali mansion (modestly known as The Shrubbery) was a cultural hub, and the family received visits from the likes of George du Maurier, James Abbott McNeill Whistler, and Algernon Charles Swinburne who, after meeting Marie Spartali, said, "She is so beautiful I feel as if I could sit down and cry."[154]

She became a sought-after model for the Pre-Raphaelite circle, but soon realized she wouldn't be content just being *in* pictures, she wanted to make them as well. As a young woman in Victorian England, Spartali Stillman wasn't exactly flooded with a wide array of options to study. Painting programs for women were doomed to subpar standards because, as I mentioned earlier, piddling details like human anatomy were considered to be inappropriate subject matter for the feminine mind. As a woman of means, she was able to work with a private tutor, PRB elder statesman Ford Madox Brown. Brown immediately recognized her talent and finessed her eye for detail into exquisitely romantic watercolors like *Love's Messenger*. Despite living six centuries after the troubadours, she was still expected to make a respectable marriage, as dictated by her father. (Some things never change.) Spartali Stillman inconveniently fell head over heels for the "notorious rake" Thomas Jones, seventh Viscount Ranelagh, whom her father deemed a most unsuitable match.[155] Instead, Mr. Spartali had his eye on the widowed (and wealthy) Dante Gabriel Rossetti for his daughter. Ford Madox Brown arranged a dinner where Rossetti could read to her the poems he'd recently retrieved from his late wife's grave. Romantic though I'm sure she found the gesture, by the end of the evening she was smitten with another man altogether: the artist and journalist and recently widowed William J. Stillman. Her father was against this match, too, but after managing to avert a greater disaster with Viscount Ranelagh, he figured he ought to quit while he was ahead. The eyes had spoken, and in 1871 Marie Spartali and William J. Stillman married. They lived for many years between Italy, where Stillman had work as a journalist, and England. They also made several trips to the United States, where he had family and she often exhibited her paintings. As a result, today the Delaware Art Museum has a treasure trove of her work.

Until recently, Spartali Stillman has remained mostly relegated to the ranks of the keen amateur. This is clearly due not to a lack of ability but rather to the restrictions of her class and era. She shunned publicity in general and had to be diplomatic in her sales. As a married woman of the upper class, she wasn't meant to earn her own living, which might imply that her husband could not support his own family.

What is initially striking about *Love's Messenger*, as Pre-Raphaelite expert Jan Marsh notes, is that the imagery seems to have come completely from Spartali Stillman's imagination. Unlike the Lady of Shallot or Ophelia or Pandora, Spartali Stillman's beauty does not come from any pre-existing source. The woman in the painting certainly has what it takes to be a heroine from Tennyson—the puffy sleeves, the red hair, the abandoned needlepoint depicting a blindfolded Eros—but she does not appear to be filled with dread; she appears content. The white dove, which represents love, has flown in the window from the open waters beyond, the realm of the unconscious. And our fair lady is feeding the bird, nourishing this messenger of love, who has arisen from her own unconscious. So perhaps the message she clutches to her breast is one that comes not from another person but from deep within herself.

To quote my favorite Victorian, Oscar Wilde, "To love oneself is the beginning of a lifelong romance."

But jealous souls will not be answered so.
They are not ever jealous for the cause,
But jealous for they're jealous. It is a monster
Begot upon itself, born on itself.

WILLIAM SHAKESPEARE, *OTHELLO*

This information is top security. When you have read it, destroy yourself.

MARSHALL MCLUHAN

O f all the Eastern spiritual concepts to take root in the West, none is as ubiquitous or as misunderstood as karma. We equate karma with a big moral abacus in the sky, an invisible hand keeping score, gleefully doling out comeuppances to miscreants and bursting in just in the nick of time with a really good reason why these two should not be joined in holy matrimony. It sounds a little like God, and a lot like a Cameron Crowe movie. In either case, it is a misunderstanding of how karma works.

Karma (Sanskrit again) translates as "action" and describes the unavoidable reality of cause and effect, and, covering all bases, effect and cause. Karma energy spurs on our frenetic tinkering to fill the space of not knowing what will happen next. It is also the single, decisive stroke that deftly brings lifetimes of planning to fruition.

Keep out of my way and we'll get along *just* fine.

Move over and let *me* do it!

Confused Karma energy is called jealousy or competition. In *Snow White*, the magic mirror's harsh tidings for the Evil Queen egg her on to eliminate the competition. In its wakeful state, however, the energy of envy is transmuted into all-accomplishing wisdom, providing us with more space and options. Instead of calling for Snow White's heart in a box, for example, the Queen could take the girl aside like Betty Grable did to Marilyn Monroe on the set of *How to Marry a Millionaire* and say, "Honey, I've had mine—go get yours."[156]

A Karma person follows their dreams—not in the upward trajectory of success but in the free-associative, intuitive sense. (For a quintessential Karma landscape, see Henri Rousseau's *The Dream*.) Karma energy follows the Thread of Ariadne, not back but forward, into the unknown. Armed with the uncanny jangle of hearing the same Alice Cooper song three times in the same day, you notice the boy with Tenniel's Red Queen (off with her head!) printed on his custom Converse as you pass down a familiar street in this unfamiliar town and stop to get directions from a man who resembles your uncle...you know, the one who always looked a bit like a white rabbit?

What. Are. The. Chances?

Karma is interdependent, ceaseless activity.

The truth of interdependence, what the Buddha realized under the Bodhi Tree, has infiltrated our psyches by countless technological avenues, but none have been quite so on-the-nose as the Internet. However, when this truth is impressed upon us rather than realized, we experience interdependence as a mortal laceration on our individuality, and not as a gateway to supreme, perfect liberation. This, in turn, often leads to paranoia and the determination to cauterize our identities into brands with a cohesive cross-platform color story. To the ego mind, interdependence feels like death. The seemingly incontrovertible reference points by which we typically garner a sense of a continuous identity—race, nationality, occupation, gender, sexuality, age— are all coming apart at the seams, not because of some attack by the liberal or conservative media, but because those reference points are innately porous and were not designed to withstand travel at the speed of light.

Karma self-generates invention of the ever newer, faster, more efficient mode to deliver it before the deadline. Karma needs that on its desk *yesterday*.

I don't really know why most things were invented, but for the sake of argument we could say "to make things better." If we accomplish remedial tasks more efficiently, then we ostensibly have more leisure time to enjoy the company of our loved ones or dabble in rock gardening. But due to some strange trait of the human mind, we also seem to innovate simply because we can. We innovate because it's better than sitting alone in a room with ourselves enjoying all of our fucking leisure time. We cannot bear the plodding space of Buddha energy, so we mindlessly tinker around, hoping to stumble onto something neat; novelty eclipses necessity. The polyrhythms created by overlapping media environments contribute to a collective mental fog, and our attention spans slowly flake away like taupe paint on the garage (it seemed like a good choice at the time).

As I explored in the work of Tayeba Begum Lipi, McLuhan explained that all tools, sped up to their extremes, reverse on themselves, resulting in effects exactly opposite to what they had been designed to do. For example, headphones, which enhance hearing, when pumped up too loud cause hearing damage. Staring into the light, which enhances vision, can cause blindness. And in the Internet age, we can see how the very tools that are meant to spread information and bring us closer together have reversed into a cesspool of conspiracy and alienation.

Even back in 1972, McLuhan saw these trends unfolding: "Separatisms are very frequent all over the globe at the present time. Every country in the world is loaded with regionalistic, nationalistic little groups. Even Belgium has a big separatist movement."[157] These regressive entrenchments are violent reactions to the shock of interdependence and the reality of no-self. McLuhan continues,

> All forms of violence are a quest for identity. When you live out on the frontier, you have no identity; you're a nobody. Therefore, you get very tough. You have to prove that you are somebody. And so you become very violent. And so identity is always accompanied by violence...Ordinary people find the need for violence as they lose their identities...Terrorists, hijackers, these are people minus identity. They are determined to make it somehow, to get coverage, to get noticed...People in all times have been this way, but in our time, when things happen very quickly, there's very little time to adjust to new situations at the speed of light.[158]

Morisot

(1841–1895)

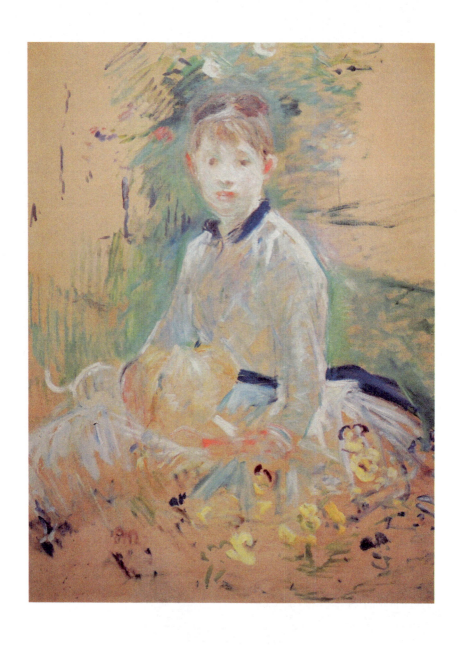

Portrait of Mademoiselle L
(Isabelle in the Garden)
Berthe Morisot

1885 | PRIVATE COLLECTION

Meteorologically speaking, wind occurs when hot air rises, leaving space into which cooler air rushes. The art world operates in much the same way. When the establishment begins to take product more seriously than practice, it becomes inflated with its own hot air, which causes it to disconnect from the earth, and in the process, mistake its own levity for superiority. Looking down from on high, the establishment begins to issue proclamations rather than perspective. Meanwhile, a cool new group rushes in to fill the vacancy that the old guard made when it abandoned innovation for constancy and credentials. This is the dynamic of Karma energy, manifesting elementally as air, as wind. Karma energy wants to either uphold its primacy or be the first to innovate. Those FOMO vibes are intense.

Berthe Morisot had no intention of being left in the dust. While she had had considerable success at the Salon de Paris (as much success as a woman who was never meant to have a career of any kind, much less as an artist, could have), she knew change was on the wind. She could feel it. Already her creative impulses were bridling at the strictures placed on art-making by the Académie. Artist friends from her social sphere were coming together to push back at the "because-I-said-so" paternalism of the official Salon. They called themselves the *Société Anonyme Coopérative des Artistes Peintres, Sculpteurs, Graveurs* (Cooperative and Anonymous Association of Painters, Sculptors, and Engravers), and among them were Monet, Cézanne, Renoir, and Degas (to name a few). It was Degas who insisted they include her in their first exhibit in 1874. "It seems to us that Mademoiselle Berthe Morisot's name and talent are too well suited to our mission to pass up," he said.[159]

More conservative artists like Pierre Puvis de Chavannes cautioned her about joining ranks with a ragtag bunch of troublemakers; if she wasn't careful, she might find herself blackballed from the Salon. But Karma energy can't stand to be left behind, and the notion that you might be caught in some passé pursuit is deadly. Morisot could have had a perfectly respectable career navigating the Salon circuit, playing it safe in the academic style, but she needed innovation and adventure. She wanted to be where the action was and jumped at Degas' invitation, becoming a founding member of the Impressionists. Sure, they were mostly derided by the press—in response to Monet's *Impression, Sunrise*, the journalist Louis Leroy, who dubbed the group "Impressionists," wrote acidly, "A preliminary drawing for a wallpaper pattern is more finished than this seascape"—but they were in it together. Of the eight official Impressionist exhibitions, she showed in seven. Morisot was the cutting edge.

The whole enterprise of Impressionist painting is shaped by, and swept up in, the changing qualities of light and air. To have a chance at capturing something so ineffable, brushstrokes have to come faster than Morse code, with the entire body operating as an eye. Impressionist painting is a nimble, improvisational dance in which the painter tries their hand at "fixing something of the passing moment," as Morisot herself put it,[160] an attempt to aggregate and arrange countless simultaneous sense impressions into a single apparent moment, a compression of impressions into a totemic now. This is Karma energy caught in paint.

Perhaps Morisot liked the thrill of riding the edge of the moment, risking tripping over it, or being dragged behind it. Perhaps she thrilled at riding the edge of propriety. She was best friends with Édouard Manet, after all, who, though never aligned with Impressionism, was no stranger to scandal. He painted naked ladies among clothed men at picnics, and gimlet-eyed hookers staring their clients down from the unassailable position of a gallery wall. Some suspected a secret romance between Morisot and Manet. He painted her more than any other model. But they could not marry because he was already married to his boyhood piano teacher, who, coincidentally, became pregnant after their lessons began. It was never quite clear whether Édouard was the father...or if his own father was the father. Sadly, it was not uncommon for "the help" to be taken advantage of by their wealthy employers. In any event, things were complicated, and when Morisot married Édouard's brother Eugène, Manet lost a model but gained a sister-in-law. For his part,

Eugène Manet, who was also a painter, stepped back to support his more talented wife, who savvily kept her maiden name professionally.

The painting thing started off as a cute idea her mother had: hire an art tutor for her three daughters, Berthe, Edma, and Yves, so they could make a birthday drawing of a sheep or something for papa. But things quickly spun out of control. No one had accounted for the girls' raw talent. Their teacher, Joseph-Benoît Guichard, warned their mother: Don't let these girls paint unless you want artists on your hands. I won't be held responsible for what's unleashed! "Do you realize what this means?" he cried. "In your upper-bourgeois milieu, this is a revolution. I might almost say, a catastrophe."[161]

Karma energy embodied is the sense of touch, and in this way is the most prurient of the Buddha families, the only one that can reach out and impact the world directly. Karma energy radiates from every nerve ending, scintillated by the Karma element of air. When the Morisot sisters expressed the desire to paint outside, *en plein air*, it was all too much for Guichard, and they were introduced to another artist who did crazy things like paint outside: Camille Corot.

Even chaperoned, which custom demanded, the sight of a well-to-do woman painting outdoors was too much for Parisian society. A woman working where the air could touch her from all sides incited children to mock her in the park. She dealt with the problem by renting a boat so she could paint in the middle of the lake, out of earshot of their taunting.

Morisot's subject matter was radical, but not wild. She painted mothers and babies and picnics, not with the adoring eye of a man but with the ambivalent eye of a woman whose lifestyle was compulsory, not chosen. As a respectable bourgeois lady, she was barred from the brothels and cabarets that her male colleagues depicted with such relish. Her personal life was not wild. She could not fully shed the shackles of her sex or status. But stylistically, her painting was the wildest, the most impressionistic of the Impressionists. As Sister Wendy puts it, "She didn't paint like a lady at all, but like a savage. Like a prisoner in chains, they said!"[162] In a style that would be adopted as radical by the Abstract Expressionists more than a half-century after her death, Morisot often left huge swaths of canvas unpainted, full of open air. This technique can be seen to marvelous effect in her *Portrait of Mademoiselle L* (a favorite model). The duty of the canvas was to hold what she had to express, not to dictate the space to be filled. If Morisot's brushstrokes are feathery, they are the feathers of a hawk; the deceptively diminutive, domestic subject matter executed by a fencing foil rather than a brush. Unencumbered by extraneous pigment, her canvases breathe in a way that she, corseted and bustled, could not.

And yet, in an art movement known for its domestic scenes of elegant ladies in soft colors, it is absurd (though not surprising) that Morisot's work was described by critics using the Three Adjectival Fs of the Apocalypse: feathery, floral, and feminine. Art historian Linda Nochlin points out that, ironically, her radical upending of painterly norms was taken as evidence of some inherent female inadequacy rather than a "'making strange' of [Impressionism's] more conventional practices."[163]

Although she ultimately acquiesced to her social status, Berthe Morisot was nevertheless keenly aware of being discounted as a woman. In her private diary she wrote, "I don't think there has ever been a man who treated a woman as an equal and that's all I would have asked for, for I know I'm worth as much as they."[164] What is striking about this entry, aside from its poignancy, is the expression of Karma wisdom. For all its frenetic scrambling, Karma energy can break through mundane competitiveness into something profound: a genuine ownership of personal mastery.

Ellsworth

(1967–present)

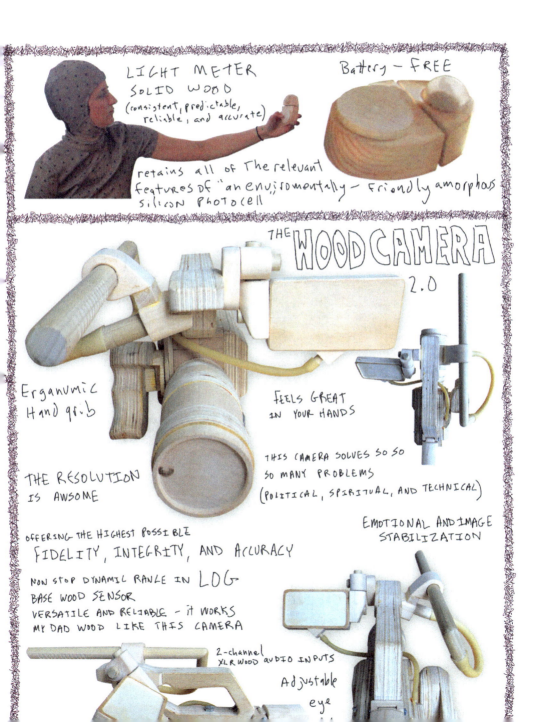

LIGHT METER
SOLID WOOD
(consistent, predictable,
reliable, and accurate)

Battery – FREE

retains all of the relevant
features of "an environmentally – friendly amorphas
silicon photocell"

THE WOOD CAMERA 2.0

Erganumic
Hand grib

FEELS GREAT
IN YOUR HANDS

THE RESOLUTION
IS AWSOME

THIS CAMERA SOLVES SO SO
SO MANY PROBLEMS
(POLITICAL, SPIRITUAL, AND TECHNICAL)

EMOTIONAL AND IMAGE
STABILIZATION

OFFERING THE HIGHEST POSSIBLE
FIDELITY, INTEGRITY, AND ACCURACY

NON STOP DYNAMIC RANGE IN LOG
BASE WOOD SENSOR
VERSATILE AND RELIABLE – it WORKS
MY DAD WOOD LIKE THIS CAMERA

2-channel
XLR WOOD AUDIO INPUTS

Adjustable
eye

Four NFTS:

A Dance for Wood Camera; Ownership Assignment Process for

Rock-Owned NFT; Location of the Rock-Owned Non-Fungible Tokens;

Put the Log Back in Analog

Michelle Ellsworth

2021 | COURTESY OF THE ARTIST

n *The Picture of Dorian Gray*, Oscar Wilde writes, "Nowadays people know the price of everything, and the value of nothing." And as if to highlight the complete subjectivity of the value that governs our economic lives, the 2020 pandemic saw a soaring stock market and a slumping economy. While many lost their jobs and small businesses shuttered, billionaires became uncomprehendingly richer and the "Investor Class" started high-hatting about town, engaging in increasingly speculative capers. Instead of investing in fusty old stocks, they began throwing their money at things called NFTS (non-fungible tokens), which are basically like one-of-a-kind digital trading cards. Journalist Sam Dean explains: "The unique digital file is stored on a blockchain network, with any changes in ownership verified by a worldwide network and logged in public."[165]

We all have different tastes, of course—some people love collecting *Star Trek* merch, for example (William Shatner's dental X-rays were an early NFT), but in large part it seems taste (or lack thereof) has little to do with the purchasing of NFTS. For that matter, taste doesn't have much to do with what a lot of art investors wind up buying. All they care about is that it is authentic and appreciable as they tuck it away in a vault, in some cases never again allowing it to see the light of day.

Sam Dean goes on: "The appeal of NFTS to collectors is obvious: Instead of relying on forensics or patchy document records to prove that a piece of art or a trading card is the real deal, the authentication is coded into the NFT file itself."[166] Dean is describing the art world fetish of *provenance*. How do we know the Van Gogh is authentic? Using auction receipts and estate bequests and pigment matching, experts try to link the painting from the present moment all the way back to the artist's studio. NFTS and cryptocurrency use blockchain to verify their authenticity, thereby making them valuable in their rarity. NFTS have been heralded by some as the death of art. Others proclaim

WOOD SD (Sanded Disk) record as much as you want. RECORDS Directly to LOG STORE footage Here and/or transfer to Hard wood drive, that Thing you did happened. Here is evidence of your labor. Impossible to use content for Deep fake Training or other post production minipulations. You did it. You did That Thing. This is all The evidence/data you need.

them an iconoclastic means by which artists reclaim agency from an antiquated and hierarchical gallery system by putting buyer and seller in direct contact.

For an artist like Michelle Ellsworth, the implications of technology loom large. "As a dancer, I'm always centralizing my physicality in relationship to these new technologies," she says. "I'm always looking [it] over, [asking] what is this? How does this sit on my body?" Like Marshall McLuhan, Ellsworth has come to see that the metaphor of technological advancement masks a real human need, and her work is an attempt to take over the means of production by addressing that need head-on. So she decided to make NFTs of her own.

In April 2021, Ellsworth choreographed a dance to music by Sean Meehan, which she then performed for wood camera. The light reader, monitor, and boom mic were also made out of wood, enabling her to "put the log back in analog."

"I did it very seriously," she says. "We rehearsed it...we had proper snacks. It took the same amount of time to shoot onto the wood camera. And I think that I danced much better with the wood camera than with the regular camera."[167] The only physical artifacts that remain of the event are the wood SD (Sanded Disc) cards.

Some ethical concerns arose in preparing the project. Firstly, the server farms that "mine" blockchain exact a heavy environmental toll. (It is estimated that the cryptocurrency Ethereum uses as much fossil fuel-based electricity as Libya.[168]) Ellsworth opted into Tezos, a green blockchain that uses proof of stake, to mint her four NFTs. Secondly, implicit in an NFT is the promise of exclusive ownership, perpetuating a hierarchical capitalist pyramid scheme. Ellsworth and her collaborator (and son), Satchel Spencer, solved the problem by deciding that "the NFT had to be owned by a rock, as opposed to a person."[169] So she printed out the key/code to the digital NFT wallet, rolled it up into a small metal capsule and placed it into a mold. Concrete was poured into the mold and the freshly cast fossil-grade rock-owner of the NFTS was then deposited somewhere between Boulder, Colorado, and Moab.

"I was definitely trying to bring a NFT into a three-dimensional world," says Ellsworth.

> But I didn't think about it with regard to money. I'm still very confused about money as an artist. I know that artists are supposed to get paid, but *everybody's* supposed to get paid. I don't think of [artists] as a special case. I *don't* want to be paid for that NFT. I don't want to participate in that...[W]hen I ingest art in one form or another it's a reconsideration. That's all I'm praying for: please help me say something that doesn't waste people's time and...maybe makes them think again, for one second, a little differently about one little thing. Just one thing. That's how art has always functioned for me. I'm so grateful.[170]

In putting the log back in analog and removing ownership from the NFT equation, Ellsworth evokes the Buddhist sage Shantideva, who admonishes us to "remain like a log" in meditation practice. While the intangible mental images we encounter are vivid and affecting, over time the notion of ownership of them naturally begins to fall away and we are less likely to be compelled into manic bartering and trading.

In ancient periods, from the Caves of Lascaux to Egypt and Sumeria, the maker was not present in the art object; its value was inherent in its scale, materials, and representation of the divine. As the millennia trundled on, some Greek artists wanted a pat on the back and noted on their vases that they had been "brought to life" by so-and-so. In the late fifteenth century, Albrecht Dürer signed his work loud and proud, going so far as to create a logo for himself and eventually bringing the first copyright infringement case to court. Throughout the Renaissance and up until the present day, emphasis increasingly shifted onto the identity and reputation of the artist, whose creative expression was itself valuable. And now, with the advent of NFTS, the arc of time has folded back on itself like an origami donkey. Rather than being an expression of God or the artist, the NFT is a totem for the money one hopes to get from bothering to make it in the first place. Now both artist and ephemeral digital object are treated like antiquated bureaucratic choreography exacted to achieve the ultimate end: The Sale. And in March 2021, Christie's sold an NFT by the artist Beeple for $69.9 million. The buyer used Ethereum's cryptocurrency Ether for the purchase. While I am in no way implying that what Beeple made is not art, it does seem that the inflated price tag wasn't so much a reflection of the artwork's value as it was an attempt to validate the value of the currency used to buy it. Intangible currency used to buy intangible objects. This must be what shopping in heaven feels like.

"When I look at [NFTS] I think, 'Oh, this is a vehicle to that other thing,'" says Ellsworth.

> I think that's why I tried to make my NFTS so labor-intensive...
> [M]aking the dance and making the wood camera and all of these
> things that went into the one JPEG, which aren't represented in any
> other way—there's no video recording, there's nothing else—it
> became actually all about the labor of making the NFT. And then
> the ownership. I think the case with me and all of the work that I'm
> making is that I'm actually not interested in the arrival or the know-
> ing or the end in itself. I don't want the end. I don't know anything
> about that. I understand [and] I like labor. I was trying to make the
> least-fixed NFT I could, both in what it was; by making a dance that
> was shot on wood camera; and that it was owned by a rock and the
> rock was gone.

Early cultures had commodity currency, actual objects whose value were self-evident (whales' teeth, shells, rats). Those currencies were exchanged for goods and services. Leather was once considered so valuable it could be used as currency—and later, when times got tough, it was boiled and eaten. Jewels and precious metals, of course, were used for trade until, eventually, paper

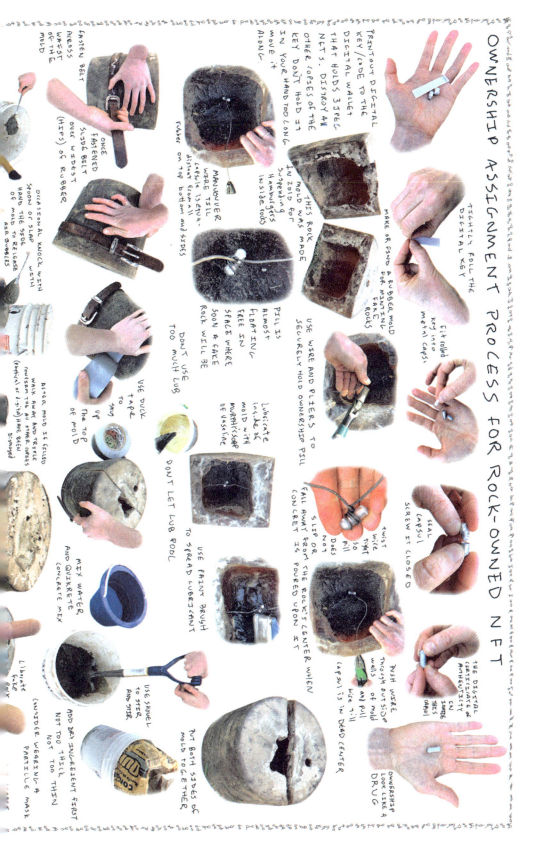

OWNERSHIP ASSIGNMENT PROCESS FOR ROCK-OWNED NFT

PRINTOUT DIGITAL KEY/CODE TO THE DIGITAL WALLET THAT HOLDS 3 STEEL NFTS. DESTROY ALL OTHER COPIES OF THE KEY. DON'T HOLD IT IN YOUR HAND TOO LONG. MOVE IT ALONG

FASTEN BELT ACROSS WAIST OF THE MOLD

ONCE FASTENED SLIDE BELT OVER WIDEST (HIPS) OF RUBBER

OCCASIONAL KNOCK WITH SPOON OR SLAP HAND THE SIDE OF MOLD TO RELEASE AIR BUBBLES

THIS ROCK WAS MADE IN 2010 FOR SCREWING HAMBURGERS INSIDE. LOOKS

MAKE OR FIND A RUBBER MOLD FOR MAKING FAKE ROCKS

MANOUVER WIRE TILL CAPSULE IS EQUAL-DISTANT FROM ALL SIDES

RUBBER ON TOP BOTTOM AND SIDES

TIGHTLY ROLL THE DIGITAL KEY

FIT ROLLED KEY INTO METAL CAPS

SEAL CAPSUL SCREW IT CLOSED

USE WIRE AND PLIERS TO SECURELY HOLD OWNERSHIP PILL

PILL IS ALMOST FLOATING FREE IN SPACE WHERE SOON A FAKE ROCK WILL BE

DON'T USE TOO MUCH LUB

USE DUCK TAPE TO SNUG UP THE TOP OF MOLD

LUBRICATE INSIDE OF MOLD WITH MURPHY'S SOAP OF VASELINE

TWIST WIRE TIGHT SO PILL DOES NOT SLIP OR FALL AWAY FROM THE ROCK'S CENTER WHEN CONCRET IS POURED UPON IT

PUSH WIRE THROUGH OUTSIDE WALLS OF MOLD AND PULL WIRE TILL CAPSUL IS IN DEAD CENTER

DON'T LET LUB POOL

USE PAINT BRUSH TO SPREAD LUBRICANT

MIX WATER AND QUIKRETE CONCRETE MIX

AFTER MOLD IS FILLED WALK AWAY AND TRIPLE CONFIRM THE ALL OTHER COPIES (PHYSICAL OR DIGITAL) HAVE BEEN DESTROYED

LIBERATE FAKE ROCK

USE SHOVEL TO STIR AND STIR

ADD DRY INGREDIENT FIRST NOT TOO THICK NOT TOO THIN

CONSIDER WEARING A PARTICLE MASK

PUT BOTH SIDES OF MOLD TOGETHER

THE DIGITAL CERTIFICATE OF AUTHENTICITY IS INSIDE THIS CAPSUL

OWNERSHIP LOOK LIKE A DRUG

money stepped in as a metaphor for those jewels. McLuhan describes the Western use of money as "store and translator of communal work and skill."[171] In other words, the paper itself acts as a bridge for joining our talents and toil to the richness that the paper money represents.

Until 1971, American currency had been backed by the gold in Fort Knox, thereby fixing all of the world's currencies to the U.S. dollar. To combat inflation caused by the Vietnam War, the "Nixon Shock" was implemented, cutting the dollar loose from gold, allowing it to float with no fixed value in a kind of free-jazz improvisation with every other currency in the international financial markets. Apparently, Nixon told his psychiatrist that when he looked into the mirror in the morning it was "as if there was no one there."[172] Why should the dollar fare better?

"From coin to paper currency, and from currency to credit card," McLuhan continues, "there is a steady progression toward commercial exchange as the movement of information itself...and approaches once more the character of tribal money."[173] In other words, the money itself is the commodity. Now, to further underline McLuhan's progression, the twenty-first century has seen the rise of cryptocurrency. Personally, I'm still working to build up enough credit to get a credit card, so I barely have any clue what cryptocurrency is or how it works. What little I do understand, however, seems to point back to McLuhan's insight that what money is moving now is not a representation of hours worked but information. And the information that cryptocurrency represents is the Libertarian ideal that we should be free from the free market, which turned out not to be quite as free as some had hoped. Libertarians are always doomed to wind up sourly nursing a flat beer in the corner of the John Wayne Saloon because their vision of personal freedom is categorically impossible, given what the Buddha realized under the Bodhi Tree: namely, everything is interdependent, there is no self, and cause and effect are unavoidable. But that hasn't stopped anyone from trying to "eke out some completely parallel world that's totally separate from the existing one," as Vitalik Buterin, the founder of Ethereum, has said.[174] Ethereum's cryptocurrency is appropriately called Ether, as it seems to relate more to the etheric plane than the physical.

This desire to amputate cause from effect and the psychic from the physical evokes Oscar Wilde's *Dorian Gray* again. In contrast with that other beautiful male archetype, Narcissus, whose inability to recognize his own reflection causes a fatal lassitude, Dorian consciously offshores the effects of his misdeeds onto an external image. In this way, Dorian is an inverted Narcissus. NFTs are heir to the Dorian Gray legacy; they seem so sleek, effortless, and eternal, while the grinding labor they require to exist is foisted upon Mother Earth in a disfiguring gasoline suck.

When Ellsworth heard Buterin's quote, her initial thought was, "'Oh, a queer future!' Like he's imagining some kind of queer futurity where we can do something differently, but the only thing he's taking forward is the idea about money, which is just a fucking story. It's not real. NFTs and cryptocurrency being unreal is no more unreal than money itself. I mean, it's never been real. The body! Oomph!"[75]

But while she is able, in retrospect, to find a capitalist critique of ownership in her NFT work, for Ellsworth even that is a metaphor to be cut through. "Actually, what I *think* is what I *did*," she said. The real inspiration for the NFT work was to bring her family together. "It was saying, 'Satch, you want to hang out? Let's eat a meal. And let's do this thing.' Ulli, my daughter, made the documentary on wood camera of the dance for wood camera, simultaneously. So it's like a family project. It's kind of like a fifteenth-century cheese farm. It feels more related to that than to anything. I just want to make cheese with my family. But I want a cow that's consenting. I want a consensual cow."[76]

Michelle Ellsworth's work is about cutting out the middleman of metaphor in meeting the immediate needs of the human being. And yet the question remains: What is the NFT metaphor attempting to address or heal? The answer, it seems, is a provenance of our own in which we truly feel authentic and valuable. The only provenance we can ever truly lay claim to is the present moment, authenticated by ourselves, our senses, like the Buddha did before us, by touching our bodies to the earth.

Artemisia

(1593–ca. 1696)

Judith Beheading Holofernes

Artemisia Gentileschi

CA. 1613 | MUSEO DI CAPODIMONTE

Every effect is set in motion by some sort of causation, but what that effect will actually wind up being is unknowable. In the documentary *Public Speaking*, Fran Lebowitz is asked whether she believes in getting even. She replies, "Do I believe in revenge? I definitely believe in revenge. People always say, 'Revenge is, you know, a dish best served cold.' It's good anytime you can get it. Any chance you have for revenge, take. Never let that pass you by. I believe in revenge. I don't believe in forgiveness, however. It might be ethnic, because forgiveness is a Christian thing. I mean, forgiveness, in fact, is Christianity. But the Jewish God is an avenging God. The Jewish God is a judge."[177]

It was the Jewish God to whom Judith of Bethulia cried out, "Strengthen me this day, Lord, God of Israel!" as she chopped off the head of the Assyrian General Holofernes with his own sword, immortalized here by the seventeenth-century Baroque painter Artemisia Gentileschi. Judith's was not a revenge killing. She was strategically dispatching with the general of the army about to obliterate her people. Yet Artemisia's *Judith* is often interpreted as a personal revenge painting. Whether this interpretation is appropriate or not, it's not hard to see why this theory came about and why it has stuck around. (An aside: normally I would refer to an artist by their last name, but for the sake of clarity I will refer to both her and her father, who was also a painter, by their first names.)

Art-making was a family affair; her father, Orazio, an associate of Caravaggio, was a well-connected history painter in Rome. Artemisia and her three brothers acted as studio assistants. Her brothers never struck out on their own, but she became a painter in her own right. The seeds of her talent somehow managed to crack open, take root, and flower, despite the inhospitable conditions seventeenth-century Rome offered a teenage girl.

Her father's colleague, Agostino Tassi (they'd been painting frescoes at the Quirinal Palace), raped her when she was seventeen. In a bizarrely convoluted scheme, Tassi was able to, with the assistance of several co-conspirators, insinuate himself into Artemisia's life. He contrived various reasons to stop by the Gentileschi home, sometimes finding her alone, sometimes finding her just out of bed. In those days young women were not allowed out of the house without a chaperone. The streets of Rome were dangerous. Rape lurked in alleyways and behind public statues, which depicted mythic rape, the gods' prerogative.

On the day Rape came as Agostino Tassi, Artemisia was not in the street, she home alone painting. He flung himself at her, threw her paintbrushes across the room, and dragged her into the bedroom as she screamed and cried. She scratched at his face and pulled his hair. She had been a virgin; she bled. Afterwards, she grabbed a knife and screamed that she would kill him. He opened his coat, daring her to strike. She threw the knife at him from across the room, just nicking him. At that time, the shame of the rape could all be wiped away if the assailant married the assailee. Artemisia became Tassi's lover, wheedled along for months by the promise of marriage, though this would never come to pass. Tassi, it turned out, was already married, though his bride had been missing for some time. The rumor was that he had hired bandits to murder her.

Rape was an assault not just on a girl but on her entire family. Left with damaged goods, Orazio's only recourse was to take Tassi to court, not for the rape but for the deflowering of his daughter. Orazio had incurred damages, as Artemisia's loss of virginity would cost him "bartering power." In order to exact recompense, it had to first be proven in court that she had been defiled. If she was proven a whore, no harm, no foul.

Over the seven months of the trial, Artemisia was put through every kind of examination and humiliation. Tassi read from letters he claimed she'd written to her many lovers, an impossibility as she could neither read nor write. But Tassi's reputation was on the line. And could you ever truly trust a woman? They had to be sure. Accompanied by the judge and two attendants, Artemisia was taken to Tassi's prison cell to undergo judicial torture to prove the veracity of her claims. The sibille was used, strips of leather wound around the fingers and thumbs, tightened to the point of breaking her painter's hands. Did she stand by her accusation against this man? "*E vero, e vero*," she cried. Tassi was found guilty of rape and banished from Rome, but given his close ties to the papal family, the sentencing was never fully upheld. All of this is recorded in four hundred pages of meticulous trial transcripts, which survive today.

Artemisia was hastily married off to the brother of the court notary who had assisted Orazio during the trial. They quickly relocated to Florence, where she became the first woman admitted to the Florentine Academy, establishing herself as a highly sought-after painter. When she returned to Rome in 1620, she was a celebrity. There's no greater revenge than success, and I wonder if, after her trial, she didn't feel some vindication returning to Rome fêted and in demand. She wasn't just a successful painter, she was a person of fascination.

By this time, she had painted the iconic scene of *Judith Beheading Holofernes* twice. The first was completed around 1613, which means she must have been painting it throughout the trial. The second was completed around 1620, on her triumphant return to Rome.

Back in Bible times, the elders of Bethulia were dithering, trying to figure out what to do about the invading Assyrian army, which was determined to wipe out the Israelites. Going over their heads and behind their backs, the beguiling widow Judith decided to take matters into her own hands. Voluptuous and perfumed, she ingratiated herself with the Assyrian general Holofernes, promising to divulge essential intel about her people if he promised to keep her safe like the big strong man that he was. Like Garbo as Mata Hari, Judith dressed to the nines to enact her subterfuge. Accompanied by her maid, Abra, she employed her feminine wiles, plying Holofernes with wine and music in a game of seduction. As he drunkenly nodded off, Judith took his sword and decapitated the boor.

Artistic treatment of biblical and mythological themes in Renaissance art can tend toward the euphemistic. John the Baptist's severed head is often presented as if it had been plated by Julia Child, while scenes of rape are coyly portrayed as overzealous squeezes, or in the case of Europa, something more akin to a rodeo, rather than devastating brutalities. No pantywaist decapitations will do for Artemisia. She wants us to feel the elbow grease. Judith is slicing through tendons, sinews, and bones here. There is a passionless determination in her task. It is thirsty work.

In the Judith saga (which appears in biblical apocrypha), having dispatched with Holofernes, she tucks the head snugly in her maid's basket. The two women escape from the camp, male military power triumphantly castrated. Judith has used the language of sexuality to execute a civic duty. The symbol of the Karma family is, after all, the double-edged sword cutting both ways through confusion. Sharpened by awareness, the sword effortlessly and radically cuts ignorance at the root. Chop, chop.

The second iteration of the scene is certainly more polished, with a few extra-gory grace notes flung in to dazzle the squinting eye. I have included Artemisia's first *Judith* not just because of its psychological proximity to the trial but because of a weird effect of time. Whatever pigment she used to paint the sword was unstable and over time has faded, leaving a shadow of a sword. We still see the ramifications of the sword's blow, but the weapon itself is in the act of vanishing; just as we feel the echoes of past hurts or genetic imprints without being able to truly point to the cause of the effect we're experiencing.

It is here that we post-modern individuals tend to read Artemisia's personal narrative into the painting. Growing up amid Rita Hayworth's *Gilda* and Angela Bassett's fiery exhale and all of the *Kill Bill*-ing, we can't help but imagine *Judith Beheading Holofernes* as a kind of pre-Freudian baroque wish-fulfillment, and it does seem clear that her Judith is a self-portrait. Rumor has it, she gave Holofernes Tassi's face. And in the intervening years, Artemisia's public expression of personal pain through her artwork has also come to serve a kind of civic function for the collective unconscious.

Recently, more cautious historians have tried to coax us away from attributing psychological narrative to artwork. While I can admire the spirit of a sober-minded approach, it does leave us twisting in the wind a bit. After all, the reason we *want* to imbue the painting with Artemisia's story is that we have already imbued her story with our own. Life is suffering and, to varying degrees, we have all been wronged, humiliated, and mutilated in the process of living, often with no means of redress and no karmic comeuppance for the apparent source of our suffering. Karma energy is highly transactional: we did X so we expect Y to happen. It wants results. It expects standards to be upheld! When our dualistic concept of tit-for-tat justice is thrown back in our faces, what to do with the desire for heads to roll?

The karmic action of the Karma family is called destroying. Because, let's face it, when pacifying, enriching, and magnetizing don't cut it, destroying will. Though it sounds operatic, destroying need not be a violent act. It might show up as connecting with a natural boundary in your life or going to bed early. It could look like politely withdrawing yourself from a fruitless, circular conversation. *Let them miss you.* Your absence may be an instructive presence in another's mind (though that's not really any of your business, of course). Then again, it might show up as a shriek. Everything is available to us. Everything is on the table.

Destroying may be a creative act, like pruning a hedge or pollarding a tree. On the spiritual path, as in horticulture, the act of cutting away obscurations is essential for fresh growth to occur. Some of us just need a little trim off the top in order to glimpse the wide-open night sky, while others of us require more drastic measures. Some of us require, if not a literal decapitation, then a symbolic one—or as the English philosopher and mystic Douglas Harding framed it, an acknowledgment of our innate headlessness. In his book *On Having No Head*, he described the experience of walking through the Himalayas in the 1930s and realizing that from an experiential point of view, he had no head. All he was in bodily possession of were some feet and legs, torso, arms, hands, and two pink clouds that he could perceive from the corner of either eye, which he called his nose. Empirically, there was no head, just a beacon of awareness that was not separate from all that it perceived from that lookout. This sentiment echoes the Dzogchen, or "Mind Only" teachings of Tibetan Buddhism, which state that everything we encounter is a manifestation of our own minds. As no less a pair than Jon Kabat-Zinn and Buckaroo Banzai both observed, "No matter where you go, there you are." Harding was encouraged to discover complementary images in the Zen tradition, citing Tai-hui: "The precious vajra sword is right here and its purpose is to cut off the head."[178] Harding writes, "Meeting you, there is for me only one face—yours—and I can never get face-to-face with you. In fact, we trade faces, and this is a most precious and intimate exchange of appearances."[179] So this is a decapitation in a way. The sword of Karma cleaves us from separateness, destroying the misperception of subject and object.

However, when we are attacked or maligned, when our reputations are besmirched, the illusion of subject and object becomes very intense. It feels as though negativity is being poured into us from an external source. It feels like someone is *doing* something to us. Consequently, we want to blame them for how they've made us feel, and make sure they're punished so that they aren't allowed to do the same thing to anyone else. But, as Wallace Shawn writes, "Revenge and punishment both imply, 'Even if I'd been you, and I'd had your life, I would never have done what you did.' And that in turn implies, 'I wouldn't have done it because I'm better than you.' But the person who says, 'I'm better than you' is taking a very dangerous step in a very dangerous direction. And the person who says, 'Even if I'd had your life, I would never have done what you did' is very probably wrong."[180] This is a true insight into the ultimate truth of karma.

When we stop blaming people, the bizarre side effect is that forgiveness becomes obsolete, proving Fran Lebowitz right (again). I remember passing an Episcopal Church in New York City whose bulletin board read "ENJOY YOUR FORGIVENESS," which just seemed to be missing the word BITCH at the end. And yet quite often that is precisely the attitude with which we approach forgiveness. We easily slip into smug self-aggrandizement for being the special wonderful person who is able to bestow forgiveness upon some less-evolved other. Destroying frees us from this cul-de-sac, revealing that fundamentally we are in absolutely no position to forgive anybody, because we are not discrete entities somehow floating outside of the situation. We are not superior. We are not separate.

Fundamentally, the karma of destroying is the realization that the negativity we experience is *ours*. It is arising in *our* mindstreams. Our feelings of anger, self-righteousness, despair or whatever are not parasitic bulbs planted in our heads by maleficent gardeners but, rather, deep-seated tendencies that already lie dormant within us like an ancient pestilence in the permafrost, which, once thawed by the heat of another's emotions, wreaks havoc across the land. Destroying sees to it that while negativity may be fierce, even chronic, it has no belfry to roost in.

Trauma is real and gentleness is of the essence. There are experiences we never get over, which follow their own migratory patterns. The sword of Karma eliminates, through a swift, compassionate blow, traumatized self-hood, while showing the trauma the respect it deserves.

The destroying that takes place in Artemisia's painting is nothing so penny-ante as personal revenge. It is a mythic depiction of wrathful compassion where both the rapist and the raped are liberated from their roles in a deft, perpetual chop that never coagulates. As Julia Kristeva writes in *The Severed Head*, "There is something beyond death, the artistic experience says, there is resurrection: it is nothing other than the life of the line, the elegance of the gesture, the grace or brutality of colors when they dare to show the human threshold. Decapitation is a privileged space. *Exultate, jubilate!*"[181]

Clarke

(1970–present)

Étaín's dream (i)
Nuala Clarke

2017 | PRIVATE COLLECTION, COURTESY OF THE ARTIST

I once heard that any two people can fall in love with each other if they just stare into each other's eyes long enough. While I cannot vouch for people, I can certainly verify this is true with pieces of art. In one of Sokuzan's "Opening the Eye-Mind" workshops (mentioned in the introduction), he had us gaze at an incandescent abstract canvas for what felt like an eternity. We looked well past the point of entertainment into the terrain of irritation, fury, boredom, and, finally, when the self-centeredness had stormed off to pout in its room, we actually saw what the artist had created. This experience is a lot like falling in love. The artist, in this case, was Nuala Clarke, with whom I spoke in her studio in County Mayo, Ireland.

KT: How do you pronounce the name of this painting?

NC: So as far as I know it's *Ā-deen's dream*.

KT: I did a little research on the myth, but because it's so ancient and mostly handed down orally, there are like three different versions and each is slightly different. Do you have a CliffsNotes version of the myth?

NC: No, I don't. I've been doing a series of goddess paintings. Some of them are Irish feminine emanations and they do seem to be related to the land, or the sea, or the sky. So my choice of her name and the word *dream* came after the painting. And it was a very loose pairing. Sort of like the painting and the story were floating beside each other. The story and my painting don't correlate, but I do think that they are describing the same thing. In the text that I've read, there's a lot of color language used to describe Étaín. There's a transformation. (One of the important things to know about this part of Ireland is that the sky keeps changing.) And I found her timeless transfigurations or transmutations to be similar to that kind of day that I was describing in that work.

KT: And there's some sort of convoluted jealousy plot in the myth, yes? Someone tries to keep Étaín away from her beloved and turns her into a pool of water, then turns her into a red fly and blows her all over the world on a gust of wind. And then Étaín, as the red fly, falls into a golden beer that gets drunk by some lady, who gives birth to the new incarnation of the fly girl. It's quite involved.

NC: "Black as the beetle's back her brows, hyacinth-blue her eyes. Pure white and tapering her fingers..." It's all this sleek language. I think it probably describes prized attributes of Irish women at the time. And, essentially, that's the plot to every Irish myth. There are multiple generations of the same people there, they've died, they're born again, they marry this one, someone comes along and smites them with a sword, and does something involving nature to them. And there's swallowing whole, and their children get turned into swans. There are very long periods of time between one wife doing something to a husband and then the offspring doing something to her...

KT: So it's almost like the land itself is keeping score and requiring some kind of atonement.

NC: Yes, like an absorption. The people must be absorbed by the land and be born again of it. And there are underworlds and overworlds and the moments between those two worlds, overlapping each other. And you get a real sense of that when you're here. Like, where I live, you can feel that, you can actually feel that. You can feel days being the same now as they were five thousand years ago, and the potential of being absorbed by the land.

KT: You were born in Ireland, but you spent many years living in the United States, and now you've moved back again. Can you talk a little bit about the move away and returning?

NC: I spent twenty years on the pavement in New York. You know, there's very much a street thing that happens there. You can spend all your time on the pavement. The last four years, the ones right before I left, my studio was three stories down in a basement, which was an absolutely amazing space, because it didn't have basement-height ceilings. For the first time, I felt I was *in* New York. I was inside the place, and I was privy to the things that were under it. Those last years I was in the city after I decided to come back to Ireland were really the most fruitful years I had there. But you know, I was young, I had just gone to art college and I'd watched all the movies—you know, Scorsese, *Desperately Seeking Susan*—I really wanted to see New York. I was a very naïve person and if I stayed in Ireland, I would have stayed that way. I wanted to know more and so I decided to move to New York.

KT: You say it was the end of that period that was the most fruitful, so what made you realize that it was time to go home?

NC: I found myself dealing with input all the time. And for years that was great, but in 2007 I came to Ireland to do a month-long residency here, in the town where I now live. I never thought of staying in New York, and I'd never thought of leaving and I'd never thought of coming back to Ireland. But as soon as I came here, I realized, "Oh, I could do what I want here." And what I wanted to do was slow down. I wanted to start examining things more deeply. Just to be able to look at things longer without having all the input coming in all the time. And so I went back to New York and I said, "I'm leaving, I'm going back to Ireland," and then for four years, people said, "I thought you said you were leaving!" It took four years to leave, but it was great that it took that long.

KT: I know what you mean about living in New York. It mostly feels like being on defense; deflecting rather than finding expression out of inspiration. What was it about reconnecting with Ireland that helped you to create *Étaín's dream*?

NC: This painting and just a few others (there's not many of them yet) are summer paintings. So they're kind of like a holiday for me. They're important, but they're not difficult paintings. They're easily absorbed. They're very closely related to a series of paintings called *Sublime Reverie*, and in those paintings I'm dealing with the idea of utopia. Utopia is *ou-topos*, which is "no-place." So it's this perfect place, which doesn't exist. And for me the perfect place is the interior—the space of a canvas or a board. It's the space of the painted work. And within that space, I can create my perfect form. I can create my utopia, which is a memory place. It's less imagined and more memory.

When I'm out and about, I'm gathering all the information through all my senses, and then I come back to the studio to work. I don't work on the landscape. So whatever is landscape about the painting is like the landscape of my body; memory of the light and the color and the form. I don't have to be tied to how something looks at all, because I consider these to be abstract, even though they have clouds and fields and things in them. Because abstraction is that which you know but can't see. There's no visible form for abstract nouns. So I'm attempting to make visible these ideas.

So this summer painting: one of the most glorious things to happen around here is when there's a certain kind of cloud, and there's green hills so you can see distance, and there's sun shining through these clouds. When these clouds move, there's a certain amount of wind, so what you see is this dark pattern moving across the landscape. The presence of the cloud gets reflected on the ground; as above, so below. There's an alchemical thing happening. And this form moves and changes shape. That's the main thing that's happening in that painting: this changing shape of cloud, darkness on the land.

KT: What also strikes me about these paintings is the use of green. Which obviously makes sense for the time of year you're describing, but it seems quite unusual for your work. What is it like for you to work with green?

NC: I've had a love-hate relationship with green. There was a time when I was using it a lot. I had lots of ways of mixing it and lots of ways of using it. And then a moment came where it was completely inappropriate. It wasn't right, it wasn't the right color. I couldn't use it for years. I couldn't stand it. After using it for years, then I couldn't use it for years. There's a particularly horrid color called celadon. It's probably one of the easiest colors to mix because it's sort of like the equivalent of mud in my view. But you can't deal with the summer here without using green. And I do love it in that context, but I just find it very difficult to use otherwise.

KT: And summer is Karma's time of year. I remember hearing somewhere, and now I don't know if this is actually true, but in Tibetan color theory, green represents all colors. So it makes sense that it would be overwhelming because it's so potent. Plus, it's like the cliché Irish color.

NC: Yeah, well, I mean look out the window in the summertime and everything's green.

KT: You mentioned alchemy earlier. Do you relate to your painting as alchemical?

NC: Yes, but I wouldn't necessarily put [*Étaín's dream*] into that category. But the person who owns this painting now had a really, really strong reaction to it. It was something that was vitally important to her, you know, from the moment she saw it. It was healing for her. For me, my work is...well, it's hard to put into words...

KT: That's why you paint.

NC: That's why I paint. And it's only something that I've started to talk about recently, but it has always been a part of the work. There are several bodies of work that I've done—particularly transformational bodies of work—where I had personal pain or grief and through the making of the work—and very specifically making it to deal with that pain and grief—that got transformed. I was transformed. It is a process that's been very real for me. Now what I'm doing is studying the potential for paintings to have that kind of purpose in the world. I'm investigating the mechanics, biology, chemistry, physics of that. Just because I know instinctively that they *are* that, but I want to be able to speak about it specifically. There's something about the way I work where I'm not making an image, I'm not making something to *look* like something. I'm making something that *is* something. And the object itself has properties that are necessary or important. It's not about reproducing the way something looks, but instead investing something into the work so that it becomes an important object in the world.

KT: You know, personally, creatively, I'm almost superstitious about *not* knowing the mechanics of what I'm doing. I feel like if the expression comes intuitively then I can trust it, but if I actually know what the levers or pulleys or ingredients are then I might fuck it up in some way. It sounds to me as if you're attempting to peek behind the curtain. I'm curious as to why that is. This piece, *Étaín's dream*, you said was kind of like taking a holiday, but then this woman sees it and it changed her life and she had to buy it. Based on your experience making the work, there would be no way of predicting the intensity of this woman's response, but now it seems you're actively exploring what those reasons might be. Do you have trepidation about finding an answer?

NC: Even though it's like a walk in the park—I'm not saying it was easy for me to make that work, but it wasn't a deep dive—I still think it's really necessary. I had to make that painting in order to then make the next one. With these summer paintings or with these *Sublime Reverie* paintings, I needed to make them so that I can do the next thing. They're like an outer layer of the landscape, or like an outer layer of the same being. It doesn't make it any less important than the inner layers that might be in pain or in a knot or need to be untied. This is an outer layer, but it still had to be done. It's like this one is almost more based on the sense of vision and what can be seen, and then other paintings are more based on what is internal; you know, proprioception, rather than in our most used and familiar sense, which is sight.

KT: The wind is really palpable for me in this piece. Looking at it, I almost feel my hair is getting ruffled and all of the carefully organized pages of my dissertation are being swept out to sea. It's a feeling of panic followed by a sense of release and joy. Karma family energy is about the joy of accomplishment as well as the energy of jealousy and competition. Could you say more about the effect location has had on your painting?

NC: The name *Étaín* can sometimes be translated as, or associated with, jealousy, so I find that quite interesting. Everything seems to fit. When I'm looking at that sky and when I'm making a piece of work like this, it's all about giddy joy, being in this extraordinary, majestic place. Completing the *Sublime Reverie* paintings, those are just a pure celebration of being alive. It's a very simple, straightforward kind of joy in the looking, in the doing, and in the looking at the work afterwards. The woman who responded, just her reaction...all of it is joyful.

KT: Hearing you talk about being back on your native soil, it sounds almost as if the weather and the landscape have a way of collapsing time and space. History seems very present.

NC: My father was born ten miles away from where I live now, but he moved to Dublin, where I was born. It was my uncle who got the farm and I remember being slightly jealous of my cousins. The city where I grew up, that was supposedly a forward motion, you know? I thought, well, I'm not supposed to want to be in the countryside. So I moved to New York City, the city of cities. And I had a great time, until, you know, I kept having this recurring idea. I'd be on a random street somewhere and I would want to stop and say, "Why am I here? Why am I here?" And it wasn't like a head thing, it was like a body—it was a *land* thing. I had been looking for a place to feel at home.

So yes, when I came back here to the Art Foundation it was as an Irish artist living in America...so sort of as an American. And then I was greeted by the man who ran the shop and the pub, who knew of me, and I was greeted as somebody who was from here. It was the most fascinating feeling. Because he had known my grandparents, I belonged here. I wasn't separate from here, I wasn't a stranger. And then I met a man who's lived here his whole life and we're about the same age and I keep wondering about all the places where we would have been in the same place at the same time. Like the one disco I went to with my cousin when we were teenagers; I keep imagining that I saw that man—Padraic, who is now my partner—leaning against the bar, that we were actually there on the same night. Padraic's father bought seed potatoes from my grandfather. My partner's father and my grandfather knew each other. And so, with my father's move to Dublin, it's like I got removed. I got blown away by the wind. And then I found my way back to the proper puddle, you know? The draw was irresistible. As much as my father tried to push us forward to something bigger and better, somehow I found my way back here. I find that really intriguing. I do feel like I belong here, that I can do my work here. Nothing to hold me back.

KT: What I've been coming to understand about the Buddha energies is that, while there's a lot of talk about transmuting or transforming negativity into positivity, on an experiential level, on a nerve-ending level, anger doesn't feel different from mirror-like wisdom. And somehow, Karma energy, which is said to show up as competitiveness and jealousy, doesn't feel different from all-accomplishing wisdom. When we aren't filling space with a lot of handwringing and noodling, the body still feels that jumpiness we call competitiveness, but it doesn't make a move until the time is right, and then it's one stroke. One gesture and it's done. The notion that the feeling of all-accomplishing wisdom energy feels the same as being jealous is fascinating to me. I mean, not to put words in your mouth, but it almost seems like when you were in New York, or your experience of being a child being moved away from this right spot—that yearning for the right spot is a kind of jealousy. Because, like, when we experience a craving, it's sometimes because the body is missing a nutrient—you wouldn't say that was bad. The body is simply telling you what it needs. So I wonder if we could even say that the body's yearning for the nutrients of the right spot feels like jealousy?

NC: I think you hit the nail on the head. Like last night, I was surprised that it was 11:00 p.m. because, of course, we have these really long daylight hours now. And I went out into the garden to take a proper look at the sliver of the moon and I felt this jealousy. And it feels like an activity and I do get overtaken by it. Sometimes when you feel jealous you feel a certain amount of loss. There's a loss feeling associated with it. That you've lost something to somebody else or to something else, and time can feel like that here.

KT: It's almost like what we're becoming aware of when we behold or remember something that's almost within our grasp, the jealousy we feel is the awareness that we've actually separated ourselves from it. And the all-accomplishing wisdom is: there is nothing to do. There is nothing to grasp because we're not actually separate from what we're beholding. So the feeling of loss or being left out is kind of an awareness of what we've done to ourselves through the convoluted process of ego-building in a way.

NC: I would agree with that completely. All this activity is necessary, and yet there is nothing to do.

Mitchell

(1925–1992)

Chord II
Joan Mitchell

1986 | TATE

Joan Mitchell was a night owl. Karma's time is midnight: the hour of completion; on the cusp of renewal; a constant becoming. Mitchell got to work as the sun set and slipped off to sleep as it rose. She described carrying her landscapes around with her, personal imprints of outer and inner terrains, which inspired her painting. Perhaps she felt more at ease opening her suitcases in the dark.

Mitchell was born in Chicago, the Windy City, a Karma place if ever there was one. When asked by friends what first made her aware of the existence of art, she said it was the view from her parents' apartment of windswept Lake Michigan. "That was the first time she ever thought about art," said painter Zuka Mitelberg, "the clouds and the sky and the wind. She wanted to paint it."[182]

Mitchell was virtually Chicago royalty. Her mother, Marion Strobel, had been an editor at *Poetry* magazine, and her father, James (everyone called him Jimmie), was a successful physician who specialized in dermatology and the treatment of syphilis (he was reportedly brought with a sack over his head to treat Al Capone's infection[183]). Jimmie was also a frustrated artist. He never forgave his daughter for being born a girl, an offense she tried to make up for by being the best at everything. Jimmie measured his love for his daughter in her academic successes and the trophies she won for high diving and ice skating (in high school she was a nationally ranked champion). Her childhood nickname was Bullet Head.

Before she reached teenagehood, Mitchell felt pressured to choose, if not a career, then a prime directive in life. While she felt drawn to both poetry and painting, her father ridiculed "dabblers" and admonished her as a "Jack of all trades, master of none." So Mitchell settled on painting, inadvertently horning in on Jimmie's jurisdiction. He constantly hammered into her that she would never be better than him because she couldn't draw and she was

a girl...a girl who walked like a boy. But just as Jimmie ridiculed and dimin-
ished his daughter, he was also obsessively invested in her accomplishments,
always pushing her to achieve. Mitchell credited her father's pathological
competitiveness as inspiration to move her work more and more toward total
abstraction, which was completely beyond any stylistic reference point he
had. "Then he couldn't even criticize what it was, you know?" Mitchell said.
"And then I felt protected. That I remember so clearly."[184]

Mitchell's mother was deaf. "I always tried to be in her head. What it
would be like not to hear anything. She had a lot of feeling."[185] Communicating
sound to a deaf person might seem an insurmountable challenge—but not for
Mitchell, who had synesthesia. Synesthesia is a permanent neurological condition whereby, when one sense field is stimulated, another also responds,
causing people to smell colors or taste shapes. This is quite the Karma condition, every sense field wearing multiple hats and putting in overtime. For us
Westerners who are used to conceptualizing the senses as discrete workers
on the assembly line of our experience, this probably seems odd, but as color
historian Michel Pastoureau writes, "In most sub-Saharan African societies...
it is of fundamental importance to know whether a color is dry or damp, soft
or hard, smooth or rough, mute or sonorous, joyful or sad."[186] Mitchell, who
was never aware of this diagnosis, exhibited four types of synesthesia. Two
were common: she experienced letters as colors ("S is red, K is blue grey, and
Y is yellow ochre...Sky is mixed up of those colors"[187]), and sounds appeared
before her as abstract color formations. Mitchell also exhibited two rare forms
of synesthesia: she experienced emotions as well as people's personalities as
color. "For her, hope was literally yellow. It wasn't that hope made her think of
yellow, but yellow was what hope was. Loneliness was dark green and clingy.
And depression was silvery white. 'Absolute horror,' she said. 'Just horror.'"[188]
She spent many years in psychoanalysis trying to correct this condition, to
no avail. Eventually, she learned to incorporate these experiences into her
painting to stunning effect. Hues informed by the residual emotion related to
a place whose remembered weather patterns evoked associations with personal pleasures and difficulties, each with their own innate synesthetic color
value coming to bear in the palette of the picture.

The intense Karma impulsion to constantly be honing, working, and winning led Mitchell to the mecca of such pursuits, New York City. There she found herself in the center of the beating heart of Abstract Expressionism, where art icons like Jackson Pollock, Philip Guston, and Mark Rothko were finding their way. This painting-as-full-contact-sport must have appealed to the athlete in Mitchell. She found mentors in other "action painters" like Willem de Kooning and Franz Kline, and her work was exhibited alongside theirs in the landmark Abstract Expressionist show *Ninth Street: Exhibition of Painting and Sculpture*, in 1951.

Mitchell also spent a lot of time socially with female artists like Grace Hartigan and Helen Frankenthaler, although an air of competition always cast a pall over their friendships. For them to form an AbEx Sisterhood would have been a death knell, relegating them to also-ran status. To compete with the guys you had to hang with the guys, getting into big dust-ups over stiff drinks, having hot affairs, and painting huge paintings. According to Mitchell's biographer, Patricia Albers, "Hartigan said that Mitchell had talent and virtuosity, but lacked 'the real thing.' Mitchell dismissed Frankenthaler, whose work involved pouring thinned pigment on raw canvas, as 'that tampon painter.'"[189] And later, when Mitchell met Niki de Saint Phalle in France, she scoffed, "So you're one of those writer's wives that paint."[190]

As is often the case with marginalized groups, the systems that benefit from their marginalization employ diversionary tactics such as putting the onus on the disenfranchised to disprove their unworthiness by way of gladiator-style competition. In the early 1950s, most galleries had a two-female quota, claiming that men ought to take priority as they had families to support. One gallerist said to Mitchell, "Joan, if only you were French, and male, and dead."[191] Inward-facing competitiveness consumes enormous reserves of creative energy, which might be better invested in, say, painting or singing, or perhaps in innovatively exposing the false premise on which the power-brokers base their seeming authority.

Backbiting notwithstanding, Mitchell could also be incredibly generous with developing artists, particularly young women. She would invite them to come and stay on her sprawling property, La Tour, in Vétheuil, France. She would pay for the plane ticket, buy their art supplies, provide studio space, and then often purchase what they produced at hugely inflated prices, hanging the work on her walls next to a de Kooning or a Kline.[192]

Graham Greene once observed that "all good novelists have bad memories. What you remember comes out as journalism; what you forget goes into the compost of the imagination."[193] This extends, if not to all painters, certainly to Joan Mitchell, whose work depicts not figurative people, places, or events but the imprints they made on her. She describes her process of expressing these emotional impressions as "transposing"—a term more evocative of music or poetry than painting. And like poets whose work gets deconstructed into oblivion by enthusiastic academics hoping to decipher "what the artist really meant to say," Mitchell frequently found herself swatting away attempts to intellectualize her paintings. In a hilarious exchange caught in the documentary film *Joan Mitchell: Portrait of an Abstract Painter*, Yves Michaud of Paris' École des Beaux Arts attempts to back her into a conceptual corner by getting her to reveal what she is trying to hide by using a particular white. She tartly replies, "You asked me that: why did I put white all around? You also asked me why I put red lines in some. You also asked me why I paint. I don't know, baby. And then we didn't speak to each other for a long time...Well [the white] doesn't have to do with Moby-Dick, okay?" A jump cut in the film shows Mitchell speaking to the filmmakers: "He knows I don't have any theory about why I paint or anything. You know? Fuck it."

This demand for intellectual meaning might, in the short term, provide us with a feeling of finally getting a handle on things, but in the long term, it seems that what we exchange for the firm ground of art theory is the art itself. We abandon the artwork for what we think about it. Through the rationalization of the transcendent, archetypes become clichés, to paraphrase Marshall McLuhan. Or, put another way, intellectualization can be a form of ignorance. Without clear intentions, interpretation is used as an intellectual gambit to protect us from the agonizing intimacy of being with the art itself. And if we feel we need a buffer just to look at some art, imagine how it must feel making it.

Mitchell was known for imbibing voluminous amounts of alcohol and smoking like a refinery. Maybe that's what she needed to do in order to dull the edge of the creative charge she received. You'll certainly get no judgment from me on that front. Spending time with her was, by all accounts, a fucking nightmare, and also delightfully enriching. This paradox leaves overwrought Karma energy furiously biting its nails because it can't believe (or can't stand) that there is nothing to fundamentally correct. There is no other person to be. We are faced with the frustrating reality that just as we don't get Brilliant Joan without Nightmare Joan, we also don't get Brilliant Us without Nightmare Us. Those apparent pairs of opposites are not separate from each other. We have the capacity to be with the paradox without coming to conclusions. As Mitchell said of Cézanne's work, "There's nothing more to say. You can't read it, you can't wonder what it's about. It is."[194]

Mitchell's ability to walk the high wire between expressing her vibrant emotional landscapes without conceptually clamping down on them is instructive to meditators. As we encounter our own emotional landscapes in our practice, we are very quick to jump in and to call it something, to contextualize it, to bundle it off back under the stairs. We try to spin our negativity like shoddy PR agents hoping to manage the fallout from a client's errant tweet. The irony is, the more we try to flap-ball-change our way out of our authentic experience, the more we entrench ourselves in predictive mental algorithms: *If you liked Schitt's Creek, try Cheers; if you liked Bitter Resentment and Recrimination, try Despondency and Dread. Or maybe this, or maybe this.* Instead, we could receive what we have coming to us the first time around, straight, no chaser.

Pema Chödrön puts this more simply: "feel the feeling but drop the story." After all, we only ever notice a feeling after it has already arisen, so to add an opinion as to whether or not we should be feeling the feeling we're feeling is just a lot of busywork. Rather than boarding the carousel of ascribing blame or a first cause to the feeling in an attempt to throw a Persian rug over it and hoping the festive pattern obscures the blood seeping through, we could instead approach the feeling, heads bowed with a little humility. We could approach this—we call it "inner" but where is it really?—landscape of feeling as though we were visitors to a small Balkan country whose indigenous customs were unfamiliar. If, while we were visiting, we happened on a festival where people in brightly colored robes and unsettling masks were carrying a strange icon on a palanquin, it is unlikely we would tell them they were doing it wrong, that this wasn't really appropriate, or the right weather, or what have you. No, we would simply observe the procession because we are in no position to comment on the causes and conditions that even led to such an event in the first place—and, quite frankly, it's none of our business. So we just observe. This, to the best of our abilities, is the same attitude we take with our own emotional landscapes during meditation.

Sometimes we show up to our meditation cushions, mind ablaze with memories of embarrassing remarks we've made. We attempt to flush the offending emotion out with a rush of narrative: *She did this, and they said that, and from now on I'm never going to blah, blah, blah.* When I find myself in such a mental maelstrom, I imagine that the concomitant narrative is unspooling like a ribbon and that I have a pair of scissors to snip it. So, in effect, I am cutting the narrative loose from the underlying feeling, which has no name and is neither good nor bad, and whose source cannot be found. I then try to locate where, in (or around) my body, the feeling shows up, like a scientist looking through a microscope in search of data. I imagine shining the spotlight of my attention on whatever part of the body the emotion or thought arises, exploring the sensual qualities of this particular feeling.

Mitchell describes the inseparability of subject and object in her painting, saying, "I become the sunflower, the lake, the tree. I no longer exist."[195] Similarly, Sokuzan suggests "become the very negativity you're trying to get rid of." In so doing, the mind that attempts to separate that which is not separate in order to get control no longer receives sustenance. Subject and object coalesce, liberating the feeling from the burden of a self. This frees us up to take a synesthetic approach to the experience of intense feeling: What does the emotion sound like? Does it move in a particular way? What is its texture (coarse, prickly, fluffy)? What is its fragrance, flavor? Staying with the moment-to-moment sensual experience of the feeling, we witness first-hand precisely what we wouldn't see if we had jumped ship for our punditry. No emotion is an impassive, implacable fact; feelings are dynamic, in flux, and at play. We may also find that without the breathless gossip, feelings are boring. The very thing that moments ago had us planning a honeymoon in Vegas or where to bury the body becomes just another thing for attention to drift away from.

A slight caveat: when engaging with this kind of exploration, it is important to remember that this is not some macho endurance test. We've all had quite enough of that. This isn't about trying to grind our faces into the dirt to prove how much unpleasantness we can take. To paraphrase Kurt Vonnegut, trauma is a tear in the time-space continuum, so from the nervous system's point of view, the difficult emotion isn't something we would be able to get some perspective on, it is happening now. Texture is such an important barometer in our practice. The experience of texture implies an awareness of some space. Even a very fine-grit sandpaper has some texture. In some sitting sessions, however, there might seem to be no texture at all, the experience of emotion as suffocatingly immediate as a sheet of Saran Wrap over the face. In such cases, the kind thing to do would be to drop the practice. This is the wisdom of the Karma of destroying again: we always have the autonomy from here into perpetuity to drop the practice if it becomes too intense or disorienting. Being aware of dropping the technique, getting up, opening the fridge, and putting whipped cream on the last slice of pie is still awareness. If we can then make it back to the cushion to ring the bell marking the end of our session at the agreed-upon time, that is a perfect practice.

The painting included here, *Chord II*, is part of a suite of seven paintings Mitchell did during what she called her "sick years,"[196] in the last decade of her life. She had gone through a very challenging period. In 1978, her partner of twenty-four years, the painter Jean-Paul Riopelle, took off with one of her protégées, or, as Mitchell put it, "he ran off with the dog walker."[197] In 1984, she was diagnosed with oral cancer and removal of the jaw was recommended. Mercifully, she got a second opinion and received radiation treatment, although it left her with a dead jawbone. The following year she underwent two hip replacement surgeries. As she regained her strength, she was able to get back to work in her studio and put herself back together piece by piece, like notes in a chord.

Out of this period of intense difficulty, Joan Mitchell managed to affirm once and for all the true message of her work: "I just think love has to do with painting," she said. "That's easy, no?"[198]

Portrait of Antonietta Gonzalez

Lavinia Fontana

1595 | CHÂTEAU DE BLOIS

Conclusion

ART IS FOR EVERYBODY.

DHARMA IS FOR EVERYBODY.

And yet would-be gatekeepers loiter at the portals of wisdom. Chögyam Trungpa referred to these gatekeepers as the Three Lords of Materialism.

The First Lord of Materialism is the Lord of Form, who hypnotizes us into believing that wealth and beautiful objects will act as protective talismans against death. We know, of course, that pharaohs, monarchs, dictators, robber barons, and Silicon Valley pests have all commissioned or invested in priceless works of art, either for their totemic significance (I own a Picasso!) or as a sound investment. To harken back to the NFT phenomena again, for the Lord of Form the predominant function of art is its ability to be acquired and the veracity of its provenance. Exclusivity trumps aesthetics. For some of us, these exhibitionistic expenditures become conflated with the art itself and we assume that art appreciation is a rich man's game, or else a pathetic attempt to get above our station. On a smaller scale, those of us who love art but can't afford the Picasso scurry to the gift shop immediately after visiting the exhibit to buy the Picasso tote bag or post card. On some level we feel unworthy of the creativity Picasso expressed, or we need to have whatever experience we had just looking authenticated, so we buy the cheap cardboard version. (I am not knocking this, by the way, as I have been known to visit a museum *solely* for the gift shop.)

The Second Lord of Materialism is the Lord of Speech, who fetishizes concepts and intellectual gambits. There's obviously nothing wrong with higher education. It's wonderful that some people are inspired to focus on art history, even boring down into the nuances of a particular period or artist's life. That work is unbelievably valuable. However, academia tends to be self-referential, specializing in germinating insular language to articulate its new insights. If you happen not to be of that world, however, these brittle linguistics can leave you feeling left on the outside. Or, worse, we might come to equate the art being discussed with the rarified, concentrically circular language used to describe it. That agreed-upon language habit creates a dynamic in which only a certain class of people are allowed to think, talk, or write about art. This attitude is not just based on an awww-shucks lack of self-confidence in the un-formally educated but actually seems to be a strategic approach to maintaining an air of exclusivity and control in the art world.

In the last seventy-five years or so we have also seen an increased pressure campaign on artists to control the narrative of their work. As if making art weren't hard enough, artists are now also expected to act as PR agents, contextualizing their work in the dialectic of refigurative post-queer abstraction or whatever. I mean, critical art-speak isn't a time-honored comic cliché of pretension for no reason. Many artists consider unofficial interpretations of their work as seditious to their brand, and go to great lengths to monitor who is allowed to discuss their work and how. But aside from it being none of the artist's business how another person responds to their work, this kind of rank-closing is a technique out of capitalism's playbook, not creativity's. This is ego's game.

The Third Lord of Materialism is the Lord of Mind, whose wheelhouse is performative spirituality. Because the true spiritual (and dare I say creative) path means the death of ego, the Lord of Mind intervenes with a display of funhouse mirrors to create a diversion (see the final reel of Orson Welles' *The Lady from Shanghai*). Ego will gladly don caftans and chunky turquoise bracelets and burn incense so long as it doesn't have to sit still long enough to see the holographic nature of the self.

Similarly, some folks like to amass art supplies, dabble in drawing classes, and even date drummers so that they can be art-adjacent without ever actually entering creativity's White Hot Center. Or we get the pompous Picasso-like artist who has taken credit for the creative force itself.

Whichever Lord of Materialism we find ourselves expressing fealty to moment to moment is based on the degree to which we doubt ourselves. The Lords of Materialism contrive to intimidate us into believing that our own objective experience of looking is untrustworthy. When we can't trust ourselves, we abdicate our sovereign authority to others, who are more often than not trying to sell us something we can't afford in one way or another. We are waiting for someone else's permission to be alive.

The great Philip Guston, who is largely responsible for figurative painting making a comeback after Abstract Expressionism, had profound insight into the creative process. It could also be applied to the spiritual path as well: "Your friends and art writers and the museum people, they're all in the studio," he said. "You're just there painting. And one by one they leave until you're really alone. That's what painting is: you wait and you prepare yourself...and then ideally *you* leave. A third hand does [the painting]...You're not through until you feel as if you're a medium through which this rhythm is passed...Otherwise you can't bear it. It's unbearable."[199]

All the same, to try and vanquish the Lords of Materialism is giving them too much credit. They are completely welcome to hang around in their terrifying robes like defanged Lovecraftian beasties. Maybe they will form a band. We, on the other hand, are already empowered as mediums through which the Five Wisdom Energies—Buddha, Vajra, Ratna, Padma, and Karma—flow and manifest themselves.

And flow these energies do. But while we have visited each in a sequential manner through the sacred form of the mandala, we benefit from remembering that even this is a metaphor. The Five Wisdom Energies, like the qualities described in McLuhan's Tetrad (see page 31), are inherent and simultaneous. They do not unfold or progress in any sort of processional orderliness. If we expect the Buddha families (or any aspect of the Dharma) to behave themselves, we have another thing coming. Despite their depiction to the contrary, life's energies are not cleanly partitioned, nor are they completely deranged. Do not ask of them sense nor nonsense—they will not humor you. The energies of life hum with the orderly chaos of creativity.

Even if we never pick up a paintbrush or duct-tape a banana to a wall, to develop an intuitive intimacy with these energies is itself an ever-unfolding creative act. We need practice, we need encouragement, we need some structure, but we have all of the tools we need to lead a creative life: our sense media, our curiosity, and our inspiration.

Acknowledgments

So many people helped me make this book, and I would like to take this opportunity to thank them all.

Firstly, I would like to thank my family, who have always encouraged me creatively. Deep love and admiration to my parents, Kevin Townley, Sr., and Ashley Stevens. A special debt of gratitude goes to my brother, Sean Townley, an incredible artist whose brilliance, sensitivity, and insight always inspires me. Love, too, to my Aunt Sue!

I want to thank my beautiful partner, Raul Luna, who not only endured my grumbling bouts of writer's block but gave me genuine and supportive feedback. I admire his bravery, too, as he learned to navigate the treacherous towers of art books I amassed while writing this book. I am lucky to live with someone so patient and kind, and who has such impeccable taste.

This book would not have been even remotely possible if it weren't for the support and encouragement of my teacher, Sokuzan; his wife, Unyo; and the rest of the community at Sokukoji Buddhist Monastery. I also received profound insight into the Five Buddha Families from the work of Judy Lief, Lama Tsultrim Allione, Khenchen Thrangu, and Irini Rockwell.

Several people helped me in researching this book:

My dear friend Dave McKeel connected me with Allison Rabinowitz, an expert in Tibetan art at Sotheby's, who helped me to better understand the construction of and culture surrounding thangkas.

Erik Bergrin and his incredible network of costume designers gave me a crash course on pre-French Revolutionary ladies' undergarments, for which I will always be grateful.

Nancy Churnin shared precious details with me about Laura Wheeler Waring.

Katherine Govier provided invaluable insight into the life of Katsushika Ōi.

Nathan Lambstrom helped me unlock Margareta Haverman's wild floral arrangements. His wife, Caitlin, always inspires me creatively.

As one of those people who only speaks one language, I was lucky to have several friends translate material for me: Maho Kawachi helped me to understand the Floating World. Meiun Maby, Whitney Rader, and Nicole Franceschini teamed up to translate a French interview with Niki de Saint Phalle. Merci!

Thanks to Bryce Weinert, Tasia Duske, and the MNT crew for providing me with so many opportunities to steep myself in art.

This book would truly be nothing without the artists featured in its pages. But a few artists and galleries really went above and beyond to support this project, and I would like to thank them: Linda Brumbach and Alisa Regas at Pomegranate Arts, Nicolas Ochart and Salon 94, Rachel Garbade and Garth Greenan Gallery, Davida Nemeroff and Night Gallery, Kathryn Miriam McSweeney and Sundaram Tagore Gallery, Tayeba Begum Lipi, Dana Sherwood, Jessica Stoller, Erica Lansner, Henrietta Mantooth, Nuala Clarke, Michelle Ellsworth, Karen Finley, Timothy Greenfield Sanders, Tré Gallery, Julia Gandrud, Christine Wang, Marilyn Minter, Mira Dancy, and Laurie Anderson.

Several wonderful people read early drafts of these essays or were generous sounding boards. I would like to especially thank Raul Luna, Bobbi and Joann, Dr. David Walczyk, Ana Maria Jomolca, Elna Baker, Alex Basco Koch, Kylie Holloway, Christopher Kilmer, Kelly Hurt, Marisa Viola, Ana Maria Delgado, Ericka Phillips, Lisa Fehl, and Maeve Higgins.

Special thanks to Jane Ursula Harris for broadening my horizons and introducing me to so many fabulous artists over the years.

I would like to thank my publishers, Susan Piver and Crystal Gandrud, who believed in me enough to ask that I write this book. I am truly, truly grateful for the chance they gave me. Many thanks to Emily Bower, Carra Simpson, and Merrie-Ellen Wilcox as well, who helped whip the manuscript into shape. And to Jazmin Welch for her fabulous designs.

Last but certainly not least, a tidal wave of gratitude to the Open Heart Project community, who listened to early talks of mine on this subject matter and whose enthusiasm gave me the courage to write.

Endnotes

1 Isaac Kaplan, "How Long Do People Really Spend Looking at Art in Museums?" artsy.net, November 7, 2017.

2 Marshall McLuhan and Quentin Fiore, *The Medium Is the Massage* (New York: Penguin Books, 1967), 25.

3 Chuck Smith and Sono Kuwayama, *Interview with Agnes Martin*, 1997.

4 Peter Schjeldahl, "Agnes Martin, a Matter-of-Fact Mystic," *New Yorker*, October 10, 2016, https://www.newyorker.com/magazine/2016/10/17/agnes-martin-a-matter-of-fact-mystic.

5 P.D. James, *Talking About Detective Fiction* (New York: Vintage Books, 2009), 75.

6 Jennifer Higgie, "Olivia Laing on Agnes Martin," *Bow Down*, November 11, 2019, podcast, 22:09, https://www.frieze.com/article/bow-down-podcast-women-art-history.

7 "Beauty Is in Your Mind," *TateShots*, June 5, 2015, 7:37, https://www.youtube.com/watch?v=902YXjchQsk.

8 Henry Martin, *Agnes Martin: Pioneer, Painter, Icon* (Tucson: Schaffner Press, 2018), 212.

9 Higgie, "Olivia Laing on Agnes Martin."

10 Mark L. Ruffalo, "Setting the Record Straight," *Psychology Today*, June 22, 2019, https://www.psychologytoday.com/intl/blog/freud-fluoxetine/201906/setting-the-record-straight-homosexuality-and-dsm.

11 "Beauty Is in Your Mind," *TateShots*.

12 SFMOMA, *Jay DeFeo's* The Rose: *The enormous painting that was "almost alive,"* video, 3:54, https://www.sfmoma.org/watch/jay-defeos-the-rose-the-enormous-painting-that-was-almost-alive/.

13 Victoria Finlay, *Color* (New York: Random House, 2012), 109–112.

14 Kassia St. Clair, *The Secret Lives of Color* (New York: Penguin Books, 2016) 43–46.

15 SFMOMA, *Jay DeFeo's* The Rose.

16 SFMOMA, *Jay DeFeo's* The Rose.

17 SFMOMA, *Jay DeFeo's* The Rose.

18 Thomas Hoving, *Greatest Works of Art of Western Civilization* (New York: Artisan, 1997), 20–21.

19 Whitney Museum of American Art, *Jay DeFeo's* The Rose, July 30, 2013, video, 7:12, https://www.youtube.com/watch?v=BkHi-XqVS8U.

20 Constantin Jelenski, *Leonor Fini* (New York: Olympia Press, 1968), 20.

21 Messy Nessy, "The Forgotten Bohemian Queen of the Paris Art World," June 9, 2015, https://www.messynessychic.com/2015/06/09/the-forgotten-bohemian-queen-of-the-paris-art-world-leonor-fini/.

22 Art Students League of New York, *Leonor Fini: Theater of Desire* with Lissa Rivera, March 1, 2019, video, 54:07, https://www.youtube.com/watch?v=sCDFuRppSiY.

23 Art Students League, *Leonor Fini*.

24 Art Students League, *Leonor Fini*.

25 The Art Story, "Leonor Fini," https://www.theartstory.org/artist/fini-leonor/.

26 Jenna Adrian-Diaz, "Why Isn't Leonor Fini as Famous as the Other (Male) Surrealists?" *Vulture*, December 5, 2018, https://www.vulture.com/2018/12/leonor-fini-a-surrealist-whose-legacy-is-being-revisited.html.

27 Art Students League, *Leonor Fini*.

28 Art Students League, *Leonor Fini*.

29 Georges Bataille, *Erotism: Death and Sensuality* (San Francisco: City Lights Books, 1986), 24.

30 Bataille, *Erotism*, 17.

31 Dongshan Liangjie (807–869), translation as used by the San Francisco Zen Center.

32 Katy Hessel. "Episode 54, Howardena Pindell," *The Great Women Artists*, March 2, 2021, podcast, https://podcasts.apple.com/gb/podcast/howardena-pindell/id1480259187?i=1000511349317.

33 Hessel, "Howardena Pindell."

34 Jillian Steinhauer, "At 77, Howardena Pindell Exorcises a Chilling Memory from Childhood," *New York Times*, October 16, 2020, https://www.nytimes.com/2020/10/16/arts/design/howardena-pindell-shed-video.html.

35 The Shed, *In Conversation: Pindell's Legacy,* https://www.youtube.com/watch?v=6gESL-9QJ1M&t=2072s.

36 I believe it was Dzongsar Khyentse Rinpoche, but don't quote me on that.

37 Gary Lachman, *Madame Blavatsky* (New York: Penguin Group, 2012), 78.

38 Adam McLean, "The Birds in Alchemy," *Hermetic Journal* No. 5 (1979), http://www.levity.com/alchemy/alcbirds.html.

39 Dongshan Liangjie (807–869).

40 Nuala Clarke, Zoom interview with the author, June 15, 2021.

41 Vic Reeves, *Gaga for Dada: The Original Art Rebels,* BBC, 2016, video, 57:12, https://www.youtube.com/watch?v=ed1NfFMkYmE.

42 Marshall McLuhan, *Culture Is Our Business* (New York: Ballantine Books, 1970), 192.

43 Tristan Tzara, *Dada Manifesto,* March 23, 1918, https://genius.com/Tristan-tzara-dada-manifesto-annotated.

44 Charles Cramer and Kim Grant, "Dada Performance," SmartHistory, https://smarthistory.org/dada-performance/.

45 *The Heart Sutra,* trans. Red Pine (Berkeley: Counterpoint, 2004), 2–3.

46 Laurie Anderson, "*Heart of a Dog: Retelling,*" interview with Jake Perlin, Criterion Collection Supplementary Interview, 2016, https://www.criterionchannel.com/videos/retelling.

47 Marina Rumjanzewa, dir., *Sophie Taeuber-Arp: A Famous Stranger,* SRF, 2021, https://www.youtube.com/watch?v=rssy40GtZzM&t=1031s.

48 Pamela B. Greene, *Be Natural: The Untold Story of Alice Guy-Blaché* (Zeitgeist Films 2018).

49 Gertrude M. Price, "This Girl Was Teacher. Now a Photo Player," *Pittsburgh Press,* April 10, 1913, 12.

50 Alexandra Alexa, "Tayeba Begum Lipi Wields Razor Blades to Address Violence Against Women," Artsy.net, August 6, 2015, https://www.artsy.net/article/artsy-editorial-tayeba-begum-lipi-wields-razor-blades-to-address.

51 Marshall McLuhan and Eric McLuhan, *The Lost Tetrads of Marshall McLuhan* (New York: OR Books, 2017), 7.

52 Sundaram Tagore Gallery, "In Conversation with Tayeba Begum Lipi," April 11, 2016, video, 3:41, https://www.youtube.com/watch?v=QQPNXyKd4Ak.

53 Georges Bataille, *The Trial of Gilles de Rais* (Amok, 1990).

54 Michel Pastoureau, *Blue: The History of a Color* (Princeton University Press, 2001), 26.

55 Niki de Saint Phalle, from "Pour le Plaisir," February 3, 1965, https://www.ina.fr/ina-eclaire-actu/video/i10337771/niki-de-saint-phalle.

56 Niki de Saint Phalle, *Traces* (Paris: Acatos Editions, 2000), 16.

57 Ariel Levy, "*Beautiful Monsters: Art and Obsession in Tuscany,*" *New Yorker,* April 11, 2016, https://www.newyorker.com/magazine/2016/04/18/niki-de-saint-phalles-tarot-garden.

58 Levy, "Beautiful Monsters."

59 Sarah Wilson, "Tirs, *Tears, Ricochets,*" in *Niki de Saint Phalle 1930–2002,* ed. Philip Sutton (Bilbao: La Fábrica, 2015), 97.

60 Niki de Saint Phalle, dir., *Tir a Malibu,* 1962.

61 Niki de Saint Phalle, *Traces* (Paris: Acatos Editions, 2000), 98.

62 Niki de Saint Phalle, *Harry and Me: The Family Years* (Weber-Bern: Benteli Publishers 2006), 127.

63 Robert L. Pincus, "Celebrated Sculptor Dead at 71," *San Diego Tribune,* May 23, 2002. https://www.sandiegouniontribune.com/sdut-celebrated-sculptor-dead-71-2002may23-story.html.

64 Laurie Anderson, *All the Things I Lost in the Flood* (New York: Rizzoli Electra, 2017), 10.

65 Laurie Anderson, dir., *Heart of a Dog* (HBO Documentary Films, 2015).

66 Anderson, *Heart of a Dog.*

67 Laurie Anderson, "*Heart of a Dog: Retelling.*"

68 Anderson, "*Heart of a Dog*: Retelling."

69 RoseLee Goldberg, *Laurie Anderson* (New York: Abrams, 2000), 180.

70 Anderson, *All the Things I Lost*, 99.

71 Anderson, *All the Things I Lost*.

72 Anderson, *All the Things I Lost*, 103.

73 "Laurie Anderson and Mohammed el Gharani: *Habeas Corpus*," *The Laura Flanders Show*, November 2, 2015, TeleSUR English, https://www.youtube.com/watch?v=-iCxxpD7xtI.

74 Anderson, *All the Things I Lost*, 102.

75 Wallace Shawn and André Gregory, *My Dinner with André* (New York: Grove Press, 1981), 77–78.

76 "Rekhmire-TT100," *OsirisNet: Tombs of Ancient Egypt*, https://www.osirisnet.net/tombes/nobles/rekhmire100/e_rekhmire100_11.htm.

77 Wall text, *Wine Additives*, Metropolitan Museum of Art, New York.

78 Richard H. Wilkinson, *Symbol and Magic in Egyptian Art* (London: Thames & Hudson, 1994), 83.

79 Barbara Mertz, *Red Land, Black Land* (New York: William Morrow, 2008), 188–194.

80 Nigel Strudwick, "Nina M. Davies: A Biographical Sketch," *Journal of Egyptian Archaeology* 90 (December 2004), 193–210.

81 Toby Wilkinson, *A World Beneath the Sands* (New York: W.W. Norton, 2020), 3.

82 Kara Cooney, *The Woman Who Would Be King* (New York: Crown Publishing, 2014), 22.

83 *Sister Wendy's American Collection*, season 1, episode 2, "*The Cleveland Museum of Art*," PBS, 1999.

84 Jan van Gool, *The New Theater of Dutch Painters, Part II*, 32–33.

85 Emil Kren and Daniel Marx, "Margareta Haverman," Web Gallery of Art, https://www.wga.hu/bio_m/h/haverman/biograph.html.

86 Lorraine Boissoneault, "There Was Never a Real Tulip Fever," *Smithsonian Magazine*, September 18, 2017, https://www.smithsonianmag.com/history/there-never-was-real-tulip-fever-180964915/.

87 Wall text, *A Vase of Flowers*, Metropolitan Museum of Art, New York.

88 Wall text, *A Vase of Flowers*.

89 Mearto, "Decoding the Hidden Meanings in Still Life Paintings," August 11, 2016, https://blog.mearto.com/2016/08/11/decoding-the-hidden-meanings-in-still-life-painting/.

90 Artspace, "A Symbolism Guide to the Spooky World of Dutch Still-Lives," October 25, 2019, https://www.artspace.com/magazine/art_101/in_depth/a-symbolism-guide-to-the-spooky-world-of-dutch-still-lives-56298.

91 George W.S. Trow, *Within the Context of No Context* (New York: Atlantic Monthly Press, 1997), 47–49.

92 Brooklyn Museum, "Madonna and Marilyn Minter," video, 1:14:00, January 30, 2017, https://www.youtube.com/watch?v=vlp-pqp6ynQ&t=671s.

93 Brooklyn Museum, "Madonna and Marilyn Minter."

94 Marilyn Minter, *How Did We Meet? Marilyn Minter in Conversation with Mary Heilmann* (New York: Gregory R. Miller & Co., 2010), 26.

95 Minter, *How Did We Meet?* 26–27.

96 "Marilyn Minter: Fine Artist," School of Visual Arts, Masters in Fine Arts Lecture Series, November 20, 2019, video, 1:24:00, https://www.youtube.com/watch?v=h2YfSyMsA5M&t=3192s.

97 "Elisabeth Vigée Le Brun: Painting Royalty, Fleeing Revolution," National Gallery, March 8, 2019, video, 6:34, https://www.youtube.com/watch?v=sqhrpkhX2uA.

98 Olivier Bernier, *Louis the Beloved* (Garden City: Doubleday & Company, 1984), 226–228.

99 Bernier, *Louis the Beloved*, 245–249.

100 Élisabeth Louise Vigée Le Brun, *The Memoirs of Madame Vigée Le Brun*, chapter 4: "Exile," https://www.gutenberg.org/ebooks/31934.

101 Benedetta Craveri, *The Last Libertines* (New York: New York Review Books, 2020), 140.

102 Craveri, *The Last Libertines*, 137.

103 Wikipedia, "Madame du Barry," last updated October 6, 2021, https://en.wikipedia.org/wiki/Madame_du_Barry#Imprisonment,_trial_and_execution.

104 Joni Mitchell, "The Three Great Stimulants," *Dog Eat Dog*, Geffen Records, 1985, LP.

105 Vigée Le Brun, *Memoirs.*

106 Bob Spiers, dir., "Birthday," *Absolutely Fabulous*, season 1, episode 5, December 10, 1992, DVD.

107 Nancy Mitford, *Madame du Pompadour* (New York: New York Review Books, 1953), 164–5.

108 Jane Ursula Harris, "Jessica Stoller Makes Porcelain Visions of the Rebellious Female Body," *Cultured Magazine*, August 10, 2020, https://www.culturedmag.com/jessica-stoller-porcelain-sculptures/.

109 Andreana Donahue, "Jessica Stoller," *Maake Magazine*, https://www.maakemagazine.com/jessica -stoller.

110 Donahue, "Jessica Stoller."

111 *Beautiful Thing: A Passion for Porcelain*, BBC Four, 2014, 59:00, https://www.youtube.com/watch? v=uHwx_iVhd1k&t=2789s.

112 *Four Reminders*, trans. Chögyam Trungpa.

113 Dana Sherwood, "Dana Sherwood Is In Wild Air," *In Wild Air*, 5, ed. 57 (2018), https://us14.campaign -archive.com/?u=bcbad40200704828occd5961e&id=7c561dc593.

114 Dana Sherwood, "The Wild and the Tame," August 25, 2017, video, 7:01, https://www.youtube.com/ watch?v=N1WhRZyWbE8.

115 Byron Katie, *The Work of Byron Katie: An Introduction* (Ojai: The Work), 9.

116 Dana Sherwood, "Eating in the Dark (Raised By Raccoons)," February 2019, www.danasherwoodstu-dios.com/selected-writings.

117 Sherwood, "The Wild and the Tame."

118 Marshall McLuhan, *The Medium Is the Massage* (New York: Penguin Books, 1967), 75.

119 "The Medium Is the Message, Part I; Marshall McLuhan," *Monday Conference*, ABC TV June 27, 1977, video, 14:22, https://www.youtube.com/watch?v=ImaH51F4HBw.

120 John Tierney, "What Is Nostalgia Good For? Quite a Bit, Research Shows," *New York Times*, July 8, 2013, https://www.nytimes.com/2013/07/09/science/what-is-nostalgia-good-for-quite-a-bit-research-shows. html.

121 The artist's family name was Katsushika, but I will refer to her in the text as she was known: Ōi.

122 Julie Nelson Davis, "Hokusai and Ōi: Art Runs in the Family," *British Museum Blog*, June 18, 2017, https://blog.britishmuseum.org/hokusai-and-oi-keeping-it-in-the-family/.

123 Ven. Robina Courtin, "Robina's Blog: Samsara and Nirvana," June 7, 2019, https://robinacourtin.com/ robina-s-blog/samsara-and-nirvana/.

124 Richard Lane, *Images from the Floating World* (New York: Putnam, 1978), 21.

125 Stephen and Ethel Longstreet, *Geishas and the Floating World* (Tuttle: Hong Kong, 1970), 123.

126 Longstreet, *Geishas*, 82.

127 Nell Dunn, *Talking to Women* (London: Henry E. Walter, 1968), 8.

128 "Interview with Derek Boshier," PaulineBoty.org, November 2019, https://paulineboty.org/inter-view-with-derek-boshier/.

129 Dunn, *Talking to Women*, 7.

130 Paul Mason, *Pop Art* (Chicago: Reed, 2003), 12.

131 Sue Tate, *Pop Art and Design* (London: Bloomsbury Academic, 2018), 153.

132 PaulineBoty.org, interview with Derek Boshier.

133 Ken Russell, dir., *Monitor: Pop Goes the Easel* (BBC, 1962).

134 John Silver, dir., "The Never Ending Story," *Sister Wendy: The Story of Painting*, season 1, episode 10, September 8, 1996, PBS.

135 Sabine Durrant, "The Darling of Her Generation," *The Independent*, March 7, 1993, 13–15.

136 "Combating Racism: Betsy Graves Reyneau, Laura Wheeler Waring and Representation of Black Achievement," National Portrait Gallery, Edward P. Richardson Lecture Series: Women, Power, and Por-traiture, November 17, 2020, video, 1:11:18, https://www.youtube.com/watch?v=cn_YX0QNyT8&t=2200s.

137 Laura Wheeler Waring personal statement, Harmon Foundation Papers, Harmon Foundation, 1928, Library of Congress, Washington, DC.

138 T. Denean Sharpley-Whiting, *Bricktop's Paris* (Albany: State University of New York Press, 2015), 85.

139 Theresa Leninger-Miller, "'A Constant Stimulus and Inspiration': Laura Wheeler Waring in Paris in the 1910s and 1920s," *Source: Notes in the History of Art* 24, no. 4 (Summer 2005), 14.

140 Leninger-Miller, "A Constant Stimulus," 22.

141 Leninger-Miller, "A Constant Stimulus," 14.

142 W.E.B. Du Bois, *The Souls of Black Folk*, ed. David Blight (1903, rpt., Boston: Bedford Books, 1997), 111.

143 Herbert Aptheker, *Correspondence of W.E.B. Du Bois, Volume II, 1934–44*; (Amherst: University of Massachusetts Press, 1976).

144 Laura Wheeler Waring personal statement, Harmon Foundation Papers, Harmon Foundation, 1928, Library of Congress, Washington, DC.

145 Laura Wheeler Waring to William E. Harmon, January. 26, 1928, Harmon Foundation Papers, Box 45.

146 "Letter to Inez Cunningham Stark from Mary Beattie Brady," November 12, 1936, Smithsonian Institute Online, https://learninglab.si.edu/resources/view/1291766.

147 "Combating Racism," National Portrait Gallery.

148 "Combating Racism," National Portrait Gallery.

149 Leininger-Miller, "A Constant Stimulus," 17.

150 Sarah Vowell, "American Goth," *This American Life*, December 1998, https://www.thisamericanlife.org/118/what-you-lookin-at/act-one-0.

151 Henri Dorra, *Symbolist Art Theories: A Critical Anthology* (Oakland: University of California Press 1994), 17.

152 Andrew Hutton, dir., *The Pre-Raphaelites: Victorian Revolutionaries*, BBC Four, 2009, video, 28:56, https://www.youtube.com/watch?v=FkWONORqHZw&t=224s.

153 Richard Davenport-Hines, *Gothic: Four Hundred Years of Excess, Horror, Evil, and Ruin* (New York: North Point Press, 1998).

154 Margaretta S. Frederick and Jan Marsh, *Poetry in Beauty: The Pre-Raphaelite Art of Marie Spartali Stillman* (Wilmington: Delaware Art Museum, 2015), 14.

155 Jan Marsh, *Pre-Raphaelite Sisterhood* (London: Quartet Books, 1985), 161.

156 Jackson McHenry, "Why Lauren Bacall Wins *How to Marry a Millionaire*," *Entertainment Weekly*, August 13, 2014, https://ew.com/article/2014/08/13/lauren-bacall-the-real-winner-in-1953s-how-to-marry-a-millionaire/.

157 "Marshall McLuhan in Conversation with Mike McManus," TVOntario, 1977, https://www.tvo.org/video/archive/marshall-mcluhan-in-conversation-with-mike-mcmanus?utm_source=TVO.

158 "Marshall McLuhan," TVOntario.

159 Marianne Mathieu, "Becoming an Artist," in *Berthe Morisot: Woman Impressionist* (New York: Rizzoli, 2018), 69.

160 Jean-Dominique Rey, *Berthe Morisot* (Paris: Flammarion, 2018), 41.

161 Mathieu, *Berthe Morisot, Woman Impressionist*, "Becoming an Artist," (New York: Rizzoli, 2018), 55.

162 John Silver, dir., "Impressions of Light," *Sister Wendy: The Story of Painting*, season 1, episode 8, August 25, 1996, PBS.

163 Linda Nochlin, *Women Artists: The Linda Nochlin Reader* (New York: Thames & Hudson, 2015), 171.

164 Anne Higonnet, *Berthe Morisot* (Oakland: University of California Press, 1995), 203.

165 Sam Dean, "What Are NFTs?," *Los Angeles Times*, March 11, 2021, https://www.latimes.com/business/technology/story/2021-03-11/nft-explainer-crypto-trading-collectible?utm_id=25690&sfmc_id=3573446.

166 Dean, "What Are NFTs?"

167 Michelle Ellsworth, Zoom interview with the author, August 4, 2021.

168 Justine Calma, "The Climate Controversy Swirling Around NFTs," *The Vere*, March 15, 2021, https://www.theverge.com/2021/3/15/22328203/nft-cryptoart-ethereum-blockchain-climate-change.

169 Michelle Ellsworth, Zoom interview with the author, August 4, 2021.

170 Michelle Ellsworth, Zoom interview with the author, August 4, 2021.

171 Marshall McLuhan, *Understanding Media* (Cambridge, MA: MIT Press, 1964), 136.

172 Adam Curtis, dir., *Can't Get You Out of My Head: Money Changes Everything* (BBC, 2021).

173 McLuhan, *Understanding Media*, 137.

174 Nick Paumgarten, "The Prophets of Cryptocurrency Survey the Boom and Bust," *New Yorker*,

October 15, 2018, https://www.newyorker.com/magazine/2018/10/22/the-prophets-of-cryptocurrency
-survey-the-boom-and-bust.

175 Michelle Ellsworth, Zoom interview with the author, August 4, 2021.

176 Michelle Ellsworth, Zoom interview with the author, August 4, 2021.

177 Martin Scorsese, dir., *Public Speaking* (HBO Documentary Films, 2010).

178 D.E. Harding, *On Having No Head* (London: Sholland Trust, 2014), 33.

179 Harding, *On Having No Head*, 20–21.

180 Wallace Shawn, *Night Thoughts* (Chicago: Haymarket Books, 2017), 53.

181 Julia Kristeva, *The Severed Head: Capital Visions* (New York: Columbia University Press, 2014), 75.

182 Mary Gabriel, *Ninth Street Women* (New York: Back Bay Books, 2018), 358.

183 Gabriel, *Ninth Street Women*, 362.

184 Marion Cajori, dir., *Joan Mitchell: Portrait of an Abstract Painter* (Arthouse Films, 1993).

185 Cajori, *Joan Mitchell*.

186 Pastoureau, *Blue*, 175.

187 Richard Shiff, *Joan Mitchell*, (New Haven: Yale University Press, 2020), 287.

188 Patricia Albers, "Joan Mitchell, Lady Painter," Brooklyn Museum, September 16, 2012, video, 1:08:31, https://www.youtube.com/watch?v=PnpR_vOAoYY.

189 Albers, "Joan Mitchell, Lady Painter."

190 de Saint Phalle, *Harry and Me*, 115.

191 Cajori, *Joan Mitchell*.

192 Albers, "Joan Mitchell, Lady Painter."

193 Robert Olen Butler, *From Where You Dream* (New York: Grove Press, 2005), 23.

194 Cajori, *Joan Mitchell*.

195 Franklin Einspruch, "Joan Mitchell Becomes the Sunflower," *New York Sun*, January 4, 2012, https://www.nysun.com/arts/joan-mitchell-becomes-the-sunflower/87633/.

196 Jane Livingston, *The Paintings of Joan Mitchell* (New York: Whitney Museum of American Art, 2002), 41.

197 Cajori, *Joan Mitchell*.

198 Cajori, *Joan Mitchell*.

199 Michael Blackwood, dir., *Philip Guston: A Life Lived* (Arthouse Films, 1980).

Image Credits

Tré Gallery
Francis and Ana, 2009
Courtesy of the artist

Artist Unknown
Mandala of Vairochana Buddha, ca. 1300-1399
Ground mineral pigment on cotton
Courtesy of the Kronos Collection

Mira Dancy (1979–)
Sawblade Sunrise, 2019
Acrylic on canvas, 76 x 90½ inches
Photo: Tim Doyon
Courtesy of the artist

Agnes Martin (1912–2004)
Morning, 1965
Acrylic paint and graphite on canvas,
71⅘ x 71⅗ inches
© Estate of Agnes Martin / DACS, 2021
Tate, London

Jay DeFeo (1929–1989)
"Painter Jay DeFeo painting *The Rose*,"
San Francisco, 1960
© Burt Glinn/Magnum Photos

Leonor Fini (1907–1996)
Les Aveugles, 1968
Oil on canvas, 28⅞ by 45⅝ inches
Courtesy of Weinstein Gallery, San Francisco
Private Collection
© 2021 Artists Rights Society (ARS), New York / ADAGP, Paris

Howardena Pindell (1943–)
Columbus, 2020
Mixed media on canvas, 108 x 120 inches
Signed and dated, verso
Courtesy of the artist and Garth Greenan Gallery, New York

Hilma af Klint (1862–1944)
Group IX/SUW, The Swan, No. 1, 1915
Oil on canvas, 59 x 59 inches
© The Hilma af Klint Foundation
Moderna Museet Malmö

Sophie Taeuber-Arp (1889–1943)
Two Triangles (Point on Point), 1931
Oil on canvas, 25½ x 21¼ inches
Philadelphia Museum of Art, Philadelphia: A. E. Gallatin Collection, 1952, 1952-61-120

Alice Guy-Blaché (1873–1968)
Two Little Rangers, 1912
Film still from the collection of EYE Film Institute Netherlands

Tayeba Begum Lipi (1969–)
My Mother's Dressing Table, 2013
Stainless steel-made razor blades,
37½ x 18½ x 39 inches
Courtesy of the artist and Sundaram Tagore Gallery, New York

Niki de Saint Phalle (1930–2002)
"Niki de Saint Phalle en 1962."
Giancarlo Botti/Gamma-Rapho via Getty Images

Laurie Anderson (1947–)
"Laurie Anderson's *Habeas Corpus* at the Park Avenue Armory," October 2, 2015
© Stephanie Berger

Nina de Garis Davies (1881–1965)
Women at a Banquet, 1925
(original ca. 1479–1425 BCE.)
Tempera on paper, $18\frac{11}{16}$ × $26\frac{3}{16}$ inches
Metropolitan Museum of Art, New York: Rogers Fund, 1930

Margareta Haverman (1693–1722 or later)
A Vase of Flowers, 1716
Oil on wood, 31¼ x 23¾ inches
Metropolitan Museum of Art, New York

Marilyn Minter (1948–)
Crystal Swallow, 2006
Enamel on metal, 96 x 60 inches
Courtesy of the artist and Salon 94, New York
© Marilyn Minter

Élisabeth Louise Vigée Le Brun (1755–1842)
Portrait of Madame du Barry, 1781
Oil on panel, 27¼ x 20¼ inches
Philadelphia Museum of Art, Philadelphia: Gift of Mrs. Thomas T. Fleming, 1984, 1984-137-1

Jessica Stoller (1981–)
Untitled (floral bust), 2019
Porcelain, glaze, china paint, 12 x 12 x 10 inches
Courtesy of the artist and P.P.O.W. Gallery,
New York

Dana Sherwood (1977–)
Feral Cakes, still
Digital video, 11:22, 2017
Courtesy of the artist and Denny Dimin Gallery,
New York

Katsushika Ōi (ca. 1800–1866)
Night Scene in Yoshiwara, ca. 1844–54
Hanging scroll, ink and color on paper,
10$\frac{2}{5}$ x 15$\frac{3}{5}$ inches
Ōta Memorial Museum of Art, Tokyo

Henrietta Mantooth (1924–)
The Human Talking and Listening Machine, 2018
Mixed media and street talk
Courtesy of the artist
Photograph of *The Human Talking and Listening
Machine* © Erica Lansner, Courtesy of Erica
Lansner

Pauline Boty (1938–1966)
The Only Blonde in the World, 1963
Oil on canvas, 50 x 62$\frac{1}{4}$ inches
Inscribed and dated verso
Tate, London

Laura Wheeler Waring (1887–1948)
The Study of a Student, ca. 1940
Oil on canvas board, 20 x 16 inches
Courtesy of the Pennsylvania Academy of the
Fine Arts, Philadelphia. Gift of Dr. Constance E.
Clayton in loving memory of her mother Mrs.
Williabell Clayton, 2019.3.69.

Marie Spartali Stillman (1844–1927)
Love's Messenger, 1885
Watercolor, tempera, and gold paint on paper,
32 x 26 inches
Delaware Art Museum, Delaware: Samuel and
Mary R. Bancroft Memorial, 1935, 1935-75

Berthe Morisot (1841–1895)
*Portrait of Mademoiselle L (Isabelle in the
Garden)*, 1885
Oil on canvas, 39$\frac{3}{8}$ x 31$\frac{7}{8}$ inches
Private collection

Michelle Ellsworth (1967–)
*Four NFTs: A Dance for Wood Camera;
Ownership Assignment Process for Rock-Owned
NFT; Location of the Rock-Owned Non-Fungible
Tokens; Put the Log Back in Analog*, 2021
Concrete, 7.6 kg, Tezos blockchain
Courtesy of the artist

Artemisia Gentileschi (1593–ca. 1696)
Judith Beheading Holofernes, ca. 1613
Oil on canvas, 62$\frac{1}{2}$ x 49$\frac{2}{5}$ inches
Museo di Capodimonte, Naples
Leemage/Corbis Historical via Getty Images

Nuala Clarke (1970–)
Étaín's dream (i), 2017
Acrylic on board, 17$\frac{7}{10}$ x 13$\frac{7}{10}$ inches
Courtesy of the artist
Private Collection

Joan Mitchell (1925–1992)
Chord II, 1986
Oil paint on canvas, 63$\frac{7}{10}$ x 38$\frac{1}{10}$ inches
© Estate of Joan Mitchell
Tate, London

Lavinia Fontana (1552–1614)
Portrait of Antonietta Gonzalez, 1595
Oil on canvas, 22$\frac{2}{5}$ x 18$\frac{1}{10}$ inches
Château de Blois, Blois

Kevin Townley is a writer, filmmaker, actor, singer, and meditation instructor. He began formally studying Buddhism in 2010 and currently practices with the Sokuko-Ji Zen community under the guidance of Kyoun Sokuzan. He has taught Buddhism and meditation for over a decade. His film and television work includes appearances in *My Super Ex-Girlfriend*, *Men in Black 3*, *The Detour*, and *Law & Order*. With his band, Bambï, Townley adapted Judith Rossner's *Looking for Mr. Goodbar* into the rock opera *GOODBAR*, performed at The Public Theater. He has written extensively for the Waterwell theater company and *Rookie* magazine. He has also led hundreds of art tours in museums across the country, including the Metropolitan Museum of Art, the Art Institute of Chicago, and Boston's Museum of Fine Arts. This is his first book. For more information and to watch his short film *Who Knows?*, visit **www.kevintownley.nyc**.

JULIA GANDRUD, *KEVIN AND JOANN (BOBBI IS JEALOUS)*, 2021